T0261808

e-Finance

e-Finance

The Electronic Revolution

Erik Banks

John Wiley & Sons, Ltd
Chichester • New York • Weinheim • Brisbane • Singapore • Toronto

Other Wiley Editorial Offices

John Wiley & Sons, Inc., 605 Third Avenue,
New York, NY 10158-0012, USA

WILEY-VCH Verlag GmbH, Pappelallee 3,
D-69469 Weinheim, Germany

John Wiley & Sons Australia, Ltd, 33 Park Road, Milton,
Queensland 4064, Australia

John Wiley & Sons (Asia) Pte Ltd, 2 Clementi Loop #02-01,
Jin Xing Distripark, Singapore 129809

John Wiley & Sons (Canada) Ltd, 22 Worcester Road,
Rexdale, Ontario M9W 1L1, Canada

Library of Congress Cataloging-in-Publication Data
Banks, Erik.
    E-finance : the electronic revolution in financial services / Erik Banks.
        p. cm.
    Includes bibliographical references and index.
    ISBN 0-471-56026-X (alk. paper)
    1. Financial services industry—Computer networks. 2. Electronic commerce. 3.
Internet. I. Title.

HG151.8 B36 2001
658.8'4—dc21
                                                                                    2001023389

British Library Cataloguing in Publication Data

A catalogue record for this book is available from the British Library

ISBN 0 471 56026 X

This book is printed on acid-free paper responsibly manufactured from sustainable forestry, for
which at least two trees are planted for each one used for paper production.

'Big Money weave a mighty web . . .'

N. Peart

To my father,

Robert Banks

Contents

Acknowledgements

Thanks are due to a number of people for helping make this book a reality. Samantha Whittaker, publishing editor at John Wiley, was instrumental in supporting this project in its earliest stages and providing thoughtful guidance at key stages along the way. Likewise, Rachael Wilkie, editor at John Wiley, provided valuable suggestions and feedback during the editing stages and Monica Twine, production editor, ensured a smooth editing process. General thanks are due to the publishing and marketing professionals at John Wiley who played a vital part in creating and distributing the book. I would also like to express my gratitude to various professionals at a number of Wall Street firms and Internet ventures who provided views and thoughts on different aspects of the topic; though many prefer to remain anonymous, their contributions are recognized and appreciated.

As always, my biggest thanks go to my wife Milena . . . for making life happy, fun and interesting.

E.B.
Greenwich, CT
December 2000

1

The Arrival of e-Commerce

e-COMMERCE IN THE INTERNET AGE

Electronic commerce, digital money, online trading, and web banking—we hear these terms on the evening news and read about them in the daily newspapers. They are elements of 21st century business that have changed the way we conduct our business and lead our lives. Though the issue is complex, we propose that electronic banking, trading and finance—key elements of the broader electronic commerce (or e-commerce) sector—have been made possible by a unique confluence of technology, creativity and capital. Technology, as outlined in the Appendix, has enabled business to be conducted in a fast, efficient and secure way; creativity has allowed entrepreneurs, start-ups, and seasoned companies to break 'old economy' paradigms—those based on traditional manufacturing and industrial production models—to deliver business solutions through new, exciting, and often radically different structures; and capital, the lubricant of every micro- and macro-economy, has provided the financial wherewithal to put these technical and human wheels in motion. These three elements, working together in a deregulating environment, have started to reshape the global economic and financial landscape. As a result, the retail and institutional financial services industry is in the midst of a dramatic transformation that is affecting all participants—providers, users, regulators and investors—in a very meaningful fashion. Electronic finance (e-finance) represents a new frontier in the creation, delivery and use of financial services.

The development and expansion of computer/communication networks—fuelled by enabling technologies such as integrated circuits (ICs), personal computers (PCs) and broadband connections—has led some observers to draw parallels between the 21st century digital revolution and the 18th/19th century Industrial Revolution—which changed the social and economic landscape of England, and then the world, so dramatically. As a result of networking, new efficiencies have been achieved, new methods of working and playing have been introduced, and new methods of organizing life and work have evolved—fundamental changes that are, in many ways, as radical and transformational as those witnessed during the Industrial Revolution. From the creation of packet-switched networks in 1969, to e-mail in 1971, the web in 1991, browsers in 1993, and popular online services in 1995, the Internet (and associated private networks, intranets and extranets) has changed the way millions of people lead their personal and professional lives. As the price of communication and computing power declines, the presence and influence of networks expands even further—indeed, the steady decline in the price of information access and transmission has been, and continues to be, central to the success of the Internet. Technical innovation has deep and lasting impact when it is affordable—the Internet, and its users, have benefited from increasingly inexpensive technology. Consider that the price of computer processing power has fallen by an average of 35% per year over the past three decades, while the cost of sending information over copper, coax, fiber or wireless has dropped by orders of magnitude—according to the Federal Reserve, the cost of sending 1 trillion bits (characters) of information over the network has declined from $150,000 in 1970 to only $0.12 in 2000, while a 20 page document can today be e-mailed for only 1 cent. Because computing and communicating power is cheap, it is available and accessible to a broad audience—this increases the connective and productive power of the network and helps transform entire aspects of financial, economic and social behavior.

Penetration and acceptance of the Internet and associated networks have been very rapid. It took 38 years for the radio to achieve widespread mass use, 13 years for the television, and 16 years for the PC—but only four years for the Internet (once it was opened to the general public). Further expansion of the Internet is expected as PC and wireless use continue to grow. The number of computers in operation globally increased from 237MM in 1995 to 428MM in 2000, and researchers expect nearly 800MM to be in use by 2005. Various forecasts already predict that Europe will be home to the largest number of computers by 2005 (260MM), followed by the US (230MM), Asia (190MM), Latin America (56MM) and Middle East/Africa (30MM). Wireless users, many of whom will access the web through their wireless devices in the future, will double to over 1B by 2004. As a result of these trends, Internet growth and activity is set to expand further over the coming years. During the mid- to late 1990s Internet traffic doubled every 100 days, and continues to accelerate; in 1995 there were approximately 39MM Internet users, by 2000 that figure had increased to 350MM and by 2005 is expected to reach over 750MM. While the US currently accounts for more than 40% of all Internet access, future growth will come from various other regions—by 2005 the US will feature

230MM Internet users, Europe 260MM, and Asia 190MM. Network hosts increased from the 'original 4' created in late 1969 to 160,000 at the end of 1989 and over 100MM at the end of 2000—and are expected to reach 1B by 2005. The number of web sites rose from a mere 130 in mid-1993 to 650,000 at the end of 1996 and 9.6MM at the end of 1999. The number of distinct web pages reached 1.5B at the end of 1999, reflecting a two-year growth rate of approximately 1.9MM pages per day; IDC, a research firm, estimates that the Internet will feature over 8B web pages by 2002. With such impressive growth and penetration rates—in such a short period of time—and with such bright future prospects, it is little wonder that many businesses, including those represented by the financial industry, have sought to take advantage of the Internet to deliver products and services.

The growing reach and influence of the Internet, fuelled by cheaper and more powerful PCs, and faster and more robust communication links, has helped spawn new ways of doing business. While technology has been an important enabler and facilitator, it has not been the sole force responsible for reshaping commerce. In order to create new business platforms, technology has been supplemented by the creative forces of businesses and entrepreneurs who have been willing to think differently, and sometimes radically, in the design and application of business methods. Prior to the mid-1990s business models were generally confined to standard 'value chains'—links in the production/service process, from logistics, to resource acquisition, design, production/manufacturing, inventory control, processing, shipping, and corporate infrastructure. By taking advantage of the commercial possibilities of the Internet these 'value chains' were—and continue to be—challenged, disassembled and reordered. With the Internet it has become possible—at least in theory—to provide small and large customers with electronic access to a broad range of information, goods and services at a cheaper price and with greater efficiency and transparency. Businesses have been able to use the Internet to reach a larger, and more geographically diverse, set of customers at very little incremental cost. In addition, they have been able to leverage technology to scale their businesses very quickly. Such is the basis of the broad field of e-commerce; as we shall note throughout this text, many of the advantages gained through this construct apply equally in the e-finance world. It is worth stressing that e-commerce is not strictly about selling goods and services through the web—though this is a part of the proposition—but about using technology to fundamentally change business processes in order to achieve speed, efficiency, innovation and customer value.

A University of Texas survey indicates that in 1996 US e-commerce accounted for $2B of a total gross domestic product (GDP) base of $7.6T—less than 0.03% of GDP. By 2002 US e-commerce is expected to account for $750B to $1T of a $10.1T economy, or 7.5–10% of GDP, and to grow even further from there. Though the US has led the way in e-commerce—

accounting for 67% of all business-to-business e-commerce revenues and 76% of business-to-consumer e-commerce revenues in 1999—nations around the world are already increasing their participation and narrowing the gap. Foreign e-commerce will be an important component of global output in the coming years; indeed, IDC predicts that by 2004 62% of e-commerce transactions will come from outside the US, with Western Europe and Japan accounting for the largest portions (35% and 16% of the total, respectively). Various research firms predict that global e-commerce will reach between $1.5T and $3T by mid-decade, with more than 90% coming from the business-to-business sector. Projecting future e-commerce revenues is a decidedly tricky task; analysts often include different sectors of the market in their definitions and typically employ different inputs to arrive at revenue growth rates (i.e. how rapidly the Internet expands, how quickly 'old economy' companies adapt their strategies, how alternate models and concepts are developed and introduced, how new technologies impact communication and distribution, and so on). Though the range of estimated future e-commerce revenues is quite large, it is clear that the sector will be a significant contributor to global output over the short- and medium-term.

e-Commerce firms operating in the 'new economy'—as it has come to be known—are redefining many of the business tenets long held 'sacred' by companies. The new economy and its successful e-commerce firms are characterized by dynamic value migration, real-time execution and fulfillment, 'webs' of alliances and partnerships, distributed work processes, and personalized, interactive customer relationships. Successful ventures are those which are capable of managing partnerships, alliances and other relationships in a flexible manner, dealing with rapid change effectively, and maintaining the highest standards of management and technical competency. Achieving commercial success on the Internet is not simple. Since many of these concepts are new or alien to well-established firms, the task of redefining and migrating business to the Internet has been, and will continue to be, doubly hard. To understand the issues and challenges involved in creating Internet platforms we explore, in this chapter, various conceptual and practical issues related to the development of e-commerce and e-finance sectors and models.

e-COMMERCE SECTORS AND MODELS

Though the field of e-commerce has only existed since the mid-1990s, it has already developed a taxonomy which helps classify and identify the functions performed by different participants in the market. For instance, it is by now well established that e-commerce is divided into three broad sectors—'business-to-consumer' (B2C), 'business-to-business' (B2B) and infrastructure. Two additional fields which offer future e-commerce potential include 'consumer-to-consumer' (C2C, sometimes also known as peer-to-peer (P2P)) and 'exchange-to-exchange' (E2E).

In B2C, businesses supply information, goods and services to individuals; individuals can purchase these goods and services directly from the B2C platform. This is the most established segment of e-commerce (though not necessarily the most profitable) and focuses heavily on access, content, traffic and consumer branding. Representative platforms in this segment, familiar to many Internet users, include Amazon, eBay, E*Trade, and so on. In the B2B sector businesses supply information, goods and services to other businesses and develop business-related exchanges to serve other businesses. Representative corporate platforms include the transaction-enabled sites of firms such as Intel, American Express, Microsoft, Ford, General Electric, Daimler Chrysler, IBM, Oracle and others; institutional buyers can transact directly with these platforms. B2B business exchanges bring together companies from identical industries (so-called vertical exchanges) or different industries (horizontal exchanges) and allow them to buy and sell goods and services in a moderated setting. Exchanges may be supplier-led, buyer-led or intermediated. Depending on the structure of the exchange, transactions can occur on the basis of auctions (sellers offer goods/services which buyers bid on), reverse auctions (buyers provide sellers with bids for specified goods/services), or matching services (brokers link buyers with sellers). In its simplest form, a buyer interested in purchasing a bulk shipment of auto parts (or Treasury bonds or any other exchangeable good) accesses the relevant electronic exchange, posts a price or lifts a seller's offer, and has the order filled; attendant fulfillment services related to payment and shipping (or transfer) are typically arranged and concluded within the exchange as well. Regardless of the structure, exchanges require an appropriate balance of buyers and sellers in order to function properly; a bias in either direction can cause the business model to fail, as supply or demand forces will act to skew prices. Vertical exchanges exist in numerous sectors, including manufacturing, utilities, construction, health care, and financial services, among others; examples include Covisint (auto parts), E2Open (electronic parts), Pantellos (energy), Transora (packaged goods) and Quadrem (mining/metals) (along with a range of financial exchanges that we discuss at length in Chapter 4). Horizontal exchanges have been created to provide distribution channels for capital equipment, excess inventory, and contract manufacturing across a range of industries; representative exchanges include Onvia and Freemarkets. E2E, a relatively new concept, is intended to promote business between, and within, exchanges. C2C, a small but emerging sector, is designed to let consumers deal directly with one another through mechanisms such as electronic auctions.

In the e-commerce infrastructure sector, technology and consulting ventures supply web ventures with the 'nuts and bolts' needed to develop and conduct Internet-based business. These companies provide consulting services, web/content enabling packages (including payment, inventory, shipping and other fulfillment services), software products, web design, wireless and broadband capabilities, security architecture, network transportation/ equipment services, and support and maintenance; infrastructure services are available to both start-up ventures and established companies. As established firms, in particular, develop e-commerce strategies and alter their business structures, existing infrastructure architecture often needs to be redesigned and reimplemented; this can be a wrenching, expensive and time-consuming exercise, particularly when legacy technology and processing platforms are well entrenched. Infrastructure companies readily assist such companies in the conversion process. Examples of companies in the infrastructure sector include Ventro, VerticalNet, Ariba, Oracle, Vignette, Commerce One, Cisco, Akamai, SAP, Inktomi, Geo Interactive, XoR, Clarus, and Digex, among others. It is worth noting that while some researchers view infrastructure companies that allow businesses to serve other businesses as B2B companies (and adjust their definitions and metrics accordingly), others define them to be separate providers of infrastructure and measure according to that definition. The categorization of e-commerce ventures into the three broad sectors described above is, of course, applicable across industries; as we shall note in greater detail later in the chapter, the financial sector features its own B2C, B2B and infrastructure providers.

Many businesses have found e-commerce to be a logical, if challenging, way of conducting and expanding business. For companies entering the e-commerce arena the value proposition—or gains to be derived—must be clear. For example, a company can use the web to reduce costs, manage supplier relationships, access and service customers, expand distribution, deliver information, streamline logistics, manage inventories and pipelines, create 'upstream' (trading partner) and 'downstream' (distributor) links, and so on. The value proposition for the customer must also be obvious—there must be a clear and compelling reason for an individual or institutional customer to use the Internet for business. Most often the enhanced value proposition relates to lower costs, greater returns, more transparent pricing, enhanced liquidity, broader selection, more rapid and convenient processing, more efficient fulfillment, and so on. Technology and marketplace dynamics change so rapidly that companies that strive to be effective and relevant constantly search for new value chain opportunities that can enhance the value proposition for themselves and their customers.

Companies entering the Internet business arena must possess a committed management view that is applied in a rigorous and disciplined manner. The e-commerce strategy must be driven from the top down and become part of everyday corporate culture—this means management must be committed to establishing a presence, being visible, offering value and convenience, and partnering/outsourcing as necessary. More than a few firms have pursued e-commerce strategies in an informal or ad-hoc fashion, leading to wasted time and resources and ineffective results. Achieving a sustainable competitive advantage is very difficult under the best of circumstances, and is virtually impossible when the approach is not properly planned, guided and driven. In practice, many companies and ventures have chosen to implement their e-commerce strategies in small steps. Commencing first with internal tactical applications, such as 'webizing' corporate functions (including human resource management, internal policies, business expenses and financial reporting), some have then moved to experimenting with the business model—primarily by targeting 'non business critical' functions with less downside risk. From there they challenge corporate standards and redesign business processes. In the final stage they may completely transform entire aspects of their business, with a view towards creating significant improvements in the value chain.

Developing an effective e-commerce platform requires the definition of a mission statement and identification of a robust business model. The business model must identify the component of the value chain that is being restructured and enhanced, and quantify the relative costs and benefits of doing so. As indicated above, the successful model provides tangible benefits to all parties involved. For established companies the development of a business model cannot, of course, be done in isolation; existing operations must be considered as part of a process that ensures the business 'scope' of the traditional and e-commerce platforms is clearly understood. Creating web-based sales, distribution, procurement or support channels can lead to 'channel conflict'—conflict that can arise when separate parts of an organization offer similar products/services through different channels, leading to 'cannibalization' of business. Avoiding or minimizing channel conflict by developing appropriate strategies is, as noted below, of paramount importance. The scalability of a business model is also critical. There is little lasting value in implementing an idea that has a very small audience or market; the potential audience for a product or service must be large enough to justify the time, investment and expense of developing it. Just as the business model must be scalable so, too, must the underlying technical architecture supporting the model—technology must be able to deliver what the business model promises. A governance process, which manages and oversees the e-commerce platform, is crucial; such a process cannot, however, be bureaucratic in nature.

There is no single 'correct' definition of the e-commerce business models that are shaping the web; many ventures and platforms cross boundaries, and analysts and researchers periodically classify them in different ways. Despite these differences, certain broad classifications can be described. At a macro level Internet players can be divided into groups focused on access, content/ context and enabling. Access platforms provide users with physical connections/entry points to the Internet and related support services; this group includes Internet service providers (ISPs), telecom providers, web hosters and middleware companies, such as America Online (AOL), Freeserve, Microsoft Network (MSN), T-Online, Tiscali/World Online, Wanadoo, and Terra Lycos. Content/context platforms provide users with information, products and services in an informational or interactive setting; this group includes electronic retailers ('e-tailers'), brokers, agents, dealers, advertisers, infomediaries, e-marketplaces and exchanges, such as Amazon, Yahoo, E*Trade, AskJeeves, LastMinute, GoTo, eBay, and QXL. Enablers facilitate the transmission of information and transactions and act as trusted, independent third parties for web commerce; this group includes clearinghouses, guarantors and security providers, such as Bottomline/Checkpoint, Guardent and Verisign. Within these three groups platforms may operate as B2C ventures, B2B ventures or providers of infrastructure. In certain cases, they may span multiple functions (acting as access and content providers, for instance).

Within the content/context subgroups we may consider more granular models. One approach divides these platforms into five different categories: vanity sites (those for personal, non-profit or altruistic ventures); informational sites (those for investor relations and product/service information); advertising sites (those for third-party promotion); subscription sites (those with specialized content and access); and storefront sites (those where users can purchase products/services and related fulfillment and support). A second approach divides business models into four slightly different categories: infomediary sites (those which collect and analyze web information/preferences in order to assist in targeted marketing); advertising sites (those which provide general, personalized or specialized access to information); merchant/'e-tailer' sites (those which provide users with products/services through virtual/ 'pure play' entities (i.e. no underlying physical store/outlet), catalog-driven entities, or physical store extensions (so-called 'bricks and clicks' or 'surf and turf')); and broker sites (those which provide users with broking or agenting services). A third approach classifies business models in a more detailed fashion: e-shop/storefront sites (those which provide advertising, goods selection and payment capabilities, primarily at the consumer level); e-mall sites (those which extend the e-shop concept by providing advertising, goods selection and payment capabilities across a wide number of e-shops (based on a single theme or a range of themes)); marketplace sites (those which provide information, analysis and aggregation across a large number of associated web platforms); e-procurement/exchange sites (those which provide tendering/ procurement facilities for goods and services, targeted especially at large companies or public/government authorities); e-auction sites (those which provide bidding facilities for goods and services, along with contract and payment capabilities); information management/infomediary sites (those which supply information and provide data management collation, analysis and search services); value chain service provider sites (those which provide niche components of the value chain, such as product creation, payment or shipping); and value chain integrator/portal sites (those which provide aggregate components of the value chain, such as information dissemination, resource acquisition/purchasing and design/manufacturing). In addition to these structures the B2B sector is sometimes defined to include additional models such as virtual/affinity communities (sites where users with common interests/themes unite), buyer/aggregators (sites where individual buyers are brought together in a consolidated fashion to obtain better prices), extranet business communities (sites where extensive private networks provide links to common interests), and so on. Naturally, various other classifications of models exist, but these are common representations. Within the e-finance world, most platforms can be classified according to one of these definitions. For instance, firms such as Bank of America and Barclays operate corporate storefronts, E-Loan and InsWeb are active as marketplaces, Citibank and American Express are broad integrator/portal sites, Financewise and finweb act as financial infomediaries, CheckFree functions as a value chain service provider, Atriax and BondBook operate as exchanges, and so on; we shall discuss these at greater length below.

e-COMMERCE IMPLEMENTATION

As indicated above, B2B and B2C e-commerce platforms often evolve through various stages. They can commence as informational sites, then introduce customer interactivity, become transaction-enabled, and then offer real-time personalized services. Indeed, many of the financial platforms discussed in this book have gone—and are going—through such evolutionary phases; some have started as infomediary sites and emerged as corporate storefronts or broad-based interactive integrator/portal sites. Others have confined themselves to a particular state, believing they can add greatest value in that form. For most companies, the e-commerce process starts with product and market transformation, which involves reinventing products/services and redefining the value proposition. For a smaller group of successful ventures it moves into a business process transformation, where new business models are created, partnerships/alliances are formed and outsourcing is undertaken. For a very select few, it culminates in a broader industry transformation, where traditional industry boundaries are redrawn and competitors are redefined. Exchanges are often created in stages as well. In the first phase, institutional buyers and sellers come together using a common web platform. Once established, the exchange expands in scope to include additional third-party/infrastructure services, including vendor certification, payment mechanisms, logistics, financing and customer support. Advanced exchanges then move into a product development/marketing phase that focuses on workflow management, optimization and fulfillment. For a select group of extremely well-developed exchanges a fourth phase focused on leading-edge business and product innovation (that becomes synonymous with industry leadership) is also possible. The essence of successful e-commerce involves rethinking and challenging value propositions—by understanding and anticipating customer needs—and then migrating business from a commoditized service, to a value-added service, to a truly unique, premium service. Defining a business model, such as one of those outlined above, forces a firm to consider attendant revenue, cost, design, technology, security and management issues. It also allows a firm to crystallize its core competencies. A business model must focus on the e-commerce business the venture is capable of pursuing in future years—it should not be seen as an opportunity to 'spread out' across an entire spectrum of businesses.

The revenue and cost dimensions of the e-commerce model must be thoroughly understood, stressed and monitored. It is worth noting that some of the services offered through the models described above appear to be 'free' to users, in the same way television and radio are 'free'. While the user may gain the benefit of some Internet service without 'paying' for it, the service provider actually attempts to generate direct or indirect revenues through alternate means—for example, by creating marketing or advertising services, developing customer information profiles for marketers, or collecting transaction/subscription fees. The e-commerce revenue paradigm is particularly complex because the web has altered established concepts of pricing. Contrary to traditional business models, for instance, the web allows for free products/services, differential pricing for the same goods, and so on. Understanding what customers are willing to pay for a particular product or service is central to unraveling the complexity surrounding revenue generation. Since the Internet is a relatively new medium it is still somewhat unclear what features like news headlines, e-mail, stock quotes, trade execution, investment advice, portfolio management, bill paying, front-to-back processing/fulfillment, and so on, are really worth to the average customer; services that can be 'bundled' or 'unbundled' add further to the complexity of the pricing function. Revenue generation within B2B exchanges is also a complicated issue. While some exchanges have been developed to bring suppliers and buyers together in order to help them 'strike deals' (and take fees), business reality is far more complex—creating a sustainable revenue flow depends very highly on the relationships between exchange participants (buyers, sellers, intermediaries), the degree to which the underlying market served by the exchange is fragmented or concentrated, the relative balance of buying and selling that occurs within the exchange, and so on; for instance, charging buyers and sellers a fee for simply bringing them together in a more efficient fulfillment setting may not necessarily be acceptable to buyers or sellers who have had a long history of dealing with each other outside the exchange structure. These pricing complexities are likely to be an ongoing challenge for all participants, particularly as competition gives rise to new ways of reconstructing the value chain and doing business. Different models obviously seek to create revenues in different ways. e-Storefronts/malls attempt to make money from product/service sales margins and advertising fees, infomediary models from advertising, subscription, partnership, and referral/transfer fees, B2B storefronts and exchanges through product/service sales margins, auction, advertising and procurement fees, and so on. As one might imagine, costs also form an essential element of any e-commerce business model. Costs of technology, development, inventory, outsourcing, fulfillment, human resources, and so on, vary from model to model; they must be justified and managed on behalf of those providing capital. New ventures, in particular, are sensitive to 'burn rates'—the speed at which funds supplied by venture capitalists and other investors are spent; if burn rates are too high, suggesting costs are moving ahead of budget, investors may take pre-emptive actions to protect their investments.

The nature of the business model generally indicates the most appropriate type of web platform design needed to perform stated tasks. A basic informational model with relatively static information is unlikely to need frequent updates or carry any sensitive user information, and therefore requires only modest technical maintenance and security once it is operational. Conversely, an informational model which relies heavily on dynamic information, such as a portal offering streaming headlines and stock quotes, requires more intricate technical construction and maintenance. A dedicated corporate storefront that offers fully interactive, transaction-enabled services demands extensive technical design that is sensitive to both security and performance—this ensures that appropriate safeguards exist to protect customer information and that transaction execution and fulfillment can be accomplished accurately and efficiently.

Technical architecture follows from design, and focuses on both the external platform that is being offered to customers and the internal platform required to deliver services and integrate legacy systems. Legacy systems are an important part of the process, as it is common for mature companies to have well-established technology focused on inventory control, payments, billing, cash management, accounting, reporting, and marketing. These operations must generally be integrated with new Internet applications, and infrastructure companies specializing in this type of work often facilitate the process. For instance, if a bank is offering customers the ability to access account balance information that resides on a legacy mainframe database, it must design and implement architecture that provides a seamless link between what the customer sees on the web and the information that resides in the mainframe database. In certain instances the incremental expense of converting or merging legacy systems into a new, integrated platform is justifiable. Other aspects of technology play an important role in the cost aspects of the business model, including minimum hardware and software requirements, ISP stability and performance standards, disaster recovery plans, system redundancy, data management, data capacity, and so on. The more intricate the platform, the greater the issues and costs.

Regardless of whether a venture is entirely new or an extension of an existing institution, the process of developing a client-facing B2B or B2C e-commerce platform goes through a reasonably standard cycle of technical definition, design and testing. In most cases the process begins with a clear definition of the product/service deliverables and the targeted audience. Thereafter, content sources are identified, risks are assessed, architecture is designed, master rollout schedules are created, and development begins. In the development phase servers are installed and tested, client connections are established and verified, content is created, Internet, intranet and extranet sites are integrated, design is finalized and beta testing is completed. A final stabilization, or quality assurance (QA), phase is standard, with a particular focus on pilot testing, and attendant support, risk, marketing, security and technical reviews. Once these have been successfully completed the platform is ready to publish in a live production environment.

Security remains central to any aspect of business model development and web design; this is particularly true for transaction-enabled e-commerce sites. Concern regarding the privacy of transactions and the input of 'sensitive' material (including credit card/payment authorizations and personal financial information) has been a major focus of businesses and consumers using the Internet for commercial transactions. Security design must achieve at least two broad goals simultaneously: it must be sufficiently robust to prevent unauthorized access to, or release of, information, but not so complex that it renders the web site inefficient. The basic security construct embedded into web platforms/browsers, particularly those involving sensitive information or transaction execution, is based on physical and transmission safeguards. Physical security around, and within, the site is centered on firewalls, intrusion detectors, and vulnerability scanners. Firewalls act as barriers between the Internet and an institution's own internal networks, and are configured to filter traffic and block access to particular sites and features. Intrusion detectors identify and deactivate 'malicious' code, viruses, Java applets/mobile code, and so on. Other dimensions of security architecture, including network access control, remote access control, password control, and so on, must also be well defined. Transmission security, focused primarily on user authentication, is a second important dimension of overall Internet security. Secure browsers generally make use of a secured sockets layer (SSL) which encrypts account information. SSL protocol provides proof that the server the user claims to be using is, in fact, the one being used. Once verified, all communications between the user and the server are encrypted. Technology is now widely available for senders and receivers to verify their identities through symmetric (private key) and asymmetric (public/private key) encryption. For example, digital certificates—or identification mechanisms issued by certificate authorities—that are asymmetric in nature contain public and private keys. The digital certificate holds a user's public key and contains non-confidential information about the user and a specific association with a private key. When the user applies the private key to data (via cryptographic operations) the data are unrecoverable until the public key is applied. If the receiver can recover data using the public key, verification is complete. In practice, the public key is downloaded from a browser or hard drive and attached to a transaction command or document; the private key resides on a hard drive and, when activated by a username and password, unlocks the user's public key access. Banks dealing in individual transactions in excess of $1MM now routinely employ digital certificates. While encryption protection has become increasingly sophisticated, it is worth noting that the more complex the encryption process, the faster system performance deteriorates. A parallel concept which accompanies security, and which is of great importance in financial transactions, is 'non-repudiation'. Digital certificates are now a recognized and approved method for demonstrating undeniable proof of participation by sender and receiver, in the event either attempts to 'repudiate' the transaction at a later date; digital certificates effectively constitute a digital 'seal of intent'.

Management coordination issues form a critical dimension of Internet business development. In certain instances, particularly for small ventures, this may simply involve close coordination and communication between a handful of principals. In larger ventures, which exist either as standalone entities or units of larger corporate conglomerates, more intensive coordination is required. The range of management issues which must be addressed is particularly broad and includes decision-making authorities, management goals, hiring, retention, compensation, performance, and so on. In instances where a new Internet venture grows up within an existing organization, particular attention must be paid to relationships between the new 'entrepreneurs' and the established 'old guard'—how they interact, cooperate, compete, manage duplicate work processes, integrate legacy technologies and workflows, and so on.

The earliest months, and even years, of most Internet businesses are spent designing a commercial opportunity, marketing a name/brand, generating revenues and engaging in necessary short- and long-term capital spending. Throughout the latter part of the 1990s most business models which obtained funding did so on the basis of revenue, rather than profit, projections. While most believed they could generate revenues with their business models, very few thought they would actually turn a profit in the early years. Even 'household' names such as Amazon, Yahoo, and others have spent many years trying to stem the flow of red ink. Venture capitalists and other investors—who were willing, in the 1990s, to fund a certain amount of losses in the early life of Internet businesses—are becoming more demanding and looking for positive returns over a much shorter time frame. This places greater pressure on e-commerce entrepreneurs to develop models that work. In the earliest stages of the e-commerce transition—primarily the mid- to late 1990s—technology was the key driver behind many business models. The reverse is now true, and models are driving technology. When the Internet came into its own as a commercial medium, browsers, hypertext links, Java applets, application program interfaces (APIs, which link databases to front-end processors) and other technology tools provided business developers with exciting ways of creating visually appealing, interactive businesses. Some of these 'technology inspired' businesses attracted customers and succeeded, but many others failed as they were built on unsound business principles or unrealistic assumptions. The second phase of the e-commerce transition, which effectively started at the turn of the 21st century, has brought a new focus. In order to generate both revenues and profits entrepreneurs now think first about their models and then about the technology needed to deliver on the models. For instance, a venture whose model focuses heavily on greater personalization/customization in order to develop stronger customer ties might embed its technology platform with a customizable interface and 'cookies' (small bits of code planted on a user's hard drive that remembers preferred settings on a site), intelligent agents (programs that scan the web for information, goods and services it believes might be of interest to the customer), and automatic alerts (e-mail messages to convey timely information of interest to the customer) as a means of developing the enhanced customer relationship; the technology thus serves the model.

B2C models were the first to move onto the web, making their migration in the mid- to late 1990s. Many new and established firms attempted to generate revenues by offering goods and services aimed at the consumer, and more than a few found it challenging. First movers (those entering the market first, in a very decisive fashion) such as Amazon, eBay, Yahoo and E*Trade gained an early advantage; others that followed found it difficult to establish a competitive advantage and generate revenues. Margins were thin (and often negative), revenues unsteady, recruiting and staffing difficult, and brand marketing a challenge. Following a shake-out in the B2C sector in the late 1990s, entrepreneurs, venture capitalists and other investors turned towards the B2B segment, only to encounter similar difficulties. Many B2B platforms, particularly so-called 'exchanges' (which were nothing more than informal forums designed to bring buyers and sellers together), were not developed properly or were based on naive assumptions regarding institutional buying/selling/fulfillment behavior and expectations. Further consolidation is expected in both sectors over the coming years, after which a core of very strong

B2C and B2B platforms (including B2B exchanges), supported by core infrastructure companies, is likely to emerge. The failure rate of Internet businesses remains very high. Though it is very early in the business cycle to know how many more web businesses will fail or succeed, certain analysts predict the failure rate could reach 75%. Despite the difficulties of the past few years, the prospects for continued growth in e-commerce are very strong, particularly in the areas of B2B, exchanges and infrastructure solutions, which can collectively tap and service a very large market. Research firms predict that before the middle of the decade nearly 1MM US companies will be actively involved in B2B e-commerce. Application of commercial models internationally will help promote further growth, and the deployment of new technologies, including those related to fiber optics and mobile/wireless, should generate additional expansion. There is a widespread belief that advances in technology—fuelled by, and in turn fuelling, the Internet—may create a prolonged e-commerce-driven economic expansion over the coming years.

e-FINANCE SECTORS AND MODELS

Financial products and services are a logical commercial business for the Internet—they are relatively homogenous, rely heavily on information and data, and require frequent customer participation; they are also easy to deliver—fulfillment of customer requirements is very straightforward (often simply a matter of electronic debits and credits), particularly when compared to consumer goods or institutional commodities which depend heavily on timely inventory management, scheduling and shipping. These facts were recognized by several pioneering ventures during the mid-1990s. They dissected the financial services value chain, determined new ways of maximizing components of the process, and developed business models and platforms to bring customers enhanced value. As indicated earlier, the e-finance world contains its own B2B, B2C and infrastructure sectors. In the B2B sector institutional clients and exchanges deal with one another across a range of financial products, some of which are very complex in nature. In the B2C sector institutions deliver retail customers a range of relatively standard, but essential, financial transactions and services. Supplementing the B2B and B2C segments is the broad area of information—news, research, prices, data and analysis—that crosses the institutional and retail worlds and drives many aspects of financial decision-making. Infrastructure services, designed to create, migrate and support B2B and B2C e-finance, are also a key element of the industry. These enablers make it possible for new ventures and established institutions to deliver operational web solutions to their institutional and retail clients in a relatively short time frame; since speed is of the essence in the Internet world, infrastructure providers have found a ready client base in B2B and B2C e-finance ventures. The migration of B2B and B2C e-finance commenced with commoditized products/services that were simple to move into an electronic environment and readily understood and used by a broad audience. These included foreign exchange and cash equity trading in the B2B sector and online equity trading and basic online banking in the B2C sector. More complex offerings, products and services followed— and are still following—including derivatives, new issues and back-end processing in the B2B sector, and electronic bill payment, mortgages and insurance in the B2C sector. All represent likely areas of future growth.

Established financial institutions and new financial ventures have selected different business models in migrating to the online world. As indicated above, there is no single, definitive method of classifying these models, but for the purposes of this discussion we consider the granular approach cited earlier. Certain institutions have created the equivalent of 'corporate storefronts', which offer new and existing retail and institutional customers the opportunity to transact in a range of products and services through proprietary web sites. For example, Merrill Lynch offers its institutional clients online services through its MLX platform, which unites trading, banking and research capabilities under one roof. Its retail clients access services through the ML Direct platform, which features online trading, funds transfer, bill paying, account management, and so on. Dresdner Bank conducts its web business through various platforms—German retail banking flows through the main Dresdner portal (and Deutsche Hypo for home mortgages) as well as the group's Advance web-only bank, while its institutional investment banking business (including trading and research) is conducted through the Dresdner Kleinwort Benson OnlineMarkets platform. Likewise, UBS conducts its institutional B2B activities through its UBS Warburg platform and its B2C business through its e-banking classic and Tradepac modules. Prior to its merger with JP Morgan, Chase conducted its web-finance activities through several platforms, including Chase Online for retail and small business web-banking, ChaseSpace for institutional banking, Chase Markets for online research, and Brown and Co for online retail trading. Many other institutions have developed similar institutional and/or retail transaction-enabled 'storefront' models. For institutions with a relatively broad base of products, the storefront model can be an effective short- to medium-term strategy as it creates a ready client contact point/ distribution channel for existing products and services. Those with a relatively narrow base of products may not be able to attract a sufficient number of new customers to create a viable business proposition; in such cases, partnerships or alliances with third parties may be required. Over the longer-term certain B2B and B2C corporate storefronts may expand their product and service offerings and assume the appearance of broader integrators/vertical portals. Those opting to limit product/service capabilities may convert into strict 'product manufacturers' or specialists, providing their products/services to platforms with greater distribution capabilities.

A second major Internet finance model is based on the value chain integrator/vertical portal platform; this is applicable in both B2B and B2C. The integrator/portal is a broad, single-industry platform that offers customers a range of features, including information, research, tools, support and fulfillment, along with links into a comprehensive range of proprietary or third-party services—in this case, financial and commercial services. Integrators (or portals, we use the terms interchangeably) may be creators of all, some or none of their own financial products. Those that produce all of their products can be thought of as web 'financial superstores'. Firms such as Citibank and American Express are examples from the B2C sector, while Citibank/Salomon Smith Barney is representative of the B2B sector. Those that are more specialized in nature may only produce a subset of the products/services they wish to offer, such as banking, insurance or trading services. To the extent they embrace open architecture and new alliances, and form links with institutions/platforms they might otherwise regard as competitors, they assume the appearance of full service portals. For example, in the B2C sector Wingspanbank, a virtual bank focused on commercial banking services, supplements its product range with alliances that cover trading (DLJ, now CSFB), mortgages (E-Loan), and insurance (InsWeb). Portals that do not create any of their own financial products rely solely on alliances and partnerships with other firms. As one might expect, these platforms are often 'non-traditional' financial service providers—including some of the technology organizations that have helped develop aspects of the web and give e-commerce its vibrancy and innovation. AOL, the ISP and content/applications provider, falls into this category through its AOL Finance site. AOL Finance features financial news, quotes and tools, and has supplemented its lack of financial product-creation abilities through alliances covering online trading (Schwab), credit cards (Bank One/First USA), and banking services (Bank of America, Citibank); AOL customers can thus enter the main portal and be directed to additional partner sites for specific financial dealing. Yahoo operates on similar principles through its Yahoo Finance module; Yahoo provides content and information and joins with financial partners to offer clients online trading (Datek), mortgages (E-Loan), insurance (InsWeb), and tax preparation/advice (H&R Block). Bloomberg, the financial information company, provides its web customers with access to online banking (Everbank), small business finance (Allied Capital), and insurance (Accuquote). Other 'non-traditional' platforms in this category include MSN Moneycentral, Intuit/ Quicken, and Virgin, among others. Though the concept of technology companies as web financial service providers may appear somewhat radical, their participation is actually quite natural—these firms possess an intimate knowledge of the Internet and its underlying technology, are accustomed to creating and delivering customer-oriented products and services, and possess well-known brand names that are capable of generating a large amount of Internet traffic. It is worth noting that non-financial portals facilitating the provision of financial services tend to do so almost exclusively at the retail, rather than institutional, level.

A third common Internet finance model is based on the 'marketplace' paradigm, where a venture offers clients 'comparison shopping' of products and services across a large number of vendors. By aggregating the product and service offerings of participating financial institutions (including those operating storefronts of their own), the marketplace platform provides clients with the 'best deal' available (based on selection, price, execution, and fulfillment). Marketplace models are intuitively appealing because they provide customers with 'one stop' comparisons, education and analysis. This obviates the need for customers to visit many individual corporate storefronts to obtain trade/service information and price quotes prior to execution. State Street's FX Connect, which brings together numerous banks to fill an institutional client's foreign exchange order at the best possible exchange rate, is an example from the B2B sector. E-Loan, which provides retail customers with mortgage information, pricing and applications from more than 70 participating financial institutions, is an example from the B2C mortgage sector. InsWeb, which performs a similar function in insurance, is an example from the B2C insurance sector.

Additional models are also actively used in the B2B sector. As indicated above, institutional dealings may occur directly between a financial institution's storefront/vertical portal and the institutional client; these may be thought of as 'one-to-one' relationships. Alternatively, dealings may occur on the basis of 'many-to-one' or 'many-to-many' through B2B marketplaces and exchanges. Many of the trading alliances formed over the past few years, such as Fxall, BondBook, and Tradepoint (which we discuss at greater length in Chapter 4), are effectively B2B exchanges, similar to those which have been developed in other industries such as auto parts, chemicals, plastics, and so on. In a financial B2B exchange, a group of institutions comes together to provide institutional clients with access to a range of products and services (pricing, execution, news, research, and analytics that are associated with one product (such as foreign exchange), or multiple products (such as government bonds and corporate bonds)); relevant fulfillment (such as confirmation generation, settlement, valuation, and so on) can also occur through exchanges. Although segments of the institutional financial markets are very efficient—certainly when compared to other industries, which are often fragmented and inefficient—there is still room to generate new efficiencies; this is especially true in the fixed income, derivative and commodity markets. Financial B2B exchanges provide benefits to both financial product 'suppliers' and institutional customers. In particular, exchanges inject greater transparencies regarding product price, supply, availability, and substitutes. Price aberrations can be reduced or eliminated through exchanges—particularly for financial instruments such as corporate bonds and derivatives that have traditionally suffered from fragmentation, lack of fungibility or bouts of illiquidity. Though B2B exchange branding is not particularly critical, the reputations and skills of the underlying institutions participating in exchanges are of great importance. Thus, an institutional customer interested in buying a large block of high yield securities on a real-time basis is likely to want to deal with an exchange supported by reputable firms known for their expertise in the high yield market. Deep expertise, rather than extremely broad coverage, is a key driver in many emerging financial B2B exchanges.

Regardless of the specific definition or categorization of Internet-based financial service models, there are several lessons to be learned from the migration process. The web, by definition, introduces price transparency, and can generate greater price erosion, once migration occurs. Platforms must be prepared to withstand the resulting revenue and margin compression if they are to succeed. In placing financial services on the web an institution can only be successful if it is heavily focused on customer personalization and satisfaction. Since technology permits institutions to discover the needs and requirements of their institutional and retail customers, they must respond accordingly; many institutions must therefore transform from pure financial service companies to true financial marketing companies. In order for financial services ventures to be effective in migrating their services, they must also be able to translate their brand equity, product/service expertise and/or alliances/partnerships into customer reach and 'stickiness'. Online finance is effective when it reaches customers and achieves some level of 'stickiness'— keeping the broadest possible audience engaged and eager to return; that, in turn, translates into more business and revenues. Product innovation also remains critical once migration has occurred. In traditional financial services, new products are generally 'commoditized' in a short period of time, leading to replication, competition and margin compression. On the Internet this process moves more rapidly, meaning that ventures which have shifted their business online need to react even faster in the creation of new products and services. Naturally, any credible financial platform making the migration must feature real-time execution and robust, scalable architecture.

With concepts of e-commerce and e-finance sectors and models in place, we consider, in Chapter 2, the creation and migration of Internet financial services that has occurred over the past few years.

TALK OF THE TRADE

API—application program interface, a software layer which connects Internet processes and platforms with proprietary or third-party 'front-end' graphical user interfaces (GUIs).

B2B—business-to-business, Internet platforms created by institutions to serve other institutions; these may include B2B corporate storefronts, integrated portals, marketplaces, exchanges or other alliances.

B2C—business-to-consumer, Internet platforms created by institutions to serve individual consumers; these may include corporate storefronts, integrated portals or marketplaces.

Burn rate—the speed at which an Internet venture spends funds provided by venture capitalists or other investors.

Cookie—code inserted into a user's hard drive which 'recalls' specific views/preferences for individual web sites, permitting customization.

Digital certificates—a digital identification mechanism used with a public key encryption system; certificates are issued by authorities after they verify that the public key belongs to the owner.

Encryption—a security mechanism designed to keep data/information private or to verify identities; encryption is governed by certain industry standards and can be constructed based on symmetric (private key) or asymmetric (private/public key) principles.

Firewall—hardware or software placed between two networks which forces all in/out traffic to pass through a central point; this allows verification, authorization and virus checking and keeps unauthorized users or 'intruders' from accessing an internal network.

First mover—a pioneering venture that makes an early, and decisive, entry into the marketplace and builds market share and brand name recognition rapidly.

Horizontal exchange—an Internet B2B exchange which allows companies from different industries to transact in excess inventory, capital equipment, contract manufacturing, and so on.

Infomediary—an Internet platform which acts as a provider of information to individual or corporate users; it can also act as an aggregator and profiler of data.

Infrastructure providers—or enablers, software, technology and consulting companies which supply B2C and B2B platforms with customized or turn-key consulting, software, content, communications, fulfillment, security and maintenance solutions.

Intelligent agents—software programs that can be programmed to search the Internet for user-specified information, services and products.

New economy—the sector of the global economy based on 'new companies' (start-up ventures or extensions of established firms) which produce goods/services/infrastructure based on new technologies and new value chain definitions.

Non-repudiation—the process of ensuring that digital transactions are agreed and accepted by both parties; digital certificates/electronic signatures are methods of confirming that both parties have willingly participated in a transaction and eliminating the possibility of subsequent denial or refusal.

Scalability—the degree to which a business model can be readily expanded to capture a larger market share.

SSL—secured sockets layer, a security construct commonly used in Internet e-commerce and e-finance.

Transaction-enabled—a web platform structure that allows customers to buy/sell goods and services online.

Value chain—the production/service process which creates value to the end-user; in traditional corporate processes individual 'links' in the chain include resource acquisition, design, inventory management, production, fulfillment, and so on.

2
The Evolution of Digital Finance

DIGITAL FINANCE BEFORE THE WEB

'Digital finance'—a broad term we define to include any type of electronic financial service or product—has been in existence for many years, and certainly predates the commercial version of the Internet. Electronic fund transfers, automatic teller machines, debit and smart cards, point-of-sale mechanisms, home PC banking/trading services and digital securities transfers have been a part of the financial landscape for decades. For instance, consumers and businesses have been accustomed to transferring funds digitally, rather than physically, for many years, debiting and crediting accounts via computers rather than physically withdrawing and redepositing currency. The electronic fund transfer (EFT)—a mechanism used to send 'digital money' across the wire, from one account to another—has been in widespread use for decades and forms the core of electronic payments between companies, governments and other institutions. More than $5T in electronic payments occurs every day—including $2T which is transferred between banks; large value electronic payment systems and clearinghouses such as SWIFT, CHIPS, ACH, CHAPS, BACS, and others are a fundamental component of the electronic payment network. Other electronic mechanisms for obtaining cash, moving funds, and completing purchases have been in use for years and are well engrained in today's society. Consumers have actively used automatic teller machines (ATMs) since the 1980s, accessing cash, depositing funds, and transferring balances with their ATM cards. Though ATMs took more than 15 years to become firmly established in consumer banking, they are now an indispensable part of retail finance; ATMs currently account for 50% of all cash-based banking transactions and have replaced many of the functions previously handled by branch-based tellers. Debit cards, which automatically debit cash balances in checking or savings accounts when a consumer makes a purchase, have been in use in the US and Europe for many years, as have point-of-sale (POS) mechanisms. Smart cards and stored value cards (monetary and token-based), embedded with ICs and capable of holding identities, authorizations, certificates, records and monetary value, were originally developed in the late 1960s and appeared in 'workable' form in the mid-1970s. They have gradually increased in popularity since that time—particularly in Europe, where more than 100MM were in circulation at the end of the 1990s.

Phone banking and PC dial-up services have been utilized by companies and consumers for the past two decades. Through basic technology, customers have been able to manage funds and payments using phone keypads and computers. PC-based online banking started in the late 1970s and early 1980s with proprietary dial-up services. Banks such as Chemical (through Pronto), Citibank (Direct Access), Chase (Spectrum), Bank One (Applause), and others offered their customers, for a monthly fee, basic home PC banking which included balance lookup, fund transfers, personal budgeting and bill payment. Despite persistent marketing attempts, proprietary home banking services never gained a widespread following, primarily as a result of high user fees and cumbersome technical platforms (which were hampered by slow response times, complicated access procedures, and uncertain security). In the mid-1980s software companies such as Meca and Intuit/Quicken introduced third-party packages designed to link customers and banks. Local banks signed up with one of these software providers and granted customers authorization to use the platform in order to access account information, transfer funds and pay bills. Intuit's bill paying platform was reasonably successful. Customers could authorize the payment of funds to a given merchant, the Quicken package would receive the customer approval and determine, via the Intuit Services Corporation (ISC), if the merchant was part of the Federal Reserve's Automated Clearing House (ACH). If it was, ISC would effect an electronic payment through the ACH and, if not, would mail a check to the merchant (note that in 1996 Intuit sold ISC to CheckFree, one of the Internet's new leaders in electronic bill paying services). In the mid-1990s online service provider AOL partnered with Intuit on a similar basis, offering AOL's customers access to Intuit's home banking services through Quicken; customers needed only to have an account with an AOL 'partner bank' to participate. Though Intuit and others improved the home banking process, the overall market for such services remained very limited until the arrival of the Internet. Nonetheless, pre-Internet electronic home banking was an important cornerstone in the overall development of digital finance—it educated customers about financial dealings in a remote, electronic setting, away from branches and tellers.

Securities transactions—including stock and bond trading—have been driven by technology for the past few decades. It has been common practice for many years to convey stock/bond orders through brokers, who transmit the information to an exchange verbally or electronically, and then revert with appropriate debits and credits to cash and securities accounts. Virtually no one takes physical possession of securities anymore—indeed, many securities now exist only in 'immobilized' or 'dematerialized' electronic form and are transferred between seller and buyer by computer. Basic electronic tools for securities investors, including delayed quote services and portfolio tracking modules, were created by third-party vendors in the mid-1980s. In addition, certain discount brokerage companies, such as Quick and Reilly and Schwab, started offering basic PC trading capabilities through dial-up services like AOL and CompuServe in the mid- to late 1980s. Schwab introduced the 'Equalizer' electronic package in 1984 and followed with its 'StreetSmart' investment management module in the late 1980s. These services, like the home PC banking packages mentioned above, were constrained by high user charges and technological hurdles, and were never widely used.

THE CREATION OF B2C AND B2B e-FINANCE PLATFORMS

While it is clear that digital finance has existed for several decades through the mechanisms cited above, the true era of Internet-enabled e-finance commenced in the mid- to late 1990s when small and large institutions began developing new web-based platforms to deliver financial services quickly and efficiently; the process started in the B2C sector and then moved into the B2B arena. As different groups began developing business models for the banking industry (such as those mentioned in Chapter 1) several clear advantages emerged and have become key drivers up to the present time. Using the Internet, ventures can employ standard Internet protocols (TCP/IP) and meta-languages (such as XML (extensible markup language) and OFX (open financial exchange), among others) to conduct electronic business flexibly and dynamically—a feat never quite achieved through the electronic data interchange (EDI); e-finance platforms allow for common connectivity in the Internet payments system and handle small customer payments more efficiently; technology allows user-friendly GUIs and tools to be developed, helping promote interest and activity among users (which is particularly important in the retail sector); new products and services can be deployed with relative ease and speed; average user cost through the network declines as more users are added; and security, through digital certificates and firewalls, can be implemented quickly and monitored easily.

As in other 'David and Goliath' stories, it was mainly small entrepreneurs and second-tier institutions, rather than Wall Street stalwarts, who pioneered the first web-based financial services. These trailblazers included relative unknowns such as Wit Capital, Web Street Securities, Security First Network Bank, CompuBank, NetBank, and Esurance, along with traditional, if small, discount providers such as Schwab, Ameritrade, Datek, and E*Trade (some of these ventures were funded by venture capitalists, incubators and angel investors, as we shall discuss in Chapter 3). Though many of these companies have since evolved into broader, and more sophisticated, platforms, all of them commenced as corporate storefronts, promoting proprietary products and services through their own company-specific web sites.

Though discount broker Schwab began providing its customers with PC trading access as early as 1984, its service was basic and cumbersome and routed through direct dial-up rather than the Internet. True online trading got its start in a rather unlikely setting—a New York micro-brewery. In 1995 Andrew Klein, founder of the Spring Street Brewery, decided to take his company public in the first initial public offering (IPO) offered through the Internet. More than 3500 Internet-savvy investors purchased shares in the fledgling company (in a $1.6MM offering), marking the first time securities had actually been sold via the web. Concerned about this activity, and the potential precedent it might establish, the Securities and Exchange Commission (SEC) investigated both the initial offering and the ongoing secondary trading; while the investigation was underway, Klein voluntarily suspended secondary trading in the brewery shares—which took place through an Internet bulletin board known as Wit-trade. After the SEC issued a no-action letter sanctioning the transaction, buying and selling resumed—true Internet-based trading had become a reality. Wit-trade itself eventually evolved into an Internet finance group known as Wit Capital, which today features an online investment bank, Wit Soundview (with its E*Offering unit specializing in private placements and IPOs).

Several other ventures were created following the SEC's decision. Web Street Securities, a pure play platform—that is, one which exists only in a computerized state, with no traditional 'brick and mortar' offices or infrastructure—commenced its operations in 1996 by offering customers a full-service information and execution platform. Several discount brokers—including E*Trade, Schwab, Ameritrade and Datek—altered their existing discount brokerage operations in the same year and migrated to the Internet. E*Trade, a discount broker founded in 1992, has always existed as an electronic platform. Between 1992 and 1996 E*Trade offered quote and trading services to investors through AOL and CompuServe. It launched its own web-based service in 1996 and, within just a few months, had shifted 40% of its business onto the Internet. By early 2000, E*Trade featured 2.6MM customer accounts and was executing more than 200,000 trades per day, making it one of the leading online traders. (In 2000 E*Trade also developed an alliance with Wit Capital, giving E*Trade customers access to Wit's IPOs and research.)

Given its long background in PC-based trading and discount services, Schwab was quick to roll out its own web-based platform in 1996 and established a leadership position in the marketplace in short order. Between 1996 and 1999 Schwab dominated the world of online trading—offering innovative online services and competitive pricing while full service brokers, such as Merrill Lynch, Morgan Stanley Dean Witter, and Paine Webber, remained on the sidelines. By 2000 Schwab boasted 3.5MM active online accounts (equal to 50% of its total client base) and was executing nearly 250,000 trades per day. Ameritrade, which started in 1975 as discount broker Accutrade, was a pioneer in offering automated brokerage services. In 1988, for instance, it introduced touch tone telephone trading and in 1995 it acquired K.Aufhauser, a brokerage firm offering PC-based trading. In 1996 Ameritrade launched its eBroker Internet brokerage and, in 1997, combined the eBroker and Aufhauser services under a new Ameritrade platform and brand name; it remains one of the market leaders in online trading. Wall Street investment bank Donaldson Lufkin and Jenrette (DLJ, now part of Credit Suisse First Boston (CSFB)) was another early online trading pioneer—it was, in fact, the only major Wall Street house to make an early entry into the market. DLJ started investigating online trading in the late 1980s and soon thereafter created basic non-Internet technology to allow investors to execute trades online; by 1992 the company was handling about 400 trades per day through its dial-up service. As web technology improved, DLJ migrated its platform to the Internet and set up a new subsidiary, DLJ Direct, to market the new service. By the start of 2000, DLJ Direct had become a reasonably active online trading firm, executing more than 40,000 trades per day. Discount brokers were particularly successful in adapting to the Internet. Most had embraced technology and new forms of customer access (via phone and PC) during the 1980s, so the migration to an Internet environment was, if not second nature, manageable. In addition, most had a long history of offering competitive pricing and managing costs—that is the essence of the discount brokerage model. Offering the same type of pricing in a low-cost Internet environment meant they did not have to alter their pricing models radically. The same was not, of course, true for full service brokers. In the international sector, platforms such as ConSors (Germany), Direct Anlage (Germany) and Fimat (France) were early entrants in their corresponding domestic markets, helping pave the way for other local online trading ventures.

The first true Internet bank was Security First Network Bank (SFNB), created in Atlanta in 1995. SFNB started out as First Federal Savings Bank of Pineville, the main savings bank of a financial holding company known as Cardinal Bancshares. In 1995 Cardinal requested approval from the Office of Thrift Supervision to change First Federal's business focus from that of a savings institution to a pure play electronic bank. Cardinal received approval in mid-1995, changed the bank's name to SFNB and commenced operations by offering web-based balance lookup, unlimited third-party bill paying, funds transfers, loans, and Federal Deposit Insurance Corporation (FDIC) insured deposits. Though SFNB was a pioneer in bringing retail banking to the web, it opted to sell itself to the Royal Bank Financial Group of Canada in 1998; nevertheless, it continues to operate as a virtual bank with independent branding. In addition to creating the first web bank platform, SFNB's management was instrumental in creating one of the first dedicated e-finance infrastructure companies. Recognizing that the underlying technological software it had developed for its own web operations could be useful to other banks interested in migrating to the Internet, SFNB's management combined its proprietary technology solutions, along with the services of two companies that it had acquired (Five Paces and SecureWare), into a new company called Security First Technologies (S1). S1 quickly became a leading infrastructure provider, offering financial institutions an Internet turnkey product known as Virtual Bank Manager (which provides software for traditional banking transactions, bill payment, digital imaging and accounting/reporting). By the end of 1996 S1 had licensed its product to 13 major financial institutions and continued expanding its client list through the end of the decade—by 2000 it featured 800 banking clients, including more than 50 of the top 100 global banks. CompuBank, based in Houston, was another early pure play pioneer. Like SFNB, it started operations by offering a broad range of traditional banking services, including bank account balances and transfers, bill payment, FDIC deposits, loans, and so on; unlike SFNB, CompuBank was the first virtual bank with a national charter (meaning it is regulated by the Office of the Comptroller of the Currency rather than the Office of Thrift Supervision). NetBank, yet another pure play, emerged on the scene in 1996 under the name of Atlanta Internet Bank—after several years of profitable operations it went public as NetBank in 2000. First Internet Bank of Indiana, another virtual bank, joined the fray in 1997 when it received its state charter; it became operational in 1998 after gaining FDIC approval. In the international sector, platforms such as Egg (UK), Advance Bank and DB24 (Germany), SE Banken (Sweden), and e-cortal (France) were e-banking pioneers, introducing interactive corporate storefronts between 1996 and 1998. In addition to storefront-based hybrid and pure play banking institutions, a number of banking marketplace platforms came into existence during the mid- to late 1990s to help unify and consolidate aspects of the banking process. Though not strictly providers of credit or other financial services, these platforms, which we discuss at greater length in Chapter 5, effectively link customers to one of several institutions providing underlying financial services. For example, loan centers such as Money.net, Loanshop, Lendnetwork, and E-Loan allow users to input specific parameters related to banking products they are interested in accessing and provide output in the form of comparative pricing and analysis across a range of institutions and products. In some instances they also process online applications on behalf of selected institutions and help monitor and close transactions. In this sense they act as conduits between users and suppliers. Specific marketplaces oriented towards credit cards, leases, automobile loans, and mortgages were a relatively early component of the web-based financial sector.

Boston asset manager Liberty Financial was an early adopter of the Internet and a pioneer in offering web-based wealth management services. In 1995 the firm created its first informational storefront site, and shortly thereafter realized it could harness considerable marketing and distribution power through the Internet. Accordingly, it developed the WebSaver Annuity platform and started marketing annuities directly to customers through the network. Through WebSaver, customers were able to purchase annuity policies online and, though they still had to mail in signed policies and payments, the platform created a faster, more efficient and cheaper process for both parties. Liberty subsequently introduced other wealth management tools and services through the web, and is an active participant in B2C services to the present time. MPower, a California-based investment management platform, was another early participant in the online wealth management arena, introducing interactive web-based wealth management capabilities as early as 1995.

Though insurance is still a relatively small part of web financial activities it is considered one of the most promising areas of growth; pioneering platforms such as Esurance have helped redefine aspects of the industry. Esurance was created in 1998 by industry professionals drawn from some of the world's leading insurance companies, including AXA, State Farm and Fireman's Fund. The company started business by offering customers access to instant online auto insurance quotes from its own product line (backed by Argonaut Group and General Reinsurance) as well as that of its competitors; Esurance also provided online policy purchase capabilities for those choosing to pay with credit cards. Broader online insurance marketplaces, including InsWeb, QuickenInsurance and Intelliquote, soon followed, offering customers quotes and coverage across the entire spectrum of insurance products (including auto, term life, homeowners, renters and health).

Earlier we noted that some pioneering ventures had the vision to change their internal structures and processes to take advantage of the new e-commerce environment and propel their businesses forward; the platforms cited above certainly fall into that category. In addition, a very select few actually reshaped, or transformed, industry boundaries through their actions and activities; some, like E*Trade, Wit Capital, Schwab and SFNB, can rightly claim to be 'industry transformers' within the B2C sector. While these pioneering ventures have succeeded in redefining key aspects of e-finance, the same has not necessarily been true of established institutions. With very few exceptions, the world's largest financial institutions failed to act as first movers in web-based finance and delayed their offerings until others had built considerable market shares and brand identification. Certain institutions did not perceive the potential opportunities offered by the web, an error that was hardly unique to the banking industry. During the earliest days of the web it was difficult for many businesses to comprehend what the web could really offer—here was a new, and rapidly changing, medium with unanswered questions/challenges and uncertain potential. Some institutions may have understood the possible economic implications of the web, but felt secure and satisfied with the very profitable 'status quo'—especially the very robust revenue streams created by 'annuity-like' businesses and prolonged bull markets. Perhaps they were too conservative and entrenched in traditional ways of doing business to make necessary changes, or did not want to introduce a competing 'in-house' business which might cannibalize an existing, and profitable, business. In certain instances they may have recognized the potential of the web but underestimated the speed at which dynamic new competitors would make inroads. Still others may have perceived the web as all too much 'hype'—an unsustainable mechanism that would soon pass out of favor. Maybe they were unwilling to tamper with legacy technology which had already proven itself stable and secure. For banks, in particular, there was very little perceived incentive in migrating existing customers to online services when the 'traditional' model had worked perfectly well over the years—and where the lack of incremental technology-driven services (e.g. balance information, fund transfers and bill paying) was unlikely to drive customers, en masse, to others on the web.

Regardless of the underlying reasons, many of the industry's largest players found themselves chasing the upstarts during the late 1990s. Once it became clear that Internet-based commerce was a powerful force that was here to stay, the philosophy of major players changed quickly. Most institutions moved from denying the need to have an Internet presence, to using the Internet as a reactive/information mechanism, to employing it as an aggressive, transaction-enabled business-gathering tool. Most came to recognize the need to create platforms that would minimize the chance of having their services 'cherry picked' by younger start-ups—while start-ups were unlikely to be able to offer all dimensions of business via the web in a short time frame, there was little preventing them from commanding meaningful shares in market niches, such as online trading, electronic bill payments, or research aggregation. Established institutions also came to realize that the Internet allowed them to create a new 'high tech' image, offer new products/services, and enlarge reach/presence without having to spend additional capital on physical expansion.

Full service brokers such as Merrill Lynch and Morgan Stanley Dean Witter hurriedly redefined their business models and worked feverishly to provide customers with services that more Internet-aggressive firms such as Wit Capital, E*Trade, Schwab, Web Street Securities and Ameritrade were supplying. Merrill Lynch had to overcome the additional 'public relations hurdle' it created when it declared in late 1998 that (sic) '[t]he do-it-yourself model of investing, centered on Internet trading, should be considered as a serious threat to Americans' financial lives'. It is particularly ironic that large Wall Street securities firms—which pride themselves on being adept, dynamic and responsive as, in fact, they are—were unable to adapt to the new business paradigm with the same agility. Most of the major firms did not develop true online capabilities until one, two or even three years after the 'first wave'. For example, Merrill Lynch launched its online trading service in mid-1999, Salomon Smith Barney and Prudential in late 1999. Morgan Stanley Dean Witter leveraged Discover's Broker Direct platform developed in late 1997 but did not rebrand or refine it until 1999. Paine Webber rolled out its PW Edge platform with research, quotes and portfolio management in 1997, but did not add online trading capabilities until the following year. At most major investment banks Internet-based institutional offerings, directed at institutional customers rather than retail clients, did not feature in daily operations until 1999 or 2000. The largest commercial banking institutions, such as Citibank, Bank One and Chase, massively overhauled their web offerings in order to address the competitive pressure generated by new banking entrants; second-tier and regional banks, which had never offered home PC banking services, were forced to develop web strategies from scratch. As with the major securities firms, most commercial banks did not feature B2B-focused web platforms until the late 1990s. Similar trends and behaviors were also evident in the international banking and securities sectors.

Only in certain instances were the largest players true leaders. For example, Bank of America and Wells Fargo had provided customers with PC-based electronic banking for several years, and were able to quickly adapt their services to fit the Internet-based model. Wells Fargo was particularly aggressive, introducing its first informational web site in 1996 and offering customers account transfer and bill payment services shortly thereafter. As indicated above, securities firm DLJ introduced its DLJ Direct brokerage services ahead of other large Wall Street players. In the insurance sector, General Electric (GE) and American International Group (AIG) kept pace with new technologies and rolled out Internet services in relatively short order. In the main, however, it was new ventures or niche players that broke the most significant ground and caused established institutions to change their strategies. Although the largest financial institutions of the world may have been slow to react to the possibilities of the web, most—as indicated above—have since realigned their strategies and are using their considerable financial muscle, relationships and reach to challenge the upstarts. The ability of firms like Merrill Lynch, Fidelity, Morgan Stanley Dean Witter, Chase, Barclays, Deutsche Bank, and others to provide compelling platforms at competitive prices means the smallest Internet firms have already come under pressure. Though it is too early to predict which platforms will emerge as long-term market leaders, it is clear that the competitive environment has become very intense.

The pure play B2C financial services model, which formed part of the 'first wave' of pioneering digital finance platforms, is a concept that is still being tested. For certain types of financial services a pure play model appears logical; this is particularly true for online trading and online financial information/ analytic tools. Such models can be cost-effective, efficient, secure and, to the extent customers do not need to rely on physical interaction with tellers, administrators, and customer service representatives, a suitable delivery mechanism. Pure plays have the advantage of being able to create platforms from scratch, without having to worry about the integration of legacy systems and well-established processes/procedures; when aspects of a pure play's infrastructure can be handled more efficiently by third-party experts, outsourcing agreements can be arranged and implemented quickly. Once operational, pure plays tend to function more cost-effectively by avoiding the corporate overheads normally associated with 'brick and mortar' operations (though fixed start-up costs can still be significant). However, in certain instances the lack of 'bricks and mortar' means that external alliances are required to supply services that cannot be provided without a physical presence—such as access to cash or 'face-to-face' customer assistance. In addition, lack of physical presence implies, with very few exceptions, less brand name recognition among potential customers. To lure customers to a pure play web platform— in order to build up brand recognition, service usage and overall 'trust'—extra incentives (such as lower fees on transactions, free execution, and higher yields on deposits) may be required. Certain online trading pure plays have been successful in 'making a mark' more rapidly than their banking counterparts—for example, sites such as Web Street Securities and E*Trade are among the most popular on the Internet. Online trading is a more dynamic and interactive experience than online banking and, while it requires customer support, does not necessarily need to grant customers immediate access to cash. Online banks need to be able to accept and deliver cash in some form and must therefore enter into an extra step by forming an alliance with an ATM or bank network, adding to the cost of the model. Though pure play banks have to enter into ATM alliances in order to properly serve customers, they are still able to save on the costs normally associated with maintaining a physical presence (again, after they have gained enough accounts to cover the fixed start-up costs). Traditional branch networks cost an average of 3.5% of assets to operate; pure play banks need to pay only 1/3 of that amount in order to provide the relevant administrative support found in branches. This means they can use the differential to pay more interest on their certificates of deposit (CDs) or lower the cost of their loans, and reinvest the balance in interest-bearing instruments to generate incremental revenues; once established, this can be a successful and profitable strategy. A hybrid structure, which includes an established institution's traditional activities as well as its Internet platform, needs to balance traditional business conducted through 'brick and mortar' operations with new online strategies. If customers migrate more business to a hybrid's web platform (which often generates lower revenues as part of the customer cost savings value proposition), but the hybrid does not reduce its 'brick and mortar' costs, it cannibalizes business and erodes its revenue and profit margins. Hybrids must also contend with legacy system integration in order to ensure smooth and accurate communication between established technology and the web portal. This type of integration can be very expensive, particularly for large financial institutions. For example, Citibank reportedly spent $500MM integrating its legacy data processing with its web platform, while Bank of America invested $1B in a similar exercise. The debate on the merits of pure plays (low cost, efficient service providers) and hybrids ('best of both worlds' providers) is expected to continue for some time.

While the B2C e-finance sector was first out of the block and has received most of the popular press coverage, the B2B e-finance sector represents a far larger and deeper market. With the exception of a handful of markets and products (such as equity trading through electronic communication networks (ECNs)), most Internet-related B2B efforts commenced in the very late 1990s; very little development occurred during the mid-1990s when the B2C sector was in the midst of its migration. As we shall note in Chapter 4, initiatives related to online bond, currency, commodity and derivative trading, and online corporate/investment banking services, are a recent phenomenon; the corporate B2B storefront platforms of new and established companies, B2B exchanges, and B2B marketplaces appeared several years after the first B2C ventures commenced operations. Despite the late start, B2B e-finance is now a growing source of activity for providers and users. Most global financial institutions are well represented in transaction-enabled B2B ventures through internally developed efforts, alliances, partnerships and/or investments. Indeed, the largest players have moved aggressively to participate in a range of ventures, seeking to 'hedge' their bets against future structural changes in the global marketplace.

Of course, certain aspects of the financial markets have traded in electronic form, if not yet in Internet form, for the better part of one to two decades. Consider, for instance, the global foreign exchange (FX) market. This market, which is dominated by interbank players and large corporate customers, turns over $1.5T on a daily basis. Since there is no central exchange for currency trading the market has evolved from a pure over-the-counter telephonic forum to one heavily reliant on connected electronic platforms supplied by vendors such as Reuters and EBS. Though corporate customers continued to use telephones even after the advent of these systems, most interbank players quickly gravitated to the electronic environment, providing bids/offers to one another and dealing directly on-screen. The earliest FX trading platforms can thus be considered the non-Internet equivalent of B2B exchanges. With the arrival of the Internet, these very platforms are now changing. As indicated later in the text various online FX initiatives, including FX Connect, Fxall, Currenex and Atriax, among others, promise to supplement, and perhaps ultimately replace, the Reuters and EBS platforms so popular in the 1980s and 1990s.

In addition to FX, certain equity and futures markets have featured electronic trading for many years. For instance, the National Association of Securities Dealers Automated Quotes (NASDAQ) market has existed as an electronic market since its creation in 1971 while others, such as the Tokyo Stock Exchange (TSE) and the London Stock Exchange (LSE), migrated from physical open-outcry trading forums to electronic trading forums during the 1980s and 1990s. Instinet, a forerunner of today's ECNs (which provide investors with direct equity market access for certain types of securities orders), commenced its operations in the late 1960s. As technology allowed Instinet to migrate from phone-driven agency execution to computerized fulfillment it refined its business focus accordingly. Instinet is, today, the world's largest ECN, routinely commanding a 10–17% share of NASDAQ's trading volume. In the futures arena, various exchanges have also migrated from physical to electronic forums over the past few years; for example, the London International Financial Futures Exchange (LIFFE) became a pure screen-driven marketplace several years ago; Marche a Terme International de France (MATIF), the French futures exchange now operating as part of Euronext, also made a conversion from physical to electronic trading during the 1990s.

Unlike B2C platforms, the structure of B2B platforms tends to draw less focus. Since many aspects of institutional finance already occur electronically (through electronic transfers of cash and securities, for instance) the need for specific infrastructure to support cash access and customer service is simply not an issue. If an investment fund is buying $10MM worth of corporate bonds online, it is primarily interested in ensuring it receives best price execution and processing support, and less concerned about whether the venture supplying the service has a 'brick and mortar' presence.

DEVELOPMENT OF e-FINANCE INFRASTRUCTURE SOLUTIONS

In addition to the 'public face' of web-based financial services there is an underlying group of infrastructure companies that help new and established companies develop the architecture and tools needed to create, port and support web products and services. Though infrastructure providers do not typically face the public directly, they are critical for those choosing to outsource/purchase the technical components needed for Internet business. There is, as one might imagine, a great deal of technological effort involved in creating, maintaining and enhancing web platforms. Many aspects of the underlying technology infrastructure needed to convey e-finance solutions are complex; 21st century web platforms must feature multitier environments, extreme flexibility, rapid scalability and seamless customer and supplier integration. The ability to alter dimensions of technology quickly is vital in an era where speed and change are part of the operating environment; turnkey infrastructure solutions can generally be implemented in a matter of weeks, while customized solutions can often be rolled out in several months.

Even the simplest informational models require a certain amount of technical planning and resources. Platforms with any dimension of interactivity, or those with full product/service offerings requiring security, real-time information, and exchange access, need considerably more technological and architectural sophistication. For established institutions, the integration of product-centric front-office applications and mainframe-based accounting and back-office systems with consolidated front-end web-based platforms is an enormous undertaking. This is especially true in the commercial banking world, which has historically been dependent on mainframe technology to manage large volumes of data, batch processes and branch information. Integration often extends beyond internal legacy systems to include links between a venture's 'sever farms' (the network access platform) and the legacy mainframes of clearing firms and other third-party processing agents. Infrastructure solutions are focused on front-end delivery mechanisms (including web platforms), APIs and back-end processing. APIs, in particular, are powerful mechanisms which allow proprietary or third-party front-ends to link with internal or external middle- or back-end processes; this enhances overall flexibility.

As a result of these complexities, many ventures have come to rely on specialist infrastructure companies capable of providing requisite technical assistance. Many of these providers were created early in the cycle (from the mid- to the late 1990s) and were thus able to provide new and established banks, securities firms, insurers and others with quick solutions needed to deliver Internet-based services to their customers—saving time, resources, and expenses, and avoiding 'ground up' reinvention. e-Finance infrastructure services include front-end Internet banking software, credit card and payment processing applications, bank transaction security, web design/media packages, web hosting and analytic solutions. Institutions such as S1 (the SFNB spin-off described earlier, focused on front-end banking applications), Sanchez (front- to back-end e-banking applications), Digital Insight (front-end banking applications, content aggregation and web services/hosting), TradingLinx (straight-through processing), CashEdge (aggregation infrastructure), ClearCommerce (online order processing), Neuvis (B2B and exchange systems architecture), BankPass (aggregation and security), Javelin Technology (exchange infrastructure), Business Logic (mixed media solutions), Derivion (electronic payment solutions), Channelpoint (insurance marketplace architecture), Ilumen (news/price collation and integration), Mutant Technology (trading application servers and solutions), and Financial Fusion (online product delivery and capital markets trading solutions), among many others, have implemented infrastructure solutions for a range of e-banking and e-trading platforms over the past few years—and have thus emerged as a vital link in the e-finance migration. Though successful e-finance infrastructure providers are now very prevalent in the industry, not every venture has triumphed. For instance, in 1996 IBM and 18 large banks formed Integrion Financial Network to provide online banking build-outs for the web. Integrion was seen as a credible vehicle to challenge solutions being developed by firms such as Intuit and Microsoft, but was hampered by internal disputes and missed deadlines; the venture folded in 2000 after failing to gain a critical mass of business.

Certain application service providers (ASPs) are included in the infrastructure category, as they supply services directly to the public but also provide turnkey or customized solutions that can be accessed by any financial venture. For instance, CheckFree's online bill payment and presentment solution is used by many top online banking platforms—the application constitutes a key component of web infrastructure; the same is true of Bottomline Technology/ Checkpoint, which acts in a similar capacity. Both ventures also offer the same payment services directly to their own customers. Espeed, which creates B2B exchange architecture and front-to-back processing for third parties, also acts as an ASP by providing trading services directly to end-customers. It is important to note that much of the infrastructural work that has been developed over the past few years has been directed at front- and middle-office functionality. Since legacy systems are still handling many aspects of the back-office, including trade capture and processing, accounting, financial reporting, transaction management, operational control, and so on, web-based solutions have not been a primary area of focus. As institutions begin dismantling or replacing components of their legacy processes, true front-to-back web solutions will become a more important dimension of overall infrastructure business.

It is reasonable to assume that, without the contributions of e-finance infrastructure providers, the creation and migration of financial products and services onto the web would have been slowed considerably. These companies provided—and, indeed, continue to provide—new and established ventures with rapid solutions, allowing platforms to be converted from informational offerings of limited use and appeal, to transaction-enabled platforms capable of attracting clients and generating new revenues. They have thus been central, if often invisible, participants in the e-finance migration process.

SELECTING e-FINANCE STRUCTURES

The expanding power of the Internet, increasing competition, declining barriers to entry, and changing regulations mean that financial services companies are redefining themselves. The choice of how to approach a web-based business has been, and continues to be, extremely challenging for both new ventures and established companies. For the latter group, in particular, a central issue relates to the development of new Internet platforms that work in tandem with already-established businesses. Institutions must avoid channel conflict, the formal term given to intracompany competition for clients. In some instances cannibalization, though temporarily destructive, can actually be a useful experience—institutions that are willing to challenge their own value chain and destroy part of it by introducing a 'competing platform' are effectively preparing themselves for competition in a new commercial environment. Most major financial institutions entering the market attempt to cope with channel conflict by considering alternate structures which can help direct or segregate business flows. The primary structures that can be employed include an independent platform (which is also applicable, of course, to new start-ups), a hybrid platform, a third-party alliance, or a 'white label' venture. Optimal structures are often derived from the specific business model under consideration—such as the corporate storefront, marketplace, or vertical portal models described in Chapter 1; this applies equally in B2C and B2B.

Financial institutions opting for an independent strategy often seek to separate their traditional and Internet services by creating a pure play. This type of strategy can be followed when an institution perceives little overlap between the two businesses and wants to introduce a separate brand to distinguish the new service; this can allow a firm to access a new segment of the client base by creating a platform with a 'younger', more technologically-oriented, image. For instance, Fidelity Investments, the US investment manager, segregated its online trading service from its traditional investment management operations and renamed it PowerStreet, in an effort to project a new and distinct image for the business. An institution may also follow this approach if it wants to minimize channel conflict. By offering products and services under an entirely different name and brand (perhaps a subset of those normally available to traditional customers), it may be able to guide and direct business flows more precisely and avoid cannibalizing existing business. One example of this structure is apparent through Wingspanbank, the Internet-only bank that operates quite independently of its parent, Bank One (which has a web-banking platform of its own). Services are appropriately segregated in order to minimize channel conflict, and management of Wingspanbank is solely responsible for operating the platform. In order to access cash Wingspanbank's customers are permitted to use Bank One's ATMs—but they cannot use any of its branch services. Bank One's customers can, likewise, only use Wingspanbank's electronic bill paying facilities—and even then must pay a fee. These branding differences and product/service restrictions help guide and target business flows and minimize chances for cannibalization. Other examples of the independent web strategy abound, and include ventures such as Cahoot (the independent web platform of Abbey National), Smile (part of the Co-op UK group), DB24 (Deutsche Bank's phone and Internet platform), Advance Bank (Dresdner Bank's pure play platform), First Direct (HSBC's UK web bank), UnoFirst (Banco Santander CH's pure play venture), and e-cortal (BNP Paribas' pure play bank), among others. The independent, or pure play, strategy has already gained a following around the world.

Through a hybrid structure an established institution offers Internet services under its existing brand name. This has the benefit of allowing a firm to utilize an established, and presumably high quality, image/brand to market services in a new fashion. Since brand equity and name recognition are extremely important in a crowded Internet world, leveraging an existing name provides instant recognition (and, hopefully, traffic) and allows marketing costs to be curtailed. The potential downside is, of course, channel conflict. By allowing customers to execute transactions and services through the web, an institution might impact its ability to offer customers its traditional services—some of which may be premium services with higher margins. While established firms might be keen to implement an Internet strategy which gives existing clients access to new tools and services—typically at a much lower cost—they risk losing clients to their new internal, and competing, platform; this can result in a meaningful decline in revenues. Managing channel conflict means managing the business model. Balancing these seemingly conflicting strategies requires considerable effort and attention, and must be viewed with a longer-term eye. It may make sense, for instance, to sacrifice short-term revenues in exchange for providing clients with a comprehensive suite of services, incorporating both new technologies and established processes/products. Ultimately, customer satisfaction will drive the long-term prosperity of an organization. Despite the potential channel conflicts, many large financial institutions have opted for the hybrid strategy. For example, Merrill Lynch, Citibank, Bank of America, Morgan Stanley Dean Witter, Credit Suisse, Lloyds TSB, Banamex and others are all active in the hybrid sector; most follow this approach for their B2C and B2B offerings.

For institutions unwilling, or unable, to bear the risk of running a new Internet platform of their own, or those interested in tapping new, and perhaps unfamiliar, market/client segments, alliance strategies emerge as viable alternatives. One such strategy is for a financial institution to team up with one or more parties to create and offer products/services jointly. This approach 'spreads' the potential risk among several institutions and presents less of a direct threat to established services. It may also serve to broaden the potential client base by developing access to clients not previously served by any of the participating institutions. One prominent example of this approach appeared in early 2000 when Merrill Lynch teamed up with HSBC to create a new, separately branded, online bank directed at a range of medium and high net worth clients located outside the US. Both institutions contributed financial and human resources, along with their well-recognized brand names, to the venture in order to develop a market that neither institution had ever exploited on its own. Other examples of alliances include NetBank's partnership with Fidelity, CompuBank's alliance with GE, E*Trade's partnership with Ernst and Young, and Web Street Securities' global alliances with ConSors, SHK Securities and CB Capitales. Even non-financial companies have created alliances of their own; for instance Intuit, with its Quicken, QuickBooks and Turbotax products, has created partnerships with both AOL and Checkfree to provide its financial solutions to a broader base of customers.

Another type of alliance strategy occurs through so-called 'white labeling'. Under this strategy one institution acts as a 'silent partner', providing relevant resources to an Internet financial services platform that carries its own identity and labeling; this allows the creation of a fresh image/brand and helps access a new, and sometimes non-traditional, client base. Since the two partners are often from different industries, the chances of experiencing channel conflict are remote. White labeling often occurs when non-financial institutions want to enter the financial arena by offering web services—it has been used to particularly good effect in the UK. For instance, in 1998 insurance company Prudential launched a white label banking service known as Egg. Though Egg commenced as a phone deposit mechanism, it gained more than 1MM customers in very short order and ultimately discontinued phone operations in favor of a full web platform; Egg now offers its customers a full range of loans, mortgages and mutual funds. Various bank/retail white label arrangements also exist, including ventures operated by Bank of Scotland/ Sainsbury and Royal Bank of Scotland/Tesco, among others.

BARRIERS TO ENTRY

As one might expect, the competitive landscape in the web-based financial arena is extremely dynamic—business models succeed or fail, companies redefine their strategies, and players move in and out of the industry. Changes in regulations also help shape the competitive landscape. The deregulation of the London stock market in 1986 (eliminating fixed commissions and dissolving the distinction between brokers and jobbers (dealers)), the passage of the Riegle–Neal Act in 1994 (allowing US banks to serve customers across state lines), the deregulation of the Tokyo stock market in the 1990s (eliminating fixed commissions and allowing the creation of discount brokers), the crumbling of the Glass–Steagall Act in the late 1990s (allowing investment and commercial banks to participate in each other's markets), along with broader financial deregulation measures taking place in other countries around the world, has led to greater 'blurring' within the traditional and e-finance environments.

Competition in e-finance is expected to accelerate over the coming years as deregulation continues to make its way around the world and new entrants enter particular areas of the market, develop new niches/product expertise or expand into new countries. Competition will also be influenced by the relative barriers surrounding the sector. The finance industry has historically been protected by—or plagued by, depending on one's perspective—high barriers to entry. In particular, those attempting to enter the financial markets, and succeed, have had to feature strong management, deep knowledge of risk, adequate financial resources, responsive customer service, robust technological infrastructure, and well-established brand name/franchise. As financial services have gravitated to the Internet some of these barriers to entry have already been eroded; this is having a profound impact on the nature of the business and the structure/composition of service providers entering the marketplace.

A strong management team is a critical requirement for every financial venture and, while recruiting talent is always a challenge, many Internet e-finance ventures have been able to lure top bankers and technologists from established institutions—this gives them an all-important management foundation. Many seasoned banking and technology professionals have opted to move to start-ups, seeking a chance to participate in an entrepreneurial, rather than traditional corporate, venture (and being tempted, perhaps, by the potential upside offered by an IPO). For established institutions seeking to develop an Internet presence the task has been relatively easy—many large firms, such as Chase, JP Morgan, Merrill Lynch, Deutsche Bank, Dresdner Bank, HSBC, Citibank, Bank of America, First Union, and others, have 'seconded' top executives to their new Internet ventures. Internet ventures that operate as risk-taking entities, or that choose not to mitigate such risks by flowing business through clearinghouses and other trust providers, tend to recruit credit and risk officers from established firms; while not a perfect substitute for having a 'home grown' risk culture, it is a workable solution in a dynamic environment. Management, human resource, and risk personnel barriers are thus surmountable.

If an Internet start-up is acting as agent, rather than principal, in the provision of risk-based financial products, a large risk capital base is not a prerequisite and presents no particular barrier. Indeed, many web firms feature only modest capital bases (in comparison with traditional firms), implying that risk-taking capabilities are limited. Only in instances where risk-taking occurs is a sufficient pool of dedicated capital an operating requirement. Pure plays or start-ups operating as risk-taking entities must pay special attention to capital required to support the entire spectrum of risks; insufficient capital can still act as a business inhibitor, if not an outright barrier to entry. Risk, broadly speaking, may take the form of credit risk from loans or derivatives executed with other entities, interest rate risk and currency risk from deposits, loans and securities investments, compliance risk from disclosures to customers, and process/transaction risk from service failures resulting from operational or technical problems. For risk-taking ventures, capital resources must be supplemented by rigorous internal control mechanisms—this, at a minimum, must include independent risk management oversight, regular audits, and control reviews of the platform's security, disaster recovery, privacy, reliability and scalability. In addition to needing capital to support potential risk-taking, sufficient financial resources are required to fund tactical and strategic operations. Financial resources devoted to the rollout and management of an Internet platform must be readily accessible and sufficiently plentiful to ensure smooth operations. This can present a barrier for certain new ventures that are attempting to secure initial rounds of funding through venture capitalists, angel investors or other sources; raising funds, as we shall discuss in Chapter 3, can be challenging without the right business model and management leadership. It can also present a challenge for ventures that have not yet achieved profitability—it becomes difficult to spend continuously without ultimately generating profits. While established financial institutions with 'deep pockets' can theoretically afford to keep funding an Internet venture for an almost indefinite period of time, the same is not true for smaller, independent entities answerable to venture capitalists or other investors.

The ability to service customers quickly and securely has been the backbone of traditional financial services for decades. Though simple in concept, this dimension is actually complex in practice. Financial ventures must have in place a robust network of customer service agents/facilities which can access customer information quickly, respond on a timely basis, and develop solutions and answers which solve problems. This barrier is, in fact, surmountable by Internet ventures—the management of information and the ability to resolve customer problems in a secure and rapid fashion are major benefits of dealing through a web-based system. To the extent an Internet venture has committed resources to customer service and architected its technology to fulfill that goal, this can actually be an opportunity rather than a hurdle. Pure play Internet ventures must still overcome the customer service barrier related to the provision of physical services normally available through 'brick and mortar' operations—such as dispensing cash or providing 'face-to-face' consultation and advice. For ventures focused on retail banking services the ability to supply customers with ATM or teller access is critical, and most often has to be accomplished through alliances or third-party deals.

The financial sector has traditionally been very reliant on technology and technical infrastructure to handle many aspects of business, including trading, reporting, processing, and control; indeed, the industry devotes considerable financial resources to the development, or purchase, of relevant platforms and solutions. This has historically been a barrier to entry—institutions requiring speed, scope and scale have had to invest large amounts of money (and often face time delays) in order to implement reasonable technical solutions. With the advent of the web, this barrier is more easily managed. Firms are able to use the Internet and its associated technologies to adapt their architecture to deliver e-finance services; alternatively, they can completely or partially outsource the process to infrastructure providers and achieve the same goals. As a result, even small ventures with limited resources are able to overcome the technological barrier that has long existed in the sector.

With these traditional barriers to entry—management, risk, financial resources, customer services, technology—appearing surmountable (particularly once initial rounds of financing have been obtained), the major focus remains on intangibles such as brand name, image and 'trust'—a category we refer to collectively as brand equity. The establishment of recognized and respected brand equity typically comes from years, and often decades, of strong customer service, leading-edge innovation, steadfast management and sound financial performance. To create the same brand equity on the Internet, in a short time frame, is not an easy task. Some ventures have attempted to prove otherwise by creating a brand, marketing the brand in a public manner to attract customers, and then trying to create a business around that brand—most, if not all, have failed through this approach. Customers need to gain experience with a venture, its products, services and support mechanism, before granting it the same level of credibility normally given to a long-established institution. Pure plays, in particular, face a barrier in establishing confidence and trust. In the financial world many customers still take comfort in seeing and visiting a physical site such as a branch office. Placing one's assets with an institution requires, for many, identification with a physical presence; this helps build confidence and trust. Strictly 'virtual' operations must overcome the barrier by convincing customers that, despite the lack of a physical presence, their assets are secure; this remains a barrier to entry—though one which is surmountable, as evidenced by the gradually growing number of web-only financial institutions. 'Trust' develops as customers become more comfortable with the security and reliability of the web, and is aided by the oversight provided by regulators. In the world of the Internet, where thousands of new ventures have been created in a short time frame, site recognition is still a major hurdle. A relatively small number of new financial ventures have established brand names that customers and other market players easily recognize—among them are Web Street Securities, E*Trade, Wingspanbank, Advance Bank, e-cortal, ConSors, Egg, Wit Capital, Island, and Archipelago. For established institutions the task is somewhat easier, but still not guaranteed to work. For instance, Citi F/I, Citibank's second Internet venture, never established the right branding or strategy and was eventually folded into the bank's Direct Access platform—which was then updated and rebranded under the Citibank Online moniker. Marketing and advertising through the Internet and traditional media channels are very important in establishing brand equity. Indeed, financial services ventures are the largest online advertisers—research firm Jupiter estimates that the financial services sector spent $1.1B in online advertising in 2000, or more than 20% of the total spent across all industries; the sector is expected to remain the dominant spender in 2005, channeling $2.4B into online ads.

While we have focused our discussion on barriers impacting B2B and B2C platforms, it is worth noting that certain financial infrastructure companies face virtually no barriers to entry. Companies that provide enabling services are effectively free to enter the financial markets if they have a technologically compelling product or service to offer. Though they are 'indirect' participants in the financial sector, they are vital players who can enter almost at will. In addition, such companies are typically (though not always) exempt from regulatory scrutiny.

Barriers to entry in e-finance have certainly been lowered—with the possible exception of brand name and image, virtually all other hurdles are quite surmountable. Even the regulatory dimension, discussed below, which can sometimes act as a barrier, has been managed by new entrants with relative ease. As a result of being able to overcome these hurdles, a large number of web-based financial service providers have emerged over the past few years; there are now thousands of transaction-enabled retail and institutional financial service platforms operating around the world—a very high growth rate over a short period of time. Naturally, building a business model, endowing it with appropriate capital and technical resources, recruiting a management team, creating a service support mechanism, and developing a brand name do not guarantee success. Many web-based financial service providers have found the e-commerce and e-finance environment difficult to navigate. A number of providers have closed down, while others have redefined and restructured segments of their business. Though barriers to entry are lower, adapting financial services to the web remains a complex task.

REGULATING e-FINANCE

Financial ventures operating as pure plays or hybrids are, and will continue to be, regulated by various authorities, including regulators normally charged with monitoring the same types of activities in the 'physical' world. This is particularly important in a competitive environment where the theoretical barriers to entry are lower than they have been in the past, and where a large number of ventures have been created in a relatively short span of time. In the US, most of the major regulators—including the Federal Reserve, Office of the Comptroller of the Currency (OCC), SEC, Office of Thrift Supervision (OTS), FDIC, and National Credit Union Administration (NCUA), among others—have opined on different aspects of Internet banking/finance activity, including the establishment of web-based platforms and the offering of e-finance products/services. Similar input has been provided by home country regulators around the world, including Japan's Ministry of Finance (MOF), the UK's Financial Services Authority (FSA), and so on. In Japan, for example, the MOF has granted official regulatory approval for established financial institutions to create and operate standalone web-based banking platforms. In the UK, the FSA has provided guidance on aspects of investment advertisement/management over the Internet and is evaluating the regulation of ECNs. Though the Internet regulatory framework will almost certainly evolve further, many global regulators have filled the void by providing general guidance and rules on markets, products, services, customer privacy, protection and security. Since the Internet encourages innovation and quick access to new products and services, many regulators have attempted to remain adaptable, in order not to discourage the 'creative spirit' which is such an elemental component of the new economy. For instance, the OTS has authorized institutions under its purview to actively engage in both product innovation and electronic delivery of financial services, though it requires prior notification before a service is released onto the web. The OCC permits national bank subsidiaries to provide services through an Internet connection, though examiners need to understand, on a site-by-site basis, the individual business models being employed. The SEC and FSA have communicated similar views, favoring less, rather than more, Internet regulation. The general approach among regulators is to keep rules and regulations to a minimum and avoid being premature in adding new dictates.

Basic measures are largely in place to protect users and providers of financial services. In a banking context—particularly as related to deposits, loans and payments—electronic services are defined broadly to include long-established mechanisms such as EFTs and electronic POS transactions, as well as the new range of online financial services. As a 'rule of thumb' many of the principles that are applied to 'paper' transactions may also apply to electronic financial service transactions. For instance, when Internet banks in the US arrange/execute EFTs which debit/credit customer accounts, the Electronic Fund Transfer Act/Regulation E apply. When stored value products (including 'micropayments' or 'e-cash', as discussed in Chapter 5) are utilized, Regulation E once again applies, and if the stored value product acts as a demand deposit, Regulation D and attendant reserve requirements move into force. For banks which advertise deposit products online, disclosure must adhere to the requirements set out in the Truth in Savings Act/Regulation DD. Loan and leasing services fall under the jurisdiction of numerous existing regulations, including the Truth in Lending Act, Consumer Leasing Act, Equal Credit Opportunities Act, and so on. Naturally, some amendments to the process are necessary. For example, no 'hardcopy' terminal receipts are required for many of the banking transactions performed online—a digital record is sufficient.

In order to properly regulate securities offerings and trading which occurs via the web, regulators such as the SEC and FSA, among others, have focused their attention on activity impacting onshore investors. For instance, the SEC has strict regulations in place regarding the registration of public offerings before they can be sold to onshore investors. Under the Securities Act of 1933, an issuer offering securities to onshore investors through interstate commerce must register the offering (through a rather lengthy and detailed process, which culminates in a registration statement) or claim an appropriate exemption; under the Investment Company Act of 1940, foreign investment companies cannot use interstate commerce to offer securities to onshore investors unless the investment company receives an order to the contrary from the SEC. Since the web is indifferent to, and unaware of, geographical boundaries, care must be taken in distinguishing between onshore and offshore purchasers. The SEC has indicated that solicitation of offshore investors in non-registered securities does not violate the regulatory dictums established under the relevant Acts, as long as issuers and dealers have implemented measures 'reasonably designed' to guard against sales to onshore persons. Since posting information on the web may constitute an offer of securities, those offering the securities must demonstrate they have adequate measures in place to prevent US onshore investors from actually participating. If they can do so, then the SEC will not view the offering as having occurred in the US for registration purposes. Though it is difficult to know a priori what measures would be considered 'adequate', certain obvious safeguards include incorporating appropriate disclaimers on the site, embedding the site with appropriate password protection which bars onshore residents from executing trades, and so on. Similar protection needs to be included when dealing with offerings from offshore investment companies. As more virtual broker/dealers are created, those dealing within the US (regardless of whether or not they feature a physical presence) must be registered under the Exchange Act. Only non-US broker/dealers which do not intend to buy or sell securities in the US are exempt from registration. In the UK, the FSA has created similar rules. For example, under Section 3 of the FSA Act any person doing investment business in the UK (which can be defined to include dealing, arranging, managing or advising) must be authorized by the FSA to engage in such business, and must become a member of a self-regulatory organization (SRO). While pure Internet access/site providers are unlikely to fall under this umbrella, those which operate a sole or joint venture on the web that actively undertakes investment business would be included and must be duly authorized. In addition, any venture distributing investment advertisements that reach the UK community, whether or not designed to do so, must also be authorized. Investment offerings and agreements issued from outside the UK which 'discourage' or 'disclaim' participation by resident investors must be similarly authorized; only those offerings which restrict access to UK persons would be considered exempt. For institutions introducing Internet financial services, regulatory agencies around the world strongly recommend having on-staff compliance officers familiar with applicable rules and regulations. This helps ensure compliance when disseminating materials and services that will be used by the public. Indeed, regulators are shoring up their own staffs to keep pace with this new dimension of financial activity.

In a 2000 survey conducted by KPMG, 78% of financial institution respondents indicated that they derived less than 10% of their revenues from the Internet; however, 30% of respondents expected to earn up to 25% of their revenues from the web over the coming years, while another 30% believed they would be able to earn more than half of their revenues from web-based business. A McKinsey study conducted in 2000 indicated that in 1999 only 2% of total financial services revenue of $340B was derived from online sources, but by 2002 up to 10% of $400B will be sourced online. It is clear from these types of estimates that e-finance will continue to increase in prominence and scale over the coming years. The financial landscape will undoubtedly change further as new dimensions of e-finance appear and the banking industry continues to reshape—though the ultimate structure of the e-finance sector has yet to be solidified, there is little doubt that it will be an increasingly vital component of global financial services.

TALK OF THE TRADE

Cannibalization—losing customer business to an alternate distribution mechanism such as an Internet platform; since Internet services offered to clients are often cheaper than traditional services, a migration of existing customers to the web platform can result in a reduction of revenues.

Channel conflict—intracompany competition that may arise from the creation of alternate sales/distribution mechanisms (such as Internet platforms) leading to cannibalization.

Corporate storefront—a corporate Internet platform which acts as the entry point for an institution's web offerings; transaction-enabled storefronts permit clients to deal in the institution's proprietary products and services.

EFT—electronic funds transfer, a standard mechanism for electronically transmitting funds between two parties.

Hybrid—an Internet strategy and structure in which an established firm supplements its traditional physical ('brick and mortar') operation with an Internet platform under an existing brand.

Legacy system—any technical platform that forms part of an established institution's operating processes; legacy systems typically have to be integrated with web-based front-end platforms to deliver full client execution capabilities.

Marketplace—an Internet model and platform that aggregates product/ service offerings from numerous providers and allows customers to search/ select based on defined criteria.

Pure play—an Internet strategy and structure based on a virtual operation which has no physical 'brick and mortar' presence.

Stickiness—a measure of a web site's ability to attract and retain customers; sticky web sites often offer new, unique or appealing content, products or services.

Stored value cards—smart cards which can be used to purchase goods/services electronically; cards are available as monetary stored value cards (an anonymous form of electronic cash (e-cash), meaning that whoever holds the card holds the value) and token stored value cards (an application-specific card which creates a record of usage).

Vertical portal—an Internet model and platform that offers the broadest range of information, products and services within a given industry.

XML—extensible markup language, a meta-language that is becoming a standard for communication on the Internet; XML is a markup and tagging language that describes web-based content—it helps power web searches and can assist programs and applications in exchanging information.

3
Financing Digital Finance

FUNDING WEB PRODUCTS AND SERVICES

The availability of capital has been, and remains, essential in helping businesses migrate e-finance products/services to the web. Though technology and entrepreneurial vision have been key drivers in the migration process, the availability of capital to fund the platforms of start-up ventures and established institutions has been critical. Developing technology to deliver Internet-based financial solutions, recruiting and retaining management, marketing products and services, and building brand loyalty are all capital-intensive endeavors. As capital providers and capital users have discovered, producing and delivering quality Internet offerings, which have reach and longevity, can be an expensive proposition; in the increasingly competitive e-commerce and e-finance sectors, creating top-tier platforms, by supplying sufficient capital, is paramount.

Before accessing capital a business model, supported by a business plan, must be in place—capital-providers demand a sound, well-planned, strategy before committing funds. Start-up ventures seeking their first round of financing must present and defend a rational and credible plan. Established companies seeking to expand to the Internet face pressures that are different, but just as great—particularly since funds needed to leverage an existing financial strategy, often on a global, cross-product, scale, can be especially large. A business model defines the operating space for a particular Internet venture and a business plan helps quantify the financial backing needed to make the venture a reality. Any supplier of capital—whether internal or external—needs to be thoroughly convinced of the model before committing capital. Business plans are a key mechanism for communicating the strategic and tactical vision behind the model, and are scrutinized in detail by capital providers to determine the viability of a venture. The business plan focuses on the operations the venture is expected to undertake, how it plans to deliver its product/service, why it is unique and distinct from others operating on the web, how it can achieve required scale, how revenues and profits will be generated, what benefits will accrue from the provision of capital, how capital infusions should be sequenced and timed, and so on. Business plans also include risk analyses, pro-forma financial projections, and stresses of those projections. The nature of the capital infusion—for instance the kind of instrument that best addresses the needs of the venture at a particular stage in its development—must also be considered. There are numerous debt and equity instruments that can be used to fund an operation. In the research, development and early distribution stages, equity warrants, common stock (voting/non-voting), and preferred stock are often selected; in growth and expansion stages notes and debentures are often added, and in the buyout stage a new round of common stock, often via an IPO, is typical; up to 80% of early stage funding is from private, rather than public, investors. The primary sources of capital available to Internet businesses include self-financing, venture capital, angel and incubator investment, corporate investment and direct investment from other institutional investors; established ventures seeking to expand onto the Internet often do so through internal corporate funding. These sources are generally supplemented or replaced in later stages by funding through the public markets (via an IPO, equity add-on or debt issue) or the private markets (via private placements).

Financing web start-ups or growth stage ventures—businesses which are not yet established, or public, operation—is a very risky proposition. One research estimate predicts that up to 75% of all Internet businesses will ultimately fail. The US Department of Commerce estimates that approximately 1MM new businesses (both 'traditional' and Internet-based) are created in the US every year; of those, 40% fail in the first year and 80% fail within five years, suggesting that the odds of creating a viable, and sustainable, business platform, supported by appropriate funding, are rather small. An Industry Standard Internet survey conducted in 2000 reflects the difficulty of getting Internet business models properly financed and operational. The survey found that out of a pool of 2.5MM business entrepreneurs, only one in five developed credible business plans. Of the 500,000 or so business plans developed and 'pitched' to venture capitalists, angel investors, corporate backers and other financiers, only 10,000 to 20,000 received funding—including about 10% devoted to wholesale and retail financial services. Only 600 or so of those went public or were acquired, meaning that the chances of going from a 'good idea' to final public market or third-party takeout equaled 0.02%. New Internet ventures thus face considerable challenges.

SELF-FINANCING

Self-financing is the more 'refined' term applied to the process of obtaining funds from informal sources—friends, family, colleagues and, as has become apparent during the Internet revolution, credit card and short-term credit providers.

Funding through this mechanism is applicable almost exclusively to very small start-up ventures rather than those with any type of scale. The maximum amount of capital likely to be raised through self-financing sources tends to be capped at relatively modest amounts—after all, there are only so many friends, relatives and credit cards one can tap—suggesting that self-financed ventures must, in their earliest stages, focus on applications which do not require major investment in infrastructure, personnel, marketing or technology. Since, as discussed in Chapter 2, some aspects of web-finance require a reasonable amount of capital, self-funded operations in the development phase tend to focus on smaller market niches. As they grow in size and scope, they may replace self-arranged funds with more robust, and dependable, institutional capital.

Though largely informal, self-financing is an important source of capital for many start-ups. Even platforms which already have access to other sources of funds may opt to supplement their resources through self-financing. According to the Industry Standard survey, 86% of all Internet start-ups use some form of self-financing (as the sole source, or one of several sources, of capital). For instance, Kiodex, the B2B commodity risk management platform which provides users with trading engines, trade matching systems and risk management services, raised over $8MM through self-financing sources in order to get its venture operational; it then supplemented these funds with institutional venture capital. Self-financing is, of course, an unreliable and often expensive source of capital. Since channels to obtain such funds are generally very informal it is difficult, in many instances, to predict when, and if, capital will be available—general inability to know precisely when a venture will have access to funds is a considerable disadvantage to those trying to get a business started or expanded. Those opting for greater 'predictability' through use of credit cards or consumer lines of credit pay a price through high interest rate charges. With many credit revolvers charging in excess of 15–20% per year on the amount borrowed, interest costs for a start-up can soon become burdensome.

VENTURE CAPITAL

Start-up or emerging outfits with a robust business model, solid business plan, and a certain amount of demonstrable experience, can periodically access sources of funds which are more reliable, and generally less expensive, than those obtained via self-financing channels. Venture capital (VC)—private risk funding channeled by investors to new or expanding ventures—is one such source of financing.

VC has been an accepted method of financing new businesses since the mid-1940s. In 1946 MIT President Karl Compton and Harvard Professor Georges Doriot sought to commercialize some of the technologies which had been developed during World War II and created American Research and

Development (ARD), a venture capital group, as a vehicle to do so. ARD, which was structured as a closed-end fund, undertook a series of investments over its life, including a $70,000 financing made to the MIT start-up outfit which ultimately became DEC; in 1971 ARD's stake was valued at $355MM. Arthur Rock, an East Coast financier working at merchant bank Hayden Stone, moved to the West Coast to invest in new technology companies and became one of the true 'pioneer' venture capitalists (VCs). He is credited with funding ventures such as Fairchild Semiconductor, Teledyne, Intel and Apple—all well known for achieving great success in the technology sector. Indeed, Rock's 1975 investment of $1.5MM in Apple was worth $100MM when the company went public in 1978, while his $300,000 investment in Intel in the late 1960s mushroomed to a value of $700MM in 1999. Other early VCs included the Rockefeller family, J.H. Whitney, Greylock and TA Associates.

During the 1950s a handful of publicly traded closed-end VC funds emerged, as did the first limited partnership fund (run by Draper, Gaither and Anderson). More such funds appeared in the 1960s and 1970s, but the scale of investment was limited to a maximum of several hundred million dollars per year. Investment capital came from the investing public—despite the fact that the projects being funded were relatively high risk—as well as large institutional investors. Widespread institutional participation appeared in 1979 after a clarification of Employee Retirement Income Security Act (ERISA) laws permitted pension funds to once again invest more liberally in venture capital and 'higher risk' situations. In the early 1970s, prior to the ERISA law change, the market featured approximately $480MM in VC funds, with individuals contributing 32%, and pensions 15%, of the total; by 1986 the amount invested had increased to $4.8B, with pensions contributing 50% of that amount. During the 1970s, when activity in VC projects was still relatively modest, pensions invested directly in VC funds; in the 1980s, as amounts and obligations increased, pensions began hiring investment advisors to help them with the task. During this period limited partnership (LP) funds emerged as the predominant structure for investing; indeed, LP funds remain one of the most popular VC investment mechanisms up to the present time. An LP fund is comprised of investors who serve as limited partners and investment managers who serve as general partners; limited partners are able to monitor the fund's performance but cannot influence the investment decisions undertaken by the general partners. VC moved to great prominence during the 1980s as the boom in PCs took hold. Based on the technology advances described in the Appendix, the estimated value of the PC industry increased from virtually zero in 1980 to $100B by 1990; approximately 70% of that was financed through various VC structures, primarily LP funds.

Many new VC firms have appeared since the early work of ARD and Arthur Rock, and the VC sector has become a widely recognized, and important, funding conduit. Modern-day VC groups take one of several

forms. VC firms may be structured as private companies or general partnerships, such as Kleiner Perkins Caufield and Byers, Accel Partners,
Benchmark Capital, Draper Fisher Jurvetson, Softbank, Sierra Ventures,
Hummer Winblad, Redpoint Partners, and others; these entities are typically
quite small, comprising only a handful of partners and small teams of analysts.
VC firms may also be established as separately capitalized subsidiaries of
large banks. There are approximately 70 such entities around the world,
including well-known names such as Morgan Capital, UBS Capital, and Citi-
corp Venture Capital. Many of these bank-related firms are more conservative in their investments than VC partnerships and often direct their capital
towards 'later stage' companies. Many large corporations also operate VC
subsidiaries of their own, often to participate in specific projects related to a
parent company's underlying business. DEC, Raychem, Memorex and others
commenced this practice in the mid-1960s, and by the early 1970s 25% of
Fortune 500 companies featured VC arms. Though many ultimately abandoned their ventures, they were responsible for helping institutionalize, at a
corporate level, the concept of strategic VC investment. Today, companies
such as Cisco, Lucent, Intel, Microsoft and others feature separately capitalized VC subsidiaries that invest in technology-focused ventures; there are
approximately 80 such entities in operation. In addition to these major VC
groups, various institutional investors and investment banks operate private
equity funds that effectively act as VC conduits. In the public sector, 180 small
business investment companies (SBICs) operate as quasi-government VC
groups, channeling seed money from local, state and federal government
programs to various start-up ventures.

Regardless of the specific organizational structure, most VCs tend to raise
and allocate funds in a similar manner. As indicated, the most common approach is to create a new LP fund on a periodic basis. Investors—typically
large institutional investors such as pension funds, insurers, and university
endowments, along with a small number of very high net worth individuals—
subscribe as limited partners in a new fund when it is established; VCs act as
general partners, giving them responsibility for the investment selection and
management process. In the US, approximately half of all investment funds
come from pensions, and a further 25% from corporations and endowments;
as a result of regulatory restrictions only a small fraction has historically come
from financial institutions, though that is beginning to change with the fall of
the Glass–Steagall Act (which previously segregated banking and securities/
investment transactions). New funds typically have a 10 year life (though they
can be extended in certain instances) and are raised as existing funds are
retired. VCs typically raise new funds every two to five years in order to have
a relatively steady flow of investment capital available for new projects; most
VCs operate two to three funds at any point in time. Though the US is the
single largest market for VC financing—raising three times more capital in a

given year than any other country—venture funding is becoming a stronger factor in countries such as Australia, France, Germany, Israel, Italy, Netherlands and the UK. VC moved to prominence in Europe in the early 1980s, and began making inroads in Asia in the late 1980s. In both regions VC has historically been used for buyouts of existing companies rather than seeding of new companies, though that practice is gradually changing—new start-ups are enjoying greater access to venture funds. In Europe, banks and pensions each provide about 25% of VC funds, while in Asia corporations provide more than 40% of funds.

Contrary to popular belief, VCs do not only finance technology-oriented start-ups. Indeed, only 25% of annual VC investments flow into true start-ups; the balance is directed towards later stage, or even established, companies. VC investments are made in a number of areas, including technology, biotechnology, medicine, manufacturing, production, marketing, and finance, among others. There are approximately 700 distinct VC funds in the US; according to a Venture One research study, between early 1998 and mid-2000 approximately $65B of VC funds were allocated to the Internet sector. An incremental $4B to $5B is invested every year, with roughly 2000 businesses receiving some form of venture funding in a typical year. Most VC funds invest in companies in specific industries, sectors, development stages, or locales. More than 2/3 of VC investments are greater than $1MM in size; though first round VC deal size varies, amounts in excess of $10MM for very promising ventures are not unusual. Second and third rounds can increase total funding well above that, assuming management and operating targets are reached. Many VC funds are actually limited by covenant on the amount they can invest in a single venture—primarily to prevent general partners from throwing 'good money after bad' in the event an investment sours. VC funds are also restricted on the amount they can invest in a given sector or asset class, other venture funds, leveraged buyouts (LBOs), and public and foreign securities; new investments are typically reviewed by fund advisory boards (which include external directors). General partners face limitations on their personal investments in funds.

The primary function of any VC outfit is to provide new, or expanding, ventures with an appropriate amount of financing to implement a business strategy. In exchange for performing due diligence, vetting business models, and providing capital, VCs typically receive a fixed annual fee plus variable compensation based on a fund's profits. Funds take an equity stake in a new company and a seat on the board so they can monitor progress and influence direction. In a typical 'stage 1' company (seed or start-up with no product, only a model), equity stakes may run to 30% or more; in a 'stage 2' company (product developed but no revenues generated), equity stakes may range from 8% to 15%; and in 'stage 3' and 'stage 4' companies (products generating revenues, then profits), equity stakes decline to 5% or 6%. VCs generally seek enough voting power in early stage companies to gain control if a venture's management is unable to deliver on its stated goals. They are also willing to partner with other VCs or capital providers on a single venture—this helps diversify risk among a number of investors, provides portfolio balance, and helps 'validate' investment decisions. Successful ventures that meet stated milestones and demonstrate an appropriate level of progress can typically tap VCs for additional rounds of financing. The concept of disbursing funds in stages helps ensure fiscal and managerial discipline within the venture; if the VC team is unsatisfied with progress being made on specific business targets, it may choose to withhold incremental funds until changes are made. In the extreme, VCs may attempt to change the venture's strategy or seek control of the outfit.

The end goal of VCs is to take ventures public through IPOs or sell them to third parties at a premium. In doing so, they can reap returns that are many multiples of capital invested. In a typical VC fund, approximately 20–35% of companies are taken public—during the 1990s VC-backed ventures accounted for 12–28% of all IPO funds raised (depending on the year in question). (From 1995 to March 2000, 370 Internet companies went public, attaining an aggregate market value of $1.5T prior to the April 2000 market correction). The remainder are sold to third parties privately, merged with other entities, liquidated, or left to run as going concerns. Once a company is taken public, the fund returns capital to investors either by a direct transfer of new, publicly traded, shares, or by liquidating the shares and transferring cash; given restrictions on liquidation, it is more common to simply transfer shares to investors. If a company is sold to a third party, cash is transferred directly to investors. The VC process can thus be seen as an entire cycle: capital is raised through a VC fund, proceeds are invested in select companies, financial performance is monitored, supplemental capital is allocated as necessary, portfolio companies are liquidated (through the IPO process or sales to a third-party), and capital is returned to investors. Until the mid-1980s a typical time horizon for VC investment ranged from five to 10 years. Since then, holding periods have shortened; most VCs now seek to exit in three to seven years.

Average target returns for successful spin-offs are approximately 500% of initial investment after three years, 1000% after five years, and more than 1000% after seven years. Historical average returns, according to a Venture Economics survey, reflect a 14.5% average annual gain over the past 27 years. Returns during the 1980s were relatively modest as an excess of capital (often supplied by inexperienced VCs) pursued low quality projects that ultimately failed. By the 1990s, as inexperienced players were shaken out of the industry and the IPO market rebounded, returns increased. Obviously, not every venture funded by VCs is a success. Since VC firms run portfolios of ventures they expect some to fail, others to provide 'average' returns, and a very small number to generate spectacular returns. This portfolio approach allows them to diversify risk and take greater chances on certain ventures than they might otherwise be willing to undertake. As indicated, VCs obtain their investment capital from a variety of sources, including private investors, large institutional investors, other industry participants, and so on. Given the rather dramatic returns many of the best-known VC firms have posted over the past few years, there has been no shortage of funds available for investment. That said, VC is medium-term and high-risk, and is unsuitable for many segments of the investing community.

Good VCs are particularly demanding in their requirements of start-up ventures. Since VC firms typically receive thousands of unsolicited business plans/ideas, they inject greater discipline into the process by requiring innovative ideas backed by solid business plans and experienced management teams. Ventures must be very scalable, able to capture a significant market audience in a relatively short time frame, and demonstrate a rational strategy for moving to profitability quickly—in one to two years, instead of three to five, or more, years. Since the IPO market is not always available as a takeout, VCs attempt to do everything in their power to ensure they are backing viable businesses. Following the Internet 'euphoria' of the late 1990s, when ventures with business models that pushed revenue and profit generation into future years had ready access to funding, VCs have become stricter in their requirements. Many VC firms demand a much quicker path to profitability, forcing new enterprises to focus on execution and delivery in a much shorter time frame. This allows them to be far more selective in the projects they back, and increases the odds that the ventures they ultimately finance will have good long-term prospects and realistic chances for an IPO takeout or third-party sale. In addition, being selective allows VCs to be more attentive to the management of their portfolio investments. This type of discipline is particularly critical in an environment where players in the system are flush with cash and start pursuing mediocre opportunities. There is certainly some evidence that an excess of investable capital leads to less restrictive partnership agreements and higher investment valuations. Short-run competition can also lead to overallocation of capital in 'hot' sectors, which is not a sustainable process in the long-term.

VCs have been, and continue to be, active in funding web-based e-finance platforms of different types. As one might expect, most capital is provided to ventures that are entirely, or relatively, new rather than those that are extensions of established institutions (which tend to obtain their funding from internal sources). For example: Softbank Venture Capital has funded E*Trade (online trading), E-Loan (online mortgage platform), limitrader (online trading systems), eCoverage (online insurance), PayTrust.com (electronic bill payment service), and Sonnet Financial (online FX services); Benchmark Capital has financed E-Loan, Epoch Partners (online investment bank), and Juniper Financial Services (online financial services); Accel Partners has financed eCoverage (online insurance) and the Moneyline network (financial infomediary); Redpoint Ventures has financed Esurance (online insurance), NextCard (online credit cards), PropertyFirst (commercial real estate), and Trading Edge (online trading); Kleiner Perkins has funded Epoch Partners, NextCard, Intuit (financial infomediary/tools), MyCFO (financial infomediary/wealth manager), and LiveCapital (online small business finance); Draper Fisher Jurvetson has funded Wit Capital (online trading and investment banking) and New Markets International (online FX trading); Sierra Ventures has financed DotBank (online banking); Hummer Winblad has financed IMX (online mortgage platform); Technology Crossover Ventures has financed IMX and Trading Edge (online fixed income venture); Morgan Stanley Dean Witter Venture Partners has funded LoopNet (commercial real estate) and PeopleFirst (online auto insurance); Sequoia Capital has funded E-Loan, Quote.com (financial infomediary), and X.com (financial management/payment services); Greylock has financed CheckFree (electronic payment services) and Visible Markets (mortgage trading); Capital Z has funded LoanTrader (online mortgage broker), iExchange (investment/ information), LendingTree (loan marketplace), PrimeStreet (small business credit marketplace), Trading Edge, and mPower (online financial advisor); Flatiron Partners has financed Patagon.com (a Latin investment portal); and so on. This is simply a sample listing of financial ventures that have received VC support over the past few years. Naturally, numerous VC firms have also funded many other dedicated software, communications and infrastructure service companies that make possible the creation of e-commerce and e-finance solutions in the Internet world.

ANGEL AND INCUBATOR INVESTMENT

While VCs are very important providers of capital, angel investors and incubators are central to the capital-raising and allocation process as well. Angel investors, in particular, are a vital source of capital for start-up ventures. Angels are typically wealthy individuals who have a high tolerance for risk and a desire to participate, directly or indirectly, in the creation of new business platforms; many angels are former entrepreneurs who have achieved financial success through their own ventures and wish to remain active in the development of new businesses. Angels are rarely passive investors, preferring to remain involved and engaged in the development of new companies. According to the Small Business Administration (SBA), there are approximately 700,000 angel investors in the US. A core of about 500,000 supply from $25B to $50B in investment funds per year—more than the VC community; nearly 60% of the capital provided is in the form of equity, the

remaining 40% a combination of loans and guarantees. Most angel investments are smaller than those made by VCs; the SBA estimates that approximately 80% of deals are under $500,000 in size. Given the sheer magnitude of
the capital being mobilized, angel investing is actually far more common than
is generally known; approximately 45% of Internet start-ups receive some
amount of capital through the angel community. Unlike VCs, most angels do
not typically provide multiple financing rounds and most expect to exit in
approximately five years. Though angels have long been perceived as more
patient and risk tolerant than VCs, there is no evidence to support that belief;
indeed, angels are very aggressive and demanding business partners. Matching angels with start-up ventures is, of course, vital. Different investors have
different expertise, temperament and styles, which may or may not suit a
given web venture. In order to avoid potential conflicts it is best for the two to
be appropriately matched at the outset. Matches can occur through the economic community, personal contacts, industry associations and web-based
matching services (such as Halo Ventures, Vcapital.com, Angel Tips, Capital
Connection Network, Garage.com, and various others).

While VCs and angels share certain similarities, they are fundamentally
different types of capital providers. At the risk of generalizing somewhat, the
following distinguishing features seem to hold true: VCs operate in the public
spotlight to a considerable extent, funding larger, but accepting fewer, deals;
angels are extremely private, tend to favor smaller ventures but are more
willing to accept a greater number of deals. VCs manage assets on behalf of
institutions, pension funds, and partnerships, while angels manage their own
funds. VCs tend to favor partly established ventures rather than pure start-ups
and are generally active only as board directors; angels fund start-up ventures
and are actively involved in the management of ventures (as employees,
directors, or consultants). There are, of course, fewer VCs than angels.
Though angels are primarily early stage investors, they are often willing to
participate as late stage investors if an IPO or third-party sale is postponed
and additional funds are required. Given their preference for anonymity,
linking angel investment with specific Internet platforms is difficult; nevertheless, angels are known to invest actively in a broad range of projects, including
financial B2B, B2C and infrastructure ventures. It is worth noting that angel
investing is still primarily a US phenomenon. Though international angel
investing is appearing in countries such as the UK, most nations around the
world do not yet have the same tradition of 'individual entrepreneurial
investment'.

Incubators provide a range of services that are designed to give start-up
ventures a chance to expand and succeed. In particular, incubators supply
ventures with seed capital, administrative services, human resource expertise,
and business plan support. By offering these services they accelerate the time
between idea generation and product/service rollout, and allow entrepreneurs

to focus on the preparation of professional business plans and the development of technology platforms. Success in these areas can be helpful in obtaining additional financing from VCs. Incubators generally provide a much smaller amount of capital than VCs, typically only $500,000 to $1MM per venture—though this depends on the specifics of individual projects; a Harvard University survey on incubators reveals that approximately 1/3 of all incubator deals involve capital injections of less than $500,000, 1/3 from $500,000 to $1MM, and 1/3 over $1MM. More than 90% of incubators focus their capital and resources on Internet strategies, with 46% specialized in specific sectors (such as B2C, B2B or infrastructure) and 20% specialized by industry.

The top incubators maintain ties to the VC community and introduce their most promising new ventures to VCs—if VCs are interested, they take greater control of the process by providing incremental funding in exchange for equity stakes and board seats. Incubators also take equity stakes in the start-ups they are 'nurturing', often as high as 25–50% (note that under the US Investment Act of 1940 no more than 40% of a public holding company's assets can be in the form of non-controlling securities of other firms, or else the company becomes regulated as an 'investment company'). The typical 'cash out' time horizon for incubators is shorter than that of VCs— most incubators go into a venture intending to exit through an IPO or buyout within two to three years, or approximately 1/3 to 1/2 the time a typical VC might remain involved. Incubators are most effective in funding and 'jump starting' ventures when the IPO market is very active and the need to introduce a product or service in a short time frame is critical. When the IPO market slows down and the urgency for rollout diminishes, other methods of financing tend to dominate and incubators find themselves under business and profit pressure (as was evident in mid-2000). Not surprisingly, Internet growth has caused the number of incubators to swell dramatically in recent years. In 1990 there were approximately a dozen recognized incubators in the US, most of them government sponsored; by 2000 the US incubator sector had expanded to more than 500 firms, most of them private (this figure includes Internet 'accelerators' and other outfits that assume incubator-like functions—accelerators, for instance, support companies with promising ideas that have been rejected by VCs because of insufficient development work). International incubators have also expanded in number, reaching more than 350 in 2000, including 250 in Europe alone. Countries such as the UK, France, Germany and the Netherlands are home to a large number of incubation outfits, providing the same type of crucial start-up financing which incubators and angels provide in the US market (as indicated, outside the UK the European marketplace does not yet feature the angel investment so common in the US). Local incubators have the advantage of being able to interpret and manage very specific local requirements, customs and barriers. As with other dimensions of the Internet, ongoing consolidation within the incubator community is widely expected; indeed, the process commenced in 2000 and will likely continue over the coming years. Incubators that are diversified across a number of industries are considered more stable and more likely to endure as the IPO market slows; in addition, those that have formed partnerships with large industrial or financial conglomerates (to help speed internal or industry innovation) may also survive and prosper.

Many top incubators help fund e-finance web platforms. For instance: ideaLab has financed iExchange (financial infomediary), eLease (leasing marketplace), and PayMyBills (electronic bill paying service); Internet Capital Group has funded Blackbird (derivatives trading service), CreditTrade (credit trading exchange), eCredit (real-time credit financing service), and MetalSite (metal trading exchange); LaunchCenter 39 has funded Investorama (financial infomediary); DivineInterventures has funded aluminium.com (aluminum trading exchange) and OilSpot.com (oil trading exchange); efinanceworks has funded BankPass (bank security infrastructure), CashEdge (account aggregator), and CoverageCorp (small business insurance marketplace); Brainspeak has financed Propex (commercial property investment service); and so on. Antfactory, a European incubator, has established strategic financing partnerships with both Citibank and Lloyds TSB to fund a series of Latin and European e-commerce ventures. Within the financial sector itself, JP Morgan (prior to its merger with Chase) created an incubator known as LabMorgan. Over the past few years LabMorgan has identified and funded promising ventures related to the financial services industry, including ADR.com (provider of international equity data and research), Creditex (credit derivatives trading service), Cygnifi (derivative risk management service), Market Axess and Tradepoint (institutional bond and equity trading platforms), and Monex (Japanese online trading firm), among others. Banks such as Deutsche Bank, National Australia Bank and various others also operate incubators of their own.

CORPORATE STRATEGIC FUNDING AND INTERNAL CORPORATE FUNDING

Corporate funding is a critical dimension of financing within the e-commerce world and most often takes one of two forms—corporate strategic funding and internal corporate funding. Corporations interested in promoting research and development, product investment and industrial expansion often make funds available to new or established ventures. Corporate partners are very significant investors, committing an estimated $7B to $10B per year to new ventures. While these corporate investors hope and expect to reap financial gains from their investments, more often they seek to fund research, product innovation or market access which will ultimately be of use in their own operations. Certain corporate strategic partners actively invest in the Internet sector, including platforms dedicated to financial services. Indeed, many of the institutional alliances and B2B exchanges that have developed in the financial services sector, discussed at greater length in Chapter 4, have been made possible by corporate strategic funding. For example: JP Morgan, Bear Stearns and Chase have funded the Market Axess bond trading platform; Instinet, JP Morgan, Morgan Stanley Dean Witter, Merrill Lynch, CSFB; and Archipelago have funded the Tradepoint equity trading platform; Goldman Sachs, Merrill Lynch, Morgan Stanley Dean Witter, and Salomon Smith Barney have financed the BondBook bond trading venture; First Union, Chase and Wells Fargo have financed the Spectrum electronic bill paying service; and so on. There are, of course, many other examples of strategic alliances and partnerships funded by consortia of established financial institutions.

Internal corporate funding is a second component of overall corporate funding, and is the primary source of capital for the e-finance platforms of established financial institutions. Internet finance ventures that are designed to supplement a bank's existing business typically have access to internal 'parent' funds—giving them a distinct advantage over small ventures that are forced to depend on less 'reliable', or certain, sources of capital from VCs, angels or incubators. Most of the established financial institutions which have created an online presence over the past few years—including Merrill Lynch, Schwab, Bank of America, Citibank, Deutsche Bank, UBS and others—have relied on internal resources to fund their ventures; these, as one might imagine, are generally very significant investments. In certain instances parent funding is supplemented by additional public market equity access. For instance, US broker DLJ spun off its DLJ Direct online trading platform through a tracking stock IPO, raising new capital in the process.

While affiliated Internet ventures have ready access to parent funds they must still develop and validate their business concepts. Parent institutions committing funding to these operations demand accountability—those responsible for developing or expanding Internet services must be prepared to go through the same type of scrutiny a start-up venture seeking VC might face. Indeed, scrutiny may be even greater since the project is likely to be large in scale and have an impact on existing business, systems architecture, human resources, and corporate organization. While financial start-ups may seek $10–50MM in initial rounds of financing, and perhaps double that in second or third rounds, Internet ventures of established companies might require many multiples of that; this is particularly true if entire legacy platforms need to be integrated or replaced, new businesses staffed, operations expanded, and so on. In fact, the sums that are being invested in the e-commerce reinvention process—to deliver new and existing customers an enhanced value proposition—are very large. For instance, BNP Paribas has stated that it plans to spend $700MM over three years to fully develop its Internet platform. Deutsche Bank has indicated that it eventually plans to commit up to $1B per year on its retail and institutional Internet operations, ING Bank intends to spend approximately $2B over three years, Credit Suisse $600MM, and so on. Tower Group, a research firm, estimates that global financial services technology spending by established firms reached $81B in 1999—including all aspects of technology, from internal trading and business systems to back-office processing systems, management software and Internet development. Spending is expected to grow at an average annual rate of 12%, reaching $114B by 2002. While only a portion of this is related to Internet expansion, it places the magnitude of the technology commitment for financial services in context.

PUBLIC AND PRIVATE REFINANCING

In certain instances capital provided through self-funding, VCs, angels or incubators can be supplemented or permanently replaced by accessing the equity markets through an IPO (or equity add-on, if an IPO tranche has already occurred). Even established companies may seek to replace parent company funding with public market equity financing, primarily if the venture is being 'spun off' from existing parent operations. In order for IPO takeouts to occur, the marketplace needs exchanges which support 'younger' companies with smaller capital bases and shorter records of financial performance. In the US, the NASDAQ is the primary marketplace for such listings; in the UK it occurs through the Alternative Investment Market, in France via Le Nouveau Marche, in Germany through the Neuer Markt, and so on.

Internet IPOs were a driving force in the equity market's technology sector expansion of the late 1990s. The general 'euphoria' surrounding public offerings of 'dot coms' and other ventures reached an extreme point in early 2000 as stock valuations for unproven ventures—with little, or no, demonstrated ability to generate earnings—escalated to new highs. Indeed, for much of the late 1990s and early 2000, valuations of Internet companies were scaled as a significant multiple of future revenues, rather than earnings, since most new ventures accessing the public markets were not (and are not) profitable on an earnings basis. Following a sharp correction, underwriters have become more sanguine about the sector and more disciplined in bringing new IPOs to market. While that has excluded—perhaps rightly—certain start-up ventures from obtaining permanent financing via the equity markets, it has not barred access to those with a robust business model. Indeed, those with a valid business model, demonstrable strategy and large market share potential, are generally not barred from the public markets. Though they may be delayed in accessing public capital in times of turmoil, a proven concept vetted by early stage investors will still be valid when the public markets reopen. Launching an IPO typically gives the major stakeholders of a venture, including founding members, VCs, incubators or angels, a windfall gain on their pre-IPO ownership stakes. Selling of ownership stakes following the IPO is typically restricted—most pre-IPO shareholders are subject to a lockout period that encourages a long-term investment view and helps ensure the venture remains a stable and viable operation. Some of the e-finance ventures funded by VCs and others have accessed the equity markets in recent years and are now publicly listed and quoted; examples include E*Trade, Wit Capital and e-Loan, among others. In addition to public equity issues, Internet ventures periodically launch public bonds and convertibles to supplement their balance sheet financing. However, since many new ventures are small and lack the financial strength to achieve strong credit ratings (which leads to lower coupon/interest charges), public debt is generally not a preferred method of refinancing.

When public markets are not available as a financing or refinancing option, certain ventures choose to access the private placement market. This market provides companies with capital from private sources, typically very large institutional investors such as insurance companies, pension funds and other asset managers. Most private placements are structured in the form of equity stakes (which are not publicly traded), mezzanine financings (ranking between debt and equity in terms of security), or debt placements (in one of various forms, including senior or subordinated obligations). Such securities tend to be perpetual or very long-term in nature and are not actively traded—though there is a limited ability to sell to another qualified institutional buyer, often through the investment bank that arranged the private placement in the first instance. As we shall discuss in Chapter 4, several Internet ventures have been formed to bring together private companies and private placement investors.

The availability of capital to fund new ventures, and extend the scope of existing firms, has been—and will continue to be—a critical element of the e-commerce process. Like technology and creativity, it is certain that the migration of financial services to the web would have been slowed without capital from the providers cited above. Equally important is the fact that these capital providers have injected discipline and fiscal responsibility into the business development process; this helps ensure that only the worthiest ventures receive the funding needed to develop and implement their ideas. With the building blocks of web-finance—technology, ideas and capital—in place, we turn our attention in Chapters 4, 5 and 6 to understanding how various ventures have redefined the B2B e-finance, B2C e-finance and financial information sectors.

TALK OF THE TRADE

Accelerators—outfits which act as incubators but focus more exclusively on ventures which have been rejected by VCs for lack of development work.

Angels—wealthy individuals who actively invest in start-up ventures, generally on an anonymous or discreet basis.

Equity add-on—an incremental (post-IPO) equity tranche floated in the public markets.

Incubators—outfits which provide start-up ventures with seed capital, administrative services and business plan support in exchange for an equity stake; once a venture has been 'incubated' to a sufficient level of readiness it is often referred to VCs for additional financing.

IPO—initial public offering, a public flotation of a company in the stock market.

LP fund—limited partnership fund, a standard VC mechanism for raising and investing in new ventures; investors supplying capital act as limited partners while VC managers directing the allocation of investment funds and managing the portfolio of investments act as general partners.

SBIC—small business investment company, a publicly-sponsored VC conduit which makes local, state or federal government seed money available to start-up ventures.

Stage 1 company—a seed or start-up venture with no product/service, only a business model.

Stage 2 company—a venture with a product/service in development, but no revenues.

Stage 3 company—a venture with a product/service that is generating revenues, but no profits.

Stage 4 company—a venture with a product/service that is generating both revenues and profits.

VC—venture capital, private investment directed towards higher risk start-up or early stage ventures; VC forms an important source of funds for many Internet ventures.

4

B2B e-Finance

THE B2B VALUE PROPOSITION

With the Internet established as a robust mechanism for the creation and delivery of information, products and services, it was simply a question of time before segments of the financial industry gravitated to the web. Though early web-finance activity appearing in the mid-1990s was pioneered by start-up ventures and small institutions, most major players soon joined in the migration. By the late 1990s many established institutions had introduced web-based strategies for the delivery of financial services and sector coverage became quite comprehensive, spanning the institutional (B2B) and retail (B2C) markets. In certain instances products and services were created largely, if not exclusively, for institutions, while in other cases they were tailored for retail customers; in select instances they were created for all market participants. In this chapter we focus our attention on Internet-based structures, products and services which are aimed primarily at the institutional marketplace. In Chapter 5 we focus on those targeted at the retail customer base, and in Chapter 6 we deal broadly with the topic of financial information—content, news, research, tools, prices, and analytics—which is used by both institutional and retail participants. Given the plethora of ventures that offer web-based financial services, it is not our intent to produce a comprehensive list of web sites/electronic platforms that exist in a given category; rather, we reference particular examples within each category for illustrative and explanatory purposes.

Though B2B e-finance platforms appeared after their B2C counterparts, they represent a much larger, more complex and more sophisticated part of the market. Successful B2B platforms capable of delivering robust financial services are poised to redesign many aspects of front- and back-office institutional finance—changing, perhaps permanently, the way such services are created and delivered. B2B providers have enhanced the institutional financial services value proposition by giving their institutional clients broader product selection, faster execution, increased price transparency, tighter dealing margins, and greater cost savings. B2B exchanges, which unite numerous financial service providers and institutional clients in a marketplace setting, have similarly changed the value proposition by consolidating fragmented markets to give clients enhanced liquidity, expanded product selection, transparent pricing, and efficient execution (many times spanning the entire length of the product/service chain, from front-office trade entry, to middle-office valuation and modeling, to back-office processing and reporting). B2B infrastructure providers have also changed the client value proposition. In particular, they offer their clients—the underlying B2B providers facing end-users—turnkey or customized solutions which enable quick ramp-up of web-based platforms and integration of legacy processes; this permits B2B platforms to save time and money on redesigning and restructuring Internet delivery mechanisms.

The web gives B2B ventures greater access to clients through a relatively simple and inexpensive contact and distribution mechanism, and simultaneously provides clients with efficient and competitive product/service execution. As a result, numerous institutional financial services have already been transferred to the web, including IPOs and new issues, equity, bond, currency and derivative trading, investment and corporate banking, and valuation/processing. Some of these services have the potential to disintermediate established players by electronically linking issuers with investors and buyers with sellers. For instance, commercial paper issuance and investment, e-bond issuance and investment, and portfolio risk management can all theoretically be conducted between suppliers/product creators and end-users through electronic mechanisms—without going through a physical or electronic intermediary; though not all of these services have resulted in disintermediation, they may in the future. Other institutional services still require the participation of intermediaries, who link parties through traditional mechanisms or network platforms; for example, IPOs, derivative trading, and corporate banking services continue to feature the physical and electronic services of intermediaries.

As institutional business moves onto the web, market structures are changing rapidly. Consolidation across markets and exchanges is accelerating and alliances/joint ventures between financial institutions—who are often fierce competitors in their traditional, non-electronic businesses—are becoming increasingly evident. As markets, products and services are redefined in the wake of the Internet boom, established players and marketplaces are actively restructuring their business strategies and models to ensure they can offer institutional clients leading-edge services and generate new revenues in instances where they are being, or might be, permanently disintermediated.

Many institutions, for example, have taken shareholdings in new multiparty Internet B2B exchanges as 'hedges' against future market consolidation. Since it is unclear—and will remain unclear for some time—which products, services and structures will ultimately endure and dominate in the e-finance environment, some institutions have wisely adopted a 'portfolio approach' by participating as shareholders or joint venture partners in a range of platforms.

As indicated earlier in the text, financial B2B services are available through corporate storefront models (where individual firms provide institutional clients with direct access to proprietary content, products and services) or through B2B trading alliances and exchanges. Corporate storefronts able to create and convey the broadest range of proprietary products and services, including research, new issues, trading and fulfillment, are, and should remain, market leaders; examples in this sector include the institutional corporate storefronts of Citibank, Goldman Sachs, Deutsche Bank, UBS Warburg, Barclays Capital, BNP Paribas, Dresdner Bank, and Merrill Lynch, among others.

The B2B exchange sector is an important, if still-evolving, part of the market. As we have noted, B2B exchanges are designed to eliminate market inefficiencies by bringing together purchasers and suppliers of products/services and letting them transact with one another in a controlled forum; examples in this area include Fxall, BondBook, Creditex, and Posit, among many others. When the general B2B exchange concept was originally introduced in the late 1990s it was seen as one of the most promising areas of e-commerce. Many 'exchanges' were assembled in a short time period to take advantage of the 'hot concept' (with high valuation potential in the event of a subsequent IPO). Some of the original exchanges have failed to work as expected (in the same way that many B2C ventures have failed), and the consolidation process has commenced. While various financial exchanges will dissolve or merge over the coming years as a result of unsound business models or extreme competition, a core of well-planned, and soundly managed, platforms should ultimately achieve a critical mass of business and thrive. Though it is too early to tell which B2B exchanges will prosper, certain determinants of survivability and success can be identified. Ventures that have strong backing from established players (including institutions that are recognized leaders in particular segments of the financial markets), those that have experienced management that understands the intricacies of both the financial industry and e-commerce, those that feature flexible, scalable architecture capable of dealing with very large institutional buying/selling, those that are capable of producing and delivering new products quickly, and those that offer true value-added services that generate incremental gains for institutional end-users are the ones most likely to succeed.

B2B infrastructure providers, such as Arcordia, Indata, Sungard, IQ Financial, eSpeed, Corillion, and many others (including those referenced in Chapter 2), play a key role in the B2B e-finance sector. While certain institutions have developed their corporate storefronts internally, many others have out-sourced the task partially or completely to infrastructure companies capable of providing front-, middle- and, increasingly, back-office solutions for conveying, managing and processing B2B transactions. The presence and participation of infrastructure companies is even more evident in the B2B exchange sector. Since many financial B2B exchanges have been created by alliances which can include several, or even dozens, of large financial institutions, they tend to rely on third-party infrastructure companies to develop and implement their underlying technological platforms; this approach is generally considered more efficient and cost-effective than trying to gain technological consensus and manage technology resources across all partners in the exchange, or tasking one or two to create and deliver the required solutions. B2B exchanges thus rely heavily on infrastructure providers and other enablers. In the future, this type of cooperative infrastructure arrangement is likely to lead to further outsourcing and sharing of back-end functions. Thus, while established financial institutions and new financial ventures may focus on product design, marketing, execution and service, the actual settlement, clearing and maintenance dimensions of the business may be subcontracted to the infrastructure community and trust providers.

Though the financial B2B sector is still in the process of definition and development, its growth prospects are very strong. By 2004, researchers expect that the US B2B finance sector will generate revenues of nearly $68B, or more than 10% of all institutional financial services revenue; incremental revenues will be generated abroad and add to the total.

IPOs AND NEW ISSUES

While many IPOs, equity add-ons, convertible new issues and debt new issues still occur in a 'traditional' manner with investment bankers, capital markets specialists and syndicate managers arranging, managing and executing different aspects of a given deal, there is an increasing move towards standardizing and automating the process using the Internet. To determine which dimensions can be handled in electronic format, consider the simplified process of bringing a new issue to market. In a typical IPO—and, with only slight variations on the theme, a typical debt or convertible bond offering—the bank acting as lead manager joins with legal and audit teams in performing due diligence on the issuer. The results of the due diligence effort are embodied in the S-1 registration statement (or its equivalent in other markets), which is filed with the SEC prior to launch. The entire due diligence and registration process typically takes two months to complete. Once filed, the lead manager takes the issuer's management on a 'roadshow'—or marketing trip—to help 'sell' the deal to investors. A typical roadshow can last several days to several weeks, and is designed to showcase management and provide answers to questions about the issuer's financial and corporate position and prospects. During the roadshow the lead manager begins collecting indications of interest (IOIs) from potential investors, which reflect the number of shares they might be interested in purchasing at different price levels. The IOI process allows the lead manager to begin gauging interest and adjusting pricing parameters. Once the roadshow is complete the deal moves into the final pricing and allocation stage. At this point the lead manager and other banks in the selling group set the IPO price and allocate shares to investors. Following deal launch, banks involved with the transaction typically provide ongoing support through secondary market-making and research coverage.

Major financial institutions have begun using web technologies to gravitate elements of the new issue business online; this reduces the time to market and lowers deal costs. Though certain aspects of the process outlined above, including due diligence and registration, remain 'manual' in nature, it is now possible to accomplish many other dimensions through the web—directly or through outsourcing. For instance, a typical full service new issue platform sponsored by a large institution might include a listing of the pipeline (or calendar) of deals appearing in the future, online links to issuer S-1 registration statements, prospectuses and other financial information, live or archived replays of electronic roadshows, analyst calls and commentary, IOI input, trade allocation, trade processing and after-market research. Secondary trading in support of IPOs or other new issues can be accomplished through associated online storefront or B2B exchange trading platforms described later in the chapter. The comprehensive, convenient and cost-effective nature of these facilities has captured the attention of clients and redefined many aspects of how the new issue business will be conducted in future years. Infrastructure providers are on hand to provide support to institutions interested in outsourcing aspects of the process. For instance, once due diligence has been completed, prospectuses and other financial documents can be prepared according to 'best practice' standards by independent providers such as e-Financial, electronic roadshows can be coordinated, conducted and archived by a range of Internet multimedia ventures, and so on. Whether developed internally or externally, the benefits of migrating new issuance online are considerable: deal-related expenses can be reduced, the information-sharing process expedited, distribution channels expanded, and time to market reduced. Prior to the development of Internet-based new issue platforms, an average IPO took four to five months from inception to pricing. By moving aspects of the process to the web the time horizon has been shrunk to less than three months, and promises to become even shorter as new efficiencies are discovered.

While many established Wall Street firms—including powerhouses such as Goldman Sachs, CSFB, Salomon Smith Barney, Morgan Stanley Dean

Witter, Merrill Lynch and others—already offer electronic IPOs and other online new issue services through their corporate storefronts, a new breed of dedicated online investment banks has been created to manage and distribute new issues to both institutional and retail customers. For example, Schwab, TD Waterhouse and Ameritrade created a new venture known as Epoch Partners to offer retail and small institutional clients greater access to IPOs. Wit Capital, one of the 'founding fathers' of online trading discussed in Chapter 2, features Internet access to new issues through its Wit Soundview/ E*Offering unit. DirectIPO has been established as a niche player to provide 'turnkey' IPO and consulting services for institutions seeking to go public; in this capacity the venture's management assumes responsibility for all aspects of a company's IPO. WR Hambrecht, a relatively new investment bank, allows investors to bid for a specific number of new shares at a given price through its OpenIPO module; the offer price is then set at the lowest price at which all bids can be cleared—bids which are greater than the offer receive a full allocation. These online ventures tend to focus primarily on small new issues (supplemented by co-management positions in large issues led by top-tier houses) and are thus creating a niche for themselves. One goal of the Internet IPO houses is to avoid placing shares with 'flippers' (speculators who buy and resell the issues on a very short-term basis) by trying to direct order flow towards a more stable investor base—typically retail or small institutional investors; in order to curtail 'flipping' a number of ventures bar access to future IPOs if investors sell within 60 days of new issue launch. To the extent they are able to successfully implement this goal, they may be able to direct future IPOs towards a 'friendlier' investor base and reduce an issuer's stock price volatility. Certain online IPO houses also provide links into research portals (described in Chapter 6) which are general in nature and broad in coverage; this allows investors to review research from multiple sources— not only from the lead manager responsible for 'selling' a given deal.

New bond flotation has also started moving onto the Internet and is changing the way in which bond underwriters—primarily the large investment banks of the world—create, price and distribute product. Bond syndication— the practice of forming groups of banks to help distribute securities to end-investors—is gradually becoming an electronic process, marking a new phase in the evolution of the bond distribution mechanism. For example, Merrill Lynch, through its MLX platform, introduced I-Deal as an electronic IOI interface/order input for financial institutions and institutional clients. Institutions simply consult the platform, investigate new issue deal specifics, submit IOIs electronically, and receive confirmation once the book has closed and the deal has priced. BondDesk, a multidealer platform discussed below, features similar 'e-syndication' facilities. WR Hambrecht features an auction-based web platform that enables investors to anonymously submit on-screen bids for investment grade bond issues and, in so doing, establish the launch price. In a novel concept, JP Morgan has introduced wireless bond syndication technology that lets authorized users participate in e-syndicates from mobile devices. From the issuer's perspective the so-called 'e-bond' is a reality. e-Bonds are securities which are created and distributed strictly through the Internet, and are supported in the aftermarket through electronic trading mechanisms. In 2000 issuers such as the World Bank, Fannie Mae, Dow Chemical and others launched e-bonds to end-investors either directly or through the Internet platforms of various dealers; this has proven a quick and efficient way of raising capital.

ELECTRONIC TRADING

Perhaps the most visible element of B2B financial services has come in the form of electronic trading. The concept of electronic trading is not, of course, new to the financial markets. There has been a move away from physical, open-outcry trading for many years, though the pace has certainly accelerated over the past few years. NASDAQ, the main US market for over-the-counter (OTC) equity trading, was an early champion of the electronic trading concept. Unlike other exchanges, it never featured a trading floor or open-outcry trading—it has always operated as a private intranet of market makers who make prices via their computers (linked by 250,000 miles of dedicated telecom pipe spread around the country, which helps ensure price synchronicity). Various open-outcry equity trading floors have gravitated towards the pure electronic trading concept over the past two decades, including the LSE, Frankfurt Stock Exchange (FSE) and TSE, among others; the New York Stock Exchange (NYSE), the world's largest exchange as measured by market capitalization, is one of the last remaining holdouts. Though the NYSE continues to feature physical trading and a well-established specialist system (that acts either as market maker or as agent between brokers), it introduced its Network NYSE platform in late 2000, permitting retail and institutional investors to engage in instantaneous, and anonymous, electronic trading (including direct input of orders for immediate execution by a specialist). Numerous futures exchanges, including MATIF (now part of Euronext), LIFFE and Sydney Futures Exchange (SFE), among others, have converted from physical to electronic trading over the past decade. While equity and futures trading has evolved from the physical to the electronic in recent years, other aspects of financial trading have always existed in electronic form. Most bond, currency, and derivatives trading has historically taken place through phones and computer terminals in a large OTC market. These markets do not feature central forums to link buyers and sellers, though indicative prices have been, and continue to be, posted on certain defined screens.

Though electronic trading has existed in various forms for a number of years, the advent of the Internet has accelerated the development of new online trading mechanisms. New 'alternative trading systems' (ATSs) have fuelled interest and activity in institutional electronic trading—many ATS market structures/mechanisms have been created over the past few years through web-based technologies, and the financial world is edging closer to the notion of liquid, 24 hour, global trading across markets and products. Most of the new market structures allow investors—who are primarily, though not exclusively, institutional—to buy and sell securities and other financial assets on a secure basis through comprehensive platforms. One of the direct by-products of increased electronic trading is price transparency. Participants have much greater access to the information and flows/orders that drive prices and bid–offer spreads, and can make economic decisions accordingly. Over time this price transparency is expected to lead to even broader participation, creating deeper liquidity and tighter margins. It may also introduce greater trading volatility as participants move in and out of markets at a faster rate; that, of course, could generate increased risk for certain types of players.

Online institutional trading in equities, bonds, currencies, commodities and derivatives is readily available through the corporate storefronts of major institutions such as Goldman Sachs, Merrill Lynch, Salomon Smith Barney, Barclays Capital, Dresdner Kleinwort Benson, Deutsche Bank, UBS Warburg, BNP Paribas, ING Barings, and many others. Such services are also available through various other joint ventures, alliances, partnerships, and exchanges—together, these form the core of the broad ATS sector (which has merited a formal definition from the SEC—per SEC Regulation ATS (300), an ATS is 'any organization, association, person, group of persons, or system: that constitutes, maintains, or provides a market place or facilitates for bringing together purchasers and sellers of securities or for otherwise performing with respect to securities the functions commonly performed by a stock exchange within the meaning of Rule 3b-16; and that does not: set rules governing the conduct of subscribers other than the conduct of such subscribers' trading on such organization, association, person, group of persons, or system; or discipline subscribers other than by exclusion from trading').

From an architectural standpoint, many of the new electronic trading platforms are highly flexible, and can be based partly or totally on Internet technology. Some electronic trading platforms feature web-enabled screens which route client orders directly to the venture providing the electronic trading and execution services. Others connect proprietary or third-party trade interfaces to routing and processing mechanisms. In the latter instance, a client first enters an order on a proprietary screen; the order is immediately translated from the client's interface into a standard communication format using a meta-language (such as OFX (open financial exchange), FIX (financial information exchange), or FpML (financial product markup language), among others). The translated order is then routed via the Internet, or some alternate network link, to a bank's electronic trading platform; after the order passes through relevant security checks it moves through a filter which identifies its internal destination and directs it accordingly. The trader receives the translated order and executes it per the instructions received; once executed, the trader reconfirms details of the trade to the client through the electronic platform. Variations on the theme exist, but this is illustrative of a typical electronic trade between an institutional client and an electronic trading venture.

One of the most interesting and significant ATS mechanisms, the electronic communications network (ECN), resulted from changes in US securities laws and has been propelled to the forefront by web-based technologies. In January 1997, following its investigation of collusive market-making practices on the NASDAQ, the SEC issued new orders requiring market makers to display, and execute, limit orders (i.e. orders to trade at a specific price) when the price posted is better than that offered by a market maker, or adds to volume being offered. The SEC ruling led to the formal creation of ECNs—order matching systems which let investors trade without market makers—and forced NASDAQ and other exchanges to include competing quotes from ECNs in their bid–offer displays. Thus, when a small order is inside the bid, it must be displayed on the quote montage next to all other institutional orders. ECNs act as de-facto electronic central agency auction markets, or central limit order books (CLOBs), matching purchase and sale orders on a strict price/time priority in exchange for a small access fee (1.5 cents/share). Execution flow through ECNs is divided into marketable and non-marketable orders. A marketable order is one that agrees with the market; for purchases the price is greater than, or equal to, the offer, and for sales it is less than, or equal to, the bid. A non-marketable order is one that disagrees with the market; for purchases the price is less than the offer and for sales it is greater than the offer. Marketable orders get checked against an ECN's limit book of unexecuted orders. If a match is made, execution occurs; if no match is made, the order goes to a market maker or another ECN. ECNs add considerable value in the case of non-marketable orders. For non-marketable orders that cannot be matched, an ECN sorts and displays them on a more detailed screen (such as the NASDAQ Level II quote montage) that reflects a range of prices, including the highest bid and lowest offer.

In order for ECNs to be truly successful, they require a critical mass of marketable and non-marketable orders; not every ECN has enough liquidity in every stock to be able to match incoming orders (a competitive advantage which market makers still retain). Certain ECNs pay for non-marketable orders in order to build up their books, while others charge execution agents for order representation in exchange for fast, spread-free transactions. The more orders an ECN represents the greater its liquidity, the better the execution service for the client; the cycle then feeds on itself. This makes intuitive sense, as an ECN with only 10 orders is bound to have a harder time finding matches than one with 1000 orders. While ECNs can certainly function without Internet-based technologies, the availability of the web as an efficient order entry, routing and information mechanism has helped spur interest and volume. ECNs have been instrumental in giving retail investors access to many of the same benefits that institutional investors have long enjoyed. In particular, small investors gain anonymous, spread-free trading when crossing directly with another customer, fair representation in the market (i.e. if an order is routed to the market and it is either the highest bid or lowest offer on the ECN, it carries the same weight as an institutional order), lower bid–offer spreads, and after-hours trading (i.e. after the close, as long as trades can be matched—note that after-hours trading is still generally limited to the largest capitalization stocks). Speed and anonymity, the great advantages of ECNs, have proven particularly useful in volatile markets, when investors seek quick, reliable and discreet execution. Given these advantages, ECNs have experienced considerable growth in business flow over the past few years, and routinely account for 20–30% of trading volume on exchanges such as NASDAQ; certain industry practitioners predict that ECNs could eventually account for 50–60% of all trading.

Instinet, owned by Reuters, was created in 1969 as a telephonic equity agency brokerage that enabled institutions and large private investors to deal with one another, directly and anonymously, without going through a 'middleman'. Though it was not known as an ECN at the time, it fulfilled the same functions as today's ECNs. Over a period of years Instinet captured a significant share of agency and after-hours volume in numerous markets (including several overseas markets). During the mid-1990s it migrated its business to the Internet and today accepts electronic orders, divides them into pieces, and sends them to multiple markets to obtain appropriate access to member liquidity; this helps ensure best-price execution. The capabilities provided by the Internet have helped expand Instinet's business; the venture, for example, now routinely handles between 10% and 17% of NASDAQ's volume. Island, owned by online broker Datek, and Tradebook, owned by financial information company Bloomberg, have also become important ECNs, handling a considerable amount of institutional and retail flows. Other equity ECNs include Archipelago (one of the four 'originally authorized' ECNs which commenced operations as a national 'limit order book' for NASDAQ stocks and now allows retail and institutional customers to access other ECNs or any other NYSE/NASDAQ market maker), Brut (which specializes in NASDAQ and small capitalization stocks), Attain (which specializes in NASDAQ stocks), NexTrade (which specializes in NASDAQ stocks), Redibook (which specializes in NYSE and American Stock Exchange issues), and Posit (which focuses more broadly on US and UK stocks). (Note that Optimark, an infrastructure provider as well as an ECN, was another early entrant into the market, trading NASDAQ and Pacific Stock Exchange issues; it featured intelligent technology which allowed participants to enter complex trading rules/orders, but was unable to achieve a critical mass of orders and has since refocused its operations on e-consulting.)

By 2000 the eight largest equity ECNs, led by Instinet, increased their share of NASDAQ market trading to 34% of total turnover. Though ECNs have made meaningful inroads into the NASDAQ and various other exchanges, they have historically avoided the NYSE with its powerful, and well-established, specialist system. That process changed in mid-2000 when Archipelago—responding to a repeal of a NYSE rule that forced member firms to trade certain stocks only on the floor of the NYSE—began handling bids and offers on the Consolidated Quote System. Archipelago commenced with a dozen NYSE stocks and then expanded its coverage; though other ECNs have since joined in, their total share of NYSE turnover is still relatively small—less than 5%, compared with more than 1/3 on the NASDAQ. It is worth noting that the ECN phenomenon is gradually spreading to the overseas markets. Though many international markets have based their execution services on the CLOB concept for several years, established exchanges have still tended to dominate most trading; accordingly, some competition is appearing from new ECNs—especially in Europe, where ventures that provide pan-European stock market access are gaining ground. Sample European ECN initiatives include Tradepoint (backed by Instinet, JP Morgan, Morgan Stanley Dean Witter, Merrill Lynch, CSFB and Archipelago), Jiway (OM and Morgan Stanley Dean Witter), ITG Europe (ITG and Societe Generale), and E-Crossnet (the asset management arms of Barclays and Merrill Lynch), among others. Certain international ventures are also attempting to tap into the US market through the ECN structure. For instance, ECN Access of Spain has an alliance with Island that allows European institutions to route US stock orders through ECN Access's gateway and into the Island book; this allows instant execution from Europe. ECN Access is deploying similar order routing mechanisms into other European markets.

As a counter to the growing market share/influence of equity ECNs, which threatens to dislodge certain Wall Street houses from their traditional role as market makers, several major firms have taken equity stakes in one or more ECNs; this positions them to benefit from any permanent structural changes in the secondary trading markets. In addition, some firms have acquired technology-focused trading firms in order to give them a broader and deeper market presence. For instance, in 2000 Merrill Lynch acquired electronic market maker Herzog Heine Geduld, while Goldman Sachs acquired Spear Leeds Kellogg—these acquisitions give the large securities firms greater capabilities in off-exchange electronic market making. Other firms are also adapting to the ECN movement. For example, Knight Trading, another large electronic NASDAQ market maker, actively employs technology to sort, match and execute incoming orders instantaneously; time previously spent in sorting and matching trades is now spent analyzing trading patterns and managing proprietary risk inventory—in the hope of generating more profits. In another defensive move Wall Street's three largest houses, Merrill Lynch, Morgan Stanley Dean Witter and Goldman Sachs, proposed the creation of a unified market for all US equities—under their proposal a CLOB would aggregate orders from every market on a single screen, thus removing the incentive to trade through other ECNs; though they have since abandoned this proposal, future changes in exchange structure are highly likely. NASDAQ itself proposed the creation of a 'SuperMontage' that would incorporate into NASDAQ the best ECN bids and offers; opponents argued that such would discourage buy- and sell-side firms from routing their orders into ECNs. After receiving a certain amount of criticism, NASDAQ restructured SuperMontage and it is now designed to display up to three ECN bids and offers and provide execution and quote display in an integrated fashion, injecting more transparency and speed into the dealing process. In addition, the SuperMontage pricing algorithm no longer penalizes ECN orders (which have often been forced behind market maker orders as a result of the small access fees ECNs charge); users can express a preference for quotes from ECNs or market makers carrying the same price by filtering out access fees. As exchanges such as NASDAQ, NYSE, and others attempt to redefine their markets and strategies, individual ECNs may begin to feel some pressure—this may force them to begin interacting with one another more directly and frequently, something they have not traditionally done. It may also hasten the consolidation process, perhaps ultimately channeling a critical mass of orders into a smaller group of more powerful ECNs.

Electronic trading is not, of course, limited to equities; the same basic model is now applied to other instruments such as bonds, FX and derivatives. Secondary bond trading, in particular, has emerged as a significant area of focus and is expected to lead to considerable changes in the global bond markets over the coming years. The prospect of trading bonds over the Internet—including government bonds, agency securities, mortgage-backed securities (MBS), asset-backed securities (ABS), corporate bonds, high yield bonds, Eurobonds/global bonds, and so on—is particularly appealing to many investors as they will gain regular access to a large number of securities which would otherwise go unquoted and untraded. Since the global fixed income market is issuer- and issue-specific, it is extremely fragmented—that makes it difficult to provide, through traditional mechanisms, active and continuous two-way prices and acceptable liquidity for a large part of the market. For instance, in the US bond market there are approximately 3MM individual issues that can theoretically be quoted on a regular or periodic basis—by way of comparison, the US equity market only features 10,000 issues; similar 'discrepancies' exist in the international debt and equity markets. Internet-based platforms can help bridge the gap, providing greater coverage of the entire universe through automated processes. In addition, electronic platforms provide greater insight into pricing and liquidity, two major areas of interest to investors. The market for debt securities is presently estimated at $15T; though only 6% of that amount was traded online in 1999, research firm Tower Group estimates that 50% of fixed income trades will occur online by 2003. To capture a share of this market, numerous leading banks offer bond trading capabilities through their corporate storefronts. In addition, many dedicated bond exchanges have been established—some of them created, or backed, by the leading bond trading houses on Wall Street, who wish to 'preposition' themselves for any permanent structural changes in the fixed income trading markets. To date these financial ventures have taken the form of multidealer network alliances/exchanges. In 1997 there were 11 online bond trading platforms, by 1999 the number had increased to 40 and, by 2000, over 80. While the move towards electronic bond trading is clear and logical, there is certain to be some consolidation in the sector over the coming years—the industry is unlikely to be able to support so many platforms. Those backed, or sponsored, by the large Wall Street bond houses are expected to emerge as stable, value-added conduits with critical mass; in addition, those with a special niche focus—such as MBS, Asian bonds, and so on—may also prosper.

BondBook was one of the first electronic bond trading platforms to be created. It was founded by Goldman Sachs, Merrill Lynch and Morgan Stanley Dean Witter, which together account for a 35% share of the fixed income market, and was joined by Salomon Smith Barney as a late stage partner. The platform allows direct trading between institutional players on an anonymous basis, giving authorized participants price transparency and dealing liquidity. Live trading in investment grade, high yield and municipal bonds commenced in late 2000, with clearing routed through Merrill Lynch's Broadcort subsidiary; post-trade information processing and reporting are planned in future phases. In order to ensure the platform does not compete against the trading desks of the sponsors, each firm commits to channeling a significant amount of primary and secondary bond inventory through BondBook. BondDesk, created through the merger of two web platforms (MuniGroup and the 'original' BondDesk), is supported by 15 major international financial institutions and structured as an integrated market-making platform for municipals, agencies, Treasuries and corporates. The venture features live prices executable against existing dealer inventory and provides 'e-syndication' capabilities for new debt issues. Bond-Connect, created by State Street and Bridge, is a B2B exchange for US and European high yield, investment grade, ABS, MBS, Treasuries, agencies and municipals. BondConnect links 85 buy-side institutions and 17 sell-side dealers through an online platform that anonymously matches and crosses secondary buy and sell orders six times per day. Market Axess is a dealer-to-client corporate bond platform backed by Bear Stearns, ABN Amro, JP Morgan, Chase, Deutsche Bank, and UBS Warburg; the site provides institutions with online research and trading capabilities and permits authorized clients to deal in primary and secondary corporate bond issues.

Other representative electronic bond trading platforms include: BrokerTec (a global fixed income interdealer broker backed by 12 major financial institutions, focused on Treasuries and Euro-denominated government securities); Bond.hub (a portal/search engine for high yield bonds, collateralized mortgage obligations (CMOs), corporate bonds and agencies which provides prices, research and links to the corporate storefronts of the sponsors, including Merrill Lynch, Goldman Sachs, JP Morgan, Lehman Brothers, Morgan Stanley Dean Witter, and Salomon Smith Barney); CoreDeal (a global corporate bond trading platform operated by the International Securities Markets Association and 13 international banks); TradeWeb (a Treasury platform operated by Goldman Sachs, Morgan Stanley Dean Witter and Lehman Brothers); Visible Markets (an ABS/MBS trading platform funded by Greylock); and Securities.hub (a research and pricing platform run by Merrill Lynch, Goldman Sachs, Morgan Stanley Dean Witter, Salomon Smith Barney, JP Morgan, and Lehman Brothers). Other sites offering similar electronic bond trading services include Tradebonds, BondClick, Limitrader, eBondTrade, and TradingEdge, among others. In mid-2000 a powerful consortium of ABS/MBS market makers—Bear Stearns, CSFB, Salomon Smith Barney, and Lehman Brothers—announced the rollout of a platform for electronic trading of ABS and MBS. A subset of the MBS market, based on the underlying pools of mortgages that are used to create MBS product, has also been the focus of web-based activity. Sites such as Ultraprise and Pedestal have created online trading markets in underlying mortgages. Through these platforms, loan pool details are collected from prospective sellers and posted to an Internet 'trading exchange'; buyers can scan the database through specific criteria (including coupon, score, pool, and so on) and submit bids over the web. The US commercial paper (CP) market has also been the focus of attention by issuers interested in dealing directly with end-investors. For example, the Direct Issuers Work Group (which includes large, active CP issuers such as Ford, General Motors, and others) has formed cpmarket, a web venture that allows them to sell their CP obligations directly to end-investors online.

In the international fixed income sector, JP Morgan, Deutsche Bank, Daiwa Securities, and several VC firms created AsiaBondPortal.com, an online platform for Asian corporate bond trading and research—including Asian and Japanese issues denominated in dollars, yen, and local currencies; the major bank partners supply the venture with bond pricing, inventory/liquidity and research. Japan's three largest securities firms, Daiwa, Nikko and Nomura, developed a joint online trading system for Japanese Government Bonds; Lehman Brothers and VC firm Softbank created a similar joint platform of their own. EuroMTS, a European electronic fixed income trading platform backed by more than two dozen international banks, has emerged as a popular trading platform for a variety of European government securities. CSFB has developed a dedicated European commercial paper (ECP) conduit known as ECPTrade which allows institutional clients to trade ECP via the web and obtain associated settlement and confirmation services. In a novel alliance, futures exchange Eurex has teamed up with six European banks in the creation of a German bond/futures trading ECN which allows customers to execute online bond and derivative (i.e. basis) trades simultaneously. While this list is obviously not exhaustive, it is representative of the scope of the electronic bond trading efforts currently in existence. As indicated earlier, it is unlikely that all of these platforms can continue to operate as viable, independent entities in the medium-term. Some consolidation, to force critical mass and deeper liquidity, is expected to occur over the coming years.

The FX market has featured true electronic trading for several years. Indeed, platforms such as Reuters FX Dealing and the EBS Electronic Broking System can rightly claim to be among the first real electronic B2B exchanges. However, these ventures have operated primarily in the interbank sphere, and have never been truly embraced by corporate customers; even after the advent of these platforms, most customers continued to deal with multiple banks on a telephonic basis. With the arrival of web-based technologies, new efforts have been placed on enticing corporate customers to trade electronically. In early 2000 approximately 5% of FX trading occurred via the Internet, but various researchers expect that figure to reach 20–25% by 2003 as new ventures capture client business. Through a typical electronic FX exchange, an authorized institutional client can login to a service and enter an order to buy or sell a particular currency for spot or forward value. Once the order is input it is immediately routed to participating banks, which then have the option of providing instantaneous quotes back to the venture; the venture immediately aggregates the quotes and displays them in a ranking from best to worst. The client then has a specified amount of time (generally a few seconds) to select which quote/bank it wants to deal with; once selected, the order is confirmed with the bank through the venture—the entire process is thus quick and efficient.

There are at least two major platforms (Fxall and Atriax), along with many smaller ventures, hoping to use the Internet to redefine the FX trading market. In 1999 a group of seven US and European banks (which ultimately expanded to 13) announced the formation of FXalliance and the creation of Fxall, an electronic FX trading service operating through the web. The original banks supporting the service—Bank of America, CSFB, Goldman Sachs, HSBC, Morgan Stanley Dean Witter, UBS Warburg, and JP Morgan—created a platform where participants can see, via the web, FX research and FX prices from multiple banks, and trade with any one they choose; the web platform also generates standard electronic confirms and settles all trades.

With the additional six partner banks who joined after the founding of Fxall, the platform now comprises institutions which jointly command a 28% share of daily FX trading activity. The second major initiative, Atriax, was announced in mid-2000 by partners Deutsche Bank, Citibank, Chase, and Reuters; 47 other banks and 25 corporate clients subsequently joined the venture. Like Fxall, Atriax is intended to offer institutional clients live FX bids/offers and real-time execution, together with relevant analytics and research support. The consortium of banks comprising Atriax control 50% of daily currency trading volume, indicating that the battle between the rival platforms may be intense. In addition to these major bank-sponsored initiatives, various other FX platforms have been created. State Street has developed FXConnect, which supplies FX rates from multiple banks to 250 approved institutional investors; participants can execute their trades online with any bank posting an executable price. Trading in spot and forward FX is available through various other platforms, including Matchbook FX and Currenex. FX options trading can be accomplished through ventures such as Volbroker, an electronic FX option service jointly owned by JP Morgan, Royal Bank of Scotland, Citibank, Deutsche Bank, Goldman Sachs, and UBS Warburg (and featuring the participation of 24 other financial institutions). Volbroker provides banks with web-based access to real-time electronic interdealer trading in FX options; the service is designed to disintermediate FX option brokers by allowing direct execution over the Internet. In a novel venture, UBS Warburg has teamed up with online retail trading firm E*Trade to provide E*Trade's clients with FX capabilities using the bank's FX2B platform. In addition to alliances and marketplaces, certain banks have also developed dedicated corporate storefront platforms that deliver FX services to specific market or client bases. For example, in 2000 ANZ, in conjunction with Reuters, created FX Online as a web FX service for the bank's European institutional and corporate customers; this supplements a similar platform ANZ has been operating in Australia since 1998. Deutsche Bank provides its mid-sized Japanese corporate customers with online FX dealing capabilities of between $2MM and $5MM in selected currencies. Fuji Bank, Sumitomo Bank, DKB Trust, and Sanwa Bank followed Deutsche Bank's lead and introduced web FX services of their own. Citibank, through Citifx, offers its customers complete FX solutions, including live prices, research, data services, analytical tools, and links into trading. As an indication of the value of this service, GE outsourced $20B of its FX requirements to Citibank's web platform in late 2000, hoping to achieve requisite cost savings and execution efficiencies.

Derivatives, which trade on formal exchanges and OTC, have become a central part of B2B finance. In the listed market, long-established exchanges like LIFFE, Chicago Board of Trade (CBOT), and the Chicago Mercantile Exchange (CME), among others, have supplemented their standard electronic trading with new Internet services. For instance, LIFFE's Internet platform, LIFFE Connect, now handles the majority of the exchange's trading volume. The CME, through its CME FIX API platform, connects a trading firm's ISP software to the exchange's order routers. The CBOT, via its Open-Direct API and Electronic Open Outcry Market, links CBOT member firms and trading floor brokers through the web. Recognizing the importance of electronic trading, the CBOT also created a separate subsidiary, eCBOT, to focus on the development of electronically-traded products and electronic delivery mechanisms.

In the OTC market, interest rate, currency, equity, commodity and credit derivatives are available through different platforms. For instance, Swapswire was created by a partnership of major banks—BNP Paribas, CSFB, Goldman Sachs, Merrill Lynch, JP Morgan, Chase, Citibank, Deutsche Bank, Morgan Stanley Dean Witter, and UBS Warburg—as a point-to-point electronic platform for interest rate derivative trading. The facility provides indicative prices and can accept IOIs from approved dealers and clients. Full trade details are published to the screen once a trade is executed, and the platform supports straight-through processing (as described later in the chapter). JP Morgan established a separate corporate storefront derivative platform known as SwapsLab, which provides US and European counterparts with full derivative dealing capabilities, including indicative market rates, pricing, execution, research, news, and analysis. The bank also offers separate storefront platforms for municipal derivatives (Muniderivatives), credit derivatives (Morgancredit), and foreign exchange and precious metals (VolCenter). Various other derivative ventures are in existence, including TreasuryConnect, which allows clients to execute currency and interest rate derivatives (including swaps, forwards, caps and floors) and Icor, which acts as an Internet B2B broker on a range of debt and equity derivatives.

Participants in the credit derivative market—which represents one of the fastest growing areas of financial derivatives—have developed numerous dedicated platforms of their own. Creditex, for instance, was established by JP Morgan, Societe Generate, Deutsche Bank, Bank of America, CSFB, Dresdner Bank, UBS Warburg, CIBC, and Morgan Stanley Dean Witter, as an electronic trading and information conduit for default swaps, default options and other credit derivative structures. CreditTrade, a corporate loan/credit derivative trading platform owned by Mutant Technology and supported by Chase and Internet Capital Group, allows authorized users to post trades in a marketplace setting and receive indicative pricing and executable quotes from institutions registered as authorized credit traders. Unlike Creditex, CreditTrade allows dealing by phone as well as the Internet. In the well-established equity derivative market, various specialized platforms have emerged. For instance, StructuredMarkets provides users with a range of OTC equity derivative services, including buy-side pricing, analytic tools and documentation templates. BuySideDirect is a platform focused exclusively on equity-linked securities trading; the venture allows institutions to initiate and execute convertible bond trades and associated stock hedges, and provides related research and commentary. Numerous banks have created their own storefront modules to deal exclusively with convertible bonds. For instance, Deutsche Bank features an online convertible bond research and trading platform known as dbconvertibles, Morgan Stanley Dean Witter operates through its ConvertBond.com offering, and so on. These platforms have a range of features, including online trading and hedging, pricing, scenario analysis and research.

OTC commodities and commodity derivatives are traded through numerous B2B storefronts, alliances and exchanges, including platforms such as Kiodex, MetalSite, MetalNet, aluminium.com, OilSpot, and International Exchange, among many others. For example, Kiodex allows users to request price quotes on a range of vanilla and exotic commodity derivatives (referencing energy products, base metals and precious metals); the site allows institutions to enter orders, execute transactions and receive confirmations (though transactions can only be executed with firms that have pre-established credit limits). International Exchange, a multiproduct commodity derivative platform, was created by a consortium of banks and commodity producers/suppliers, including Deutsche Bank, Goldman Sachs, Morgan Stanley Dean Witter, Societe Generale, BP Amoco, Shell and Totalfina Elf, to promote web trading in OTC energy and metals derivatives. In Japan, e-Commodity was developed by Tokyo General, Taiyo General and Softbank as the first local online commodity trading exchange.

Given the creativity of bankers and financial engineers, it comes as no surprise that electronic forums have been created to foster trading in other financial and non-financial assets such as hedge fund shares, bandwidth, and weather derivatives. Though such efforts constitute a very small fraction of institutional online trading business, it is indicative of what creative thought and technology can produce. PlusFunds.com, backed by JP Morgan, Merrill Lynch, CSFB and four other investors, was developed in 2000 as a platform to provide institutional investors with greater access to information and trading liquidity in hedge funds. Hedge funds, which are offshore funds investing in a broad range of assets on a leveraged basis, have traditionally been secretive about their underlying positions and strategies. Though recent regulatory attempts to force a greater amount of disclosure have been a step in the right direction, many funds are still rather opaque to the outside world. Accordingly, the PlusFunds platform supplies investors with additional information about specific funds and their risk parameters, and provides a timely view of their risk performance. Equally important, the site establishes trading links for investors wishing to trade in the underlying shares of Bermuda Stock Exchange-listed hedge funds. Other platforms, such as HedgeWorld, provide similar capabilities. Several ventures emerged in the late 1990s to develop trading in bandwidth, or communications transmission capacity. This appears to be a logical strategy—so much information is flowing through networks that the ability to reallocate it based on supply and demand forces can improve pricing and transmission efficiencies. Though the market is still relatively small and volumes are low, its growth prospects appear strong. Bandwidth exchanges bring together buyers and sellers so they can negotiate, in a common setting, customized transmission deals. In a typical transaction, a telecommunications provider can log onto one of the specialized exchanges and commit to selling excess bandwidth during a particular month based on a price set by the exchange (reflecting supply and demand). A buyer of bandwidth can purchase the capacity from the exchange and, on a prespecified date, deliver the data to be transmitted to the seller, who then distributes the information along its network. Band-X, formed in 1997, trades four types of communications bandwidth, including clear channel leased, clear channel owned, international wholesale and Internet. Arbinet, RateXchange, Asia Capacity Exchange, and Chapel Hill BroadBand were created to perform similar buying/selling functions, while Enron, the energy supplier and trading company, has introduced bandwidth trading of its own. Weather derivatives are a relatively new dimension of the institutional financial world, but are gaining ground rapidly. Catastrophe Risk Exchange (Catex) was created as an online derivatives exchange specializing in catastrophe and weather derivatives; it services most of the major participants in the marketplace, including insurers, reinsurers, financial institutions and corporations. Reinsurance company SwissRe features its elrix.com Internet-based trading system for reinsurance auctions related to earthquake, windstorm and marine coverage. Enron Weather, a dedicated platform created by Enron, specializes in the creation of weather derivative solutions. Since many of these 'new derivative' areas are nascent, dealing standards and conventions are virtually nonexistent. To overcome this barrier users most often post, through web exchanges, the indicative terms and conditions of deals they are interested in executing; derivative providers then respond with specific acceptances or counterproposals.

It is worth noting that the deregulation of financial markets, blurring of market and product barriers, and development of ATSs and other B2B conduits have forced traditional exchanges to adapt their structures and strategies in order to remain relevant, viable and competitive in the 21st century. Many of the world's leading exchanges have already altered their operating structures (changing, for instance, from mutual organizations to publicly-owned and traded companies), entered into alliances or mergers with former competitors, or introduced new products/dealing mechanisms. For example: the German and Swiss futures exchanges merged to form Eurex; the Belgian, Dutch and French exchanges have created Euronext; Eurex and the CBOT have created the A/C/E futures trading alliance; the CME and TSE are developing new derivative products on a joint basis; and so on. In the US, the NYSE has demutualized and introduced its Network NYSE electronic trading platform, while NASDAQ has arranged a private placement and created the SuperMontage concept. In Asia, the Hong Kong and Sydney exchanges became public companies several years ago, while the Singapore exchange floated itself in late 2000. Consolidations and structural changes have not been limited to exchanges, but extended to the back-end entities that clear and settle their trades; for example, Deutsche Borse and Cedel have created the new ClearStream settlement house and Euroclear and French settlement house Sicovam have established a new entity of their own. Further amalgamations, driven by the rapidly changing environment, are a virtual certainty. Such changes, coupled with consolidations in the overall ATS sector as the market focuses its activity on a core of electronic platforms, means that the face of institutional electronic trading will continue to evolve over the coming years.

INVESTMENT BANKING AND CORPORATE BANKING SERVICES

Investment and corporate bankers have entered the 21st century along with their sales and trading colleagues. Though investment banking is still, at its core, a relationship business driven by personal contacts and face-to-face negotiations, certain aspects of the discipline are now being conducted in 'electronic form'. Various institutions have unified dimensions of their investment banking services through their corporate storefronts. For instance, Chase has developed a dedicated web platform for its investment banking clients known as ChaseSpace; the site gives institutional clients access to research, streaming audio/video reports, market commentary, securities prices and other deal-related information. Merrill Lynch's customers can do the same through MLX, Dresdner Bank's clients can do so through Dresdner Kleinwort Benson Online Markets, and so on.

In addition to the IPO and new issue services mentioned earlier in the chapter, other key areas of online investment banking center on matching buyers and sellers of businesses, and linking users and providers of private capital. For instance, Merrill Lynch and CapitalKey Advisors created M&A Online Advisors, an electronic forum to service small business mergers and acquisitions (M&A) in the sub-$30MM range. The platform employs web technologies and proprietary databases to match clients selling businesses with potential buyers registered through a central database. The underlying screening and matching process is very automated, resulting in time and cost savings. Once matches are identified, investment bankers intercede and provide the necessary professional advice to ensure transactions close smoothly. CapitalKey itself is a technology-based investment bank that develops and implements appropriate systems and information management processes to leverage financial opportunities. Online capital raising services are available from major Wall Street firms, as well as newer institutions such as Epoch Partners, Wit Capital/Soundview, OffRoad Capital, EarlyBirdCapital, Direct Stock Market, DirectIPO and others, through their storefront platforms. Many are active in direct private offerings (DPOs), raising capital on a private placement basis for small, private companies; for instance, ventures such as OffRoad Capital and Direct Stock Market match small companies seeking capital with private investors interested in investing in emerging firms in deals of up to $15MM.

Traditional corporate banking services have also migrated to the web over the past few years. Though many commercial banks focused their initial efforts on the provision of banking services to the general public (as we shall discuss in Chapter 5), the largest players have started using web technology to deliver banking services to their corporate customers—this appears to be a sound strategy, as more than 60% of US companies have online access and are actively using the web to conduct aspects of their business; a growing number of international businesses, especially those in Europe and Japan, are also becoming active Internet users. Migrating corporate banking services to the web, though conceptually appealing, has not been easy. While the relationship between a financial institution and a retail customer can normally be channeled through a single point of contact, the same is not necessarily true for corporate customers. Financial institutions often have multiple points of contact with a corporate customer, depending on the nature of the service provided by the bank and the specific department within a customer's organization charged with handling the service; for instance, investment management, cash management and treasury services might be handled by three different units within a bank and three different units within the client's organization. Coordinating these contacts can be challenging. In addition, integrating legacy systems within corporate banking can be complex, as individual institutional business units often use different front- and back-end systems (in retail organizations, customer-based legacy technology is often quite unified). Financial institutions are overcoming these hurdles by improving internal coordination and point contact, and integrating or unifying aspects of their technology; as a result, corporate banking services are moving onto the web.

Web-based corporate banking services are centered on several key areas, including cash management, electronic bill payment and presentment (EBPP), treasury management, trade finance, leasing, credit lines, and purchasing/procurement. In the cash management segment, platforms are available for corporate customers seeking a range of products and services— in their broadest implementation these include non-US and multicurrency payments, FX transactions, receivables processing, and cash reporting. Within the EBPP sector, most major banks allow their corporate customers to electronically receive and review bills and authorize payments (a topic we discuss at greater length in Chapter 5). Corporate banking platforms also act as payment conduits between companies participating in non-financial exchanges. For instance, a seller of a particular commodity might access a bank's online database through an exchange to determine if a particular buyer has the credit capacity/limit to make good on a payment for the commodity. Alternatively, a buyer of the commodity might access a bank through the exchange to open a credit line to effect a purchase. In the purchasing/ procurement sector, certain large banks provide their clients with electronic assistance in arranging web-based inventory purchases and fulfillment. In treasury management, many web platforms offer corporate customers electronic access to short-term investment and liability management services, including commercial paper funding/investment, overnight deposits/funds, and so on. Since corporate treasurers often employ FX, swaps, futures and options to manage their financial risks, risk management/hedging strategies based on these instruments can be structured, valued and executed online. Trade finance has emerged as another logical area for 'electronic intervention'. Trade finance is a heavily documentary process involving letters of credit, bills of exchange, bills of lading, and other credit instruments related to the shipping, importing, exporting and financing of goods. The manual nature of the documentary process lends itself to automation, and various international banks provide standard electronic templates for different aspects of the business. These documents, accompanied by digital signatures, can be distributed electronically to relevant trade participants, saving on time and expense. Online leasing services are available to corporate customers through numerous platforms which act as web-based lease brokers, linking customers searching for particular types of equipment or capital leases with financial institutions or corporations supplying leases. Some platforms simply provide quotes based on user-defined criteria (such as equipment, category, amount, tenor, and so on), while others actually match up lessor and lessee in an online marketplace model setting.

Corporate banking products and services can be obtained in 'unbundled' form through corporate storefront platforms, or in a consolidated fashion from institutions offering unified corporate banking modules. For example: Citibank offers its corporate customers billing, cash management, custody, and trade finance services; Deutsche Bank offers cash management, portfolio management and custody applications; First Union provides corporate reporting and cash management services; Wachovia supplies corporate reporting and payment products; FleetBoston Financial features letter of credit, trade finance and reconciliation services; Chase offers loan syndication, purchasing, trade finance, and treasury management services; Bank of America features treasury management and capital markets services; Royal Bank of Scotland offers payment/reconciliation, export collection, letter of credit, and cash management services; while Svenska Handelsbanken and ABN Amro offer treasury and trade-related services. In 2001 a banking consortium which includes Banco Santander CH, Commerzbank, Royal Bank of Scotland, San Paolo IMI and Societe Generale will introduce an online platform for corporate customers which allows them to deal in treasury and capital markets products (including FX, syndicated loans and interest rate derivatives). Certain corporate banking platforms are extending their reach by offering online payment and information capabilities for non-financial exchange participants (as described above); banks such as ABN Amro, Standard Chartered, Citibank, Chase and select others have created infrastructure to accommodate such dealings. Dedicated leasing ventures are becoming increasingly popular; platforms such as E-lease, Access Lease, GE Capital, and LeaseExchange are emerging as important participants in the lease market. In certain instances major banks have partnered with technology providers to create dedicated corporate banking services. For example, Citibank and Bottomline Technology have produced an online corporate billing system, Bank One has partnered with EDS, billserv and InvoiceLink to produce a joint invoice/payment solution, and so on.

Small business banking is becoming an important focal point for various web-banking service providers as well. Many established institutions have realized that small business web banking represents an important, and largely untapped, segment of the industry; the small business banking market is already technologically wired (with Internet penetration that exceeds 70%) and lends itself to higher fees and larger balances than the retail market—making it a potentially attractive source of revenues. In the US, various research studies estimate that the market for immediately accessible consumer accounts is approximately 10MM; more will undoubtedly be added at future points, but that is a readily identifiable core which can be captured over the short-term. By way of contrast, there are roughly 23MM small business accounts that can be readily migrated to the web. US small business web banking currently accounts for 5% of $50B in small business banking revenues; by the middle of the decade it is expected to grow to as much as 30%. Similar trends are also becoming apparent in the small business markets of Europe, Asia and Latin America. Most small business web-banking platforms offer EBPP, fund transfers, cash management, treasury management, factoring/accounts receivable management, leasing, and credit extensions. Established financial institutions such as Chase, Citibank, Wells Fargo, Barclays, Deutsche Bank, HSBC, Societe Generale, National Australia Bank and Banamex, among others, have tailored their storefront platforms to cater exclusively to small businesses. For instance, Citibank, through its bizzed.com site, provides small companies with financial products, credit lines, billing and procurement services; Bank of America, through its biztro.com platform, and

FleetBoston, through OfficeLink, provide their clients with similar functionality. Barclays, through a partnership with ISP FreeServe, offers a comprehensive suite of small business credit and infrastructure services, while Banamex caters to small enterprises in Mexico via its Bancanet venture. Leasing, a key component of small business requirements, is provided by numerous non-bank platforms; some, such as GE Small Business Services, offer comprehensive loan and lease services tailored expressly for the small business community.

While the largest banking institutions dominate small business banking on the web, certain niche players are expanding their presence as well. Within the credit segment, various platforms offer online application and pre-qualification on credit facilities normally offered to the small business community, including business lines of credit, commercial real estate loans, multifamily housing loans, government contract loans, equipment leases, SBA loans, permanent working capital, business acquisition loans and refinance loans. Ventures such as Presidential Online and Allied Capital specialize in small business financing and have designed their offerings accordingly. In the credit extension arena, a number of non-bank financial platforms have adopted the marketplace model and emerged as conduits between small business owners and authorized lenders. These intermediaries offer clients the opportunity to apply for credit online (including loans, credit cards, leases, revolvers, and so on), provide credit scoring for an applicant (based on various credit scoring models as well as publicly available credit reports), and forward a credit recommendation to one of the participating financial institutions. The financial institution can elect to accept the intermediary's recommendation or alter/reject it; if it wishes to proceed, it makes funds available to the applicant via the intermediary. By offering this type of service applicants get a very quick response, financial institutions have much of the pre-screening/scoring work done for them by a trusted third party, and the intermediary has an opportunity to generate a fee. LiveCapital, one such marketplace intermediary, has established lending relationships with 30 financial institutions and has become one of the top 20 originators of US business financing—proving that the model is effective and value-added. E-credit provides a similar service, linking borrowers and lenders and providing automated credit scoring.

A small, though growing, area of services which crosses the boundary between real estate and financing is found in various commercial real estate platforms, such as RealtyIQ, EquityCity, LoopNet, CityFeet, PropertyFirst.com and Commercial Real Estate Online. These entities link customers and real estate companies/lenders, and provide access to commercial property surveys, documentation, space/listings, development specifications, financial statements, financing availability, and so on. Many standard commercial real estate brokerage functions are now being handled through such platforms, forcing traditional brokers to form partnerships and alliances in order not to miss out on business opportunities.

In other areas of financial and corporate cooperation, a number of foreign banks have forged alliances with local corporate and infrastructure providers to develop B2B exchanges. For instance, in Spain Banco Santander CH actively participates in European supply chain and procurement networks, in Taiwan Chinatrust Commercial has been at the forefront in promoting investment in B2B companies and infrastructure, in Brazil Banco Bradeso is investing in B2C e-commerce companies, while in Australia National Australia Bank has developed the O2-e incubator to develop business-related Internet services. Similar arrangements exist among banks in Malaysia, Mexico and other countries. Local banks have taken on this leadership role given their relative familiarity with technology and their ability to act as conduits/dealmakers in matching suppliers and users of capital for Internet expansion.

OTHER SERVICES: PROCESSING, VALUATION, CLEARING AND SETTLEMENT

Though back-end services are not as 'high profile' as new issues, investment banking or trading, they are an equally important dimension of the financial world. Many of the services required to support e-finance lend themselves, not surprisingly, to automation—including processing trade tickets, creating electronic confirms/documentation, reporting trade settlements/fails, preparing management control reports, computing valuations, managing collateral, and so on. Electronic prime brokerage, which encompasses securities lending, financing, collateral management, custody and settlement, along with external services related to electronic clearing and settling of trades, have also become an important part of the e-finance processing sector. Many of these back-end processing capabilities are provided by B2B infrastructure ventures.

Straight-through processing (STP) is a concept that is being promoted by many financial ventures and infrastructure providers. STP is designed to minimize human intervention in the trading and settlement process by creating a seamless front-to-back process. In its fullest implementation—which requires particularly robust and cohesive architecture—a trade input on the screen by a trader flows automatically through all of the front-, middle- and back-office processes with no additional input or intervention. The ability to create a credible STP chain results in a more efficient, secure and controlled business environment. The most comprehensive electronic STP modules—some linked directly into the Internet (or some alternate network), others making use of Internet-based technologies—feature a range of capabilities. These typically include trade entry/blotter management, ticket and confirm generation, documentation creation and storage, accounting, cash management/cashiering, clearing and settling, compliance monitoring, regulatory reporting, financing, collateral management, margin management, new account handling, order handling, tax reporting and portfolio/risk reporting. Certain providers link an institution's processes directly to clearing entities, exchanges, execution agents, trade/order routing systems, and pricing suppliers, in order to provide as much real-time capability as possible. Various infrastructure providers are turning to the use of meta-languages (such as FIX, XML and FpML) in order to provide greater connectivity between B2B alliances/exchanges and middle/ back-office processes required to support the underlying business. For example, FpML (developed by JP Morgan, PriceWaterhouse Coopers, Chase, Infinity and Sybase) is intended to simplify middle- and back-end functions in financial derivatives trading by using a common language to describe products and the way they interact with different processes.

While some infrastructure platforms provide STP for an entire range of products, including equities, bonds, foreign exchange, futures, money market funds, mutual funds, Treasuries, agencies, derivatives, and so on, others specialize in product niches. Service providers such as Arcordia, Indata, Ascendant, TradingLinx, and Sungard provide broad-based STP platforms in either turnkey or customized form, with complete or partial outsourcing. ADP offers web-based trade processing services—including trade entry, confirmation, settlements, limits monitoring, payments and risk management—for foreign exchange, money market instruments and derivatives; Sungard's eFinity platform provides similar functionality. Those that promote partial solutions employ interface engines to merge product-specific Internet-based applications with back-end legacy systems and processes; for instance, IQ Financial and SS&C specialize in workstation/PC and web-based STP derivative solutions. Others provide partial or specific, rather than complete, processing. For example, JP Morgan spin-off Cygnifi supplies a web-based product focused on derivatives support, including valuations, processing and post-trade risk assessment; this is of use to smaller institutions who deal in derivatives but do not want to run the expense of creating and maintaining their own derivatives back-office infrastructure. Various platforms deliver web-enabled risk solutions that can be employed for overall valuation and risk control purposes. For example, Algorithmics, eRisks, Integrity Treasury, Intermark Solutions, Brady, Innova, NetRisk and Richmond, among others, offer Internet risk products which include risk reporting, analysis, valuation, stress testing, and value-at-risk computation, for both cash and derivative products. These can be used to supplement, or verify, risk computations obtained from third-party or proprietary front-office analytic platforms.

The prime brokerage area—which has emerged as an important facet of business for many major financial institutions over the past few years—has also made its way onto the web. The prime broker function, a 'front to back' suite of institutional services, generally includes trade execution, financing, securities lending, collateral valuation, trade settlement, custody and risk reporting. Many of these services lend themselves to web technologies, and numerous global financial institutions have already incorporated such offerings into their overall platforms. Under a typical prime broker relationship, an institutional client can execute trades electronically through a prime broker platform, borrow directly against portfolios of securities, obtain electronic confirms and safe-custody statements, and receive online updates of portfolios, collateral and risk positions. Bundling these services together in an electronic environment provides great convenience, and cost savings, to customers; it also gives financial service providers an opportunity to build relationships and cross-sell other products. Firms such as Goldman Sachs, Morgan Stanley Dean Witter, Nomura and others feature prime broker services through their corporate storefronts.

In addition to the complete or partial STP and back-end processing efforts detailed above, which are primarily internal to institutions, new virtual platforms have been created to offer users the full benefit of clearing and settlement services—which are typically external to institutions. Clearing services verify that financial transactions between buyers and sellers are properly communicated and concluded, and that appropriate margining and netting occurs. The clearer receives trade information from an exchange or individual participants, verifies details related to the trade, and then issues legally binding confirmations to both parties; as part of the clearing process margin balances and netting arrangements are reviewed and adjustments are made. Settlement services come into play once a trade has been confirmed. Specifically, the settlement agent ensures that securities or other assets are received from the seller and payment is made by the buyer; in practice such receipts and payments tend to occur electronically rather than physically (the exception being physical settlement of commodities and other hard assets).

Settlement through an independent third party obviates the need for either party to be exposed to the other, and eliminates the need for credit risk capacity. If electronic trading exists to provide customers with pricing, matching and liquidity, clearing exists to provide margining, netting and position management/verification, and settlement exists to ensure delivery and payment security. Recognizing the importance of clearing and settlement in the financial arena, new dedicated web ventures have been established to facilitate the process. For instance, UK-based CapClear has been created as a virtual clearinghouse to clear trades for B2B exchanges, ECNs and other ATS alliances. While established exchanges have traditionally featured their own clearinghouse functions (often through independently capitalized subsidiaries), these new Internet ventures provide similar clearing/settlement support for many of the pure electronic exchanges and alliances that have been developed over the past few years.

TALK OF THE TRADE

ATS—alternative trading system, any alternate forum for trading securities which brings together buyers and sellers; the ATS sector includes corporate storefronts, ECNs, B2B exchanges and other trading alliances.

Clearing—the process of verifying that a financial transaction between a buyer and seller is properly executed; clearers receive trade information, confirm details, issue legally binding confirms, and ensure that appropriate margining and netting occurs.

CLOB—central limit order book, a central repository of trades which allows matches to occur on a strict price/time priority basis; certain established exchanges operate as CLOBs.

DPO—direct private offering, a direct private placement arranged on behalf of small private companies.

Due diligence—the process of reviewing and analyzing the financial state of a company planning to issue securities; results of due diligence are contained in associated prospectuses and registration documents.

ECN—electronic communication network, an exchange-like mechanism that matches buy and sell orders anonymously, by strict price and time, without the involvement of a 'middleman'; ECNs inject price transparency and cost savings into the trading process.

FIX—financial information exchange, a meta-language that simplifies communication between financial products, participants and processes.

Flipper—an investor that purchases shares at IPO launch with the intent of reselling them quickly, in the hope of securing a short-term gain.

FpML—financial product markup language, a meta-language designed to simplify communication between financial products, participants and processes.

IOI—indication of interest, an investor's indication of the amount of securities likely to be purchased at varying price levels; IOIs, while not firm orders, provide syndicate managers with a sense of book size and investor appetite for a new deal.

Level II montage—a detailed quote screen for NASDAQ stocks which reflects active bids and offers from every market maker and ECN posting prices; Level II quotes are typically offered to users as a premium service.

OFX—open financial exchange, a meta-language designed to simplify communication between financial products, participants and processes.

Pipeline—the calendar, or schedule, of forthcoming IPOs and new issues.

Prime brokerage—a comprehensive 'front-to-back' service provided to institutional clients, which typically includes electronic trade execution, financing, clearing, settlement, custody, collateral/position valuation, and risk reporting.

Roadshow—a marketing trip held in advance of a new issue launch during which company management discusses financial performance/outlook and responds to investor questions and comments.

Settlement—the process of ensuring securities/payments are properly exchanged between buyers and sellers; settlement agents act as neutral third parties, verifying that both parties to the trade perform on their obligations.

STP—straight-through processing, an automated process covering front-, middle- and back-office functions; true STP allows a trade to be entered in a front-office system and flow through all middle- and back-office functions (including control and reporting) with no additional manual intervention.

5
B2C e-Finance

THE B2C VALUE PROPOSITION

The Internet has captured the imagination, and business, of consumers. The B2C sector, though challenging for companies creating platforms and trying to generate revenues and profits, has gained a loyal following among people who are pressed for time and want to accomplish useful tasks in a more efficient and cost-effective manner, at any time of day or night—true '24 by 7' coverage. Many aspects of personal financial services are well suited to the web as they are relatively homogenous and simple to deliver; they can be crafted to create efficiencies and cost savings for customers and generate new revenue opportunities for suppliers. As a result, the development and deployment of B2C e-finance services has been a major priority for entrepreneurs, established banks and 'non-traditional' providers—retail-based online trading, online banking, wealth management, and insurance represent an integral, and expanding, part of the financial B2C sector. Additional information services (including news, quotes, research ideas, tools, planners, and calculators), which enrich the personal financial experience, are widely available to retail customers through a variety of dedicated and integrated platforms; we shall discuss these services at greater length in Chapter 6. While certain online platforms focus on specific market niches or segments, such as trading, banking, credit services, or insurance, numerous others have expanded their offerings to reach the widest possible audience. The intent for some ventures is to serve as a retail customer's 'one stop' online financial manager, supplying a broad range of services, products, execution and advice. Firms such as Schwab, Merrill Lynch, Salomon Smith Barney, Morgan Stanley Dean Witter, Citibank, Barclays, UBS, and ING, among others, make available to their customers online trading, online banking, wealth management, mortgages, credit lines, credit cards, and insurance. They are, in essence, replicating on the Internet the suite of services they have long offered in the 'physical' world.

B2C providers have changed the retail financial services value proposition by giving consumers timely and efficient delivery and fulfillment on various banking, trading and investment products and services. While B2C storefront and vertical models generate cost savings and execution efficiencies on proprietary or allied products/services, B2C marketplace models create informational and pricing transparencies that can lead to more informed wealth-related decisions. B2C infrastructure providers enhance the value proposition for new and established financial ventures by supplying the underlying mechanics needed to create effective web-based businesses in a short period of time. The prospects for growth in the B2C financial sector are very strong. In the US alone, research estimates suggest that B2C financial service revenues will exceed $150B by 2004; in addition, though the international B2C e-finance sector has lagged that of the US, it is becoming a powerful force in countries such as the UK, France, Germany, Mexico, Japan, Hong Kong and Korea, and promises to contribute significantly to overall B2C e-finance revenues over the coming years.

ONLINE TRADING

Online trading has revolutionized and popularized the concept of web-based retail financial services. Though electronic banking existed on home PCs well before the Internet became part of the 'mainstream', it was the development of useful, flexible and secure online trading mechanisms—which dealt with an exciting part of the financial markets—that created consumer interest in web-based financial services. Online trading was, and remains, the B2C e-finance 'killer app', and has been instrumental in developing the 'stickiness' that many business models require in order to prosper. This enthusiasm and interest is hardly surprising given that individual investors have become far more active in the management of their investment and retirement assets over the past few years; concern over the availability of retirement income coming from government sponsored programs, together with liberalization of investment rules allowing for more flexible and active participation by individuals, have helped fuel the process. Many investors have taken a keen interest in self-directed financial management, reducing their reliance on financial planners, advisors and brokers; over the past few years many individuals have grown accustomed to developing investment strategies, following markets, stocks, bonds and mutual funds, and rebalancing their portfolios. The introduction of online trading, and associated informational tools like quotes, research, and portfolio management modules, simply solidified a trend that was becoming increasingly evident in the 'physical' world. The ability to 'unbundle', self-direct and customize services has been a winning combination both offline and online.

Online trading is typically offered through the corporate storefront model
(where an institution provides customers with its own online trading services),
or a vertical portal model (where a venture offers customers its own, or third-
party, online trading services, in parallel with other financial services). As
indicated in Chapter 2, Wit Capital was one of the 'founding members' of the
online trading movement, and was followed thereafter by Schwab, E*Trade,
Web Street Securities and Ameritrade. Wit Capital (which has slowly moved
from online trading to online investment banking) is still considered a storefront model, while Schwab and E*Trade have gradually assumed the
appearance of broader vertical portals. By the end of 1995, the US market
featured 12 online trading houses, two years later the number had grown to
about 30, and in early 2000 had soared to over 115. Just as in the institutional
electronic trading sector discussed in Chapter 4, it seems unlikely that the US
marketplace can support over 100 online trading firms on a permanent basis—
some will invariably sell out or merge, and others will close down operations;
Forrester Research estimates that 75% of existing ventures will be acquired,
or fold, by 2005. The mere fact that so many ventures have been created,
however, is at least partial verification that the concept is appealing and
useful. This belief is supported by trading/account volume and growth figures.
Research groups have estimated that, from a standing start in 1994, 20% of all
US retail trades were executed via the web in 1997, 30% in 1998, and 45% in
1999; the number is expected to exceed 60% by 2002. The number of US
online accounts increased from less than 5MM in 1997 to 8MM in 1998 and
16MM in early 2000; Forrester Research, Jupiter and IDC predict the US will
feature between 25MM and 30MM online retail accounts before the middle of
the decade. Online trading assets increased from $200B in 1997 to $1.15T in
2000; according to Jupiter, assets are expected to reach $3T by 2002 and $5.4T
by 2005. Discount and pure play entities that have established a strong brand
name and presence—such as E*Trade, Ameritrade, TD Waterhouse, Schwab,
and Web Street Securities—as well as those with strong parent support—such
as Merrill Lynch, Morgan Stanley Dean Witter, Salomon Smith Barney,
Fidelity and CSFB/DLJ—dominate the market and are likely to remain
leaders as competition increases. In 2000 Schwab led the way, commanding a
20% share of all US online trading, followed by E*Trade (16%), TD Waterhouse (13%), Ameritrade (11%), Datek (10%), and Fidelity/PowerStreet
(10%); the remainder was split among the large full service firms. Though full
service firms were slow to enter the market, they started challenging the
original discount and pure play ventures in the late 1990s, and accounted for
approximately 20% of all accounts by early 2000.

While online trading commenced primarily as a US-based phenomenon
(where the percentage of stock ownership among the investing public is as
high as 50%), it has already spread globally, especially in Europe; more than
3MM European accounts were active in 2000, and researchers expect more

than 17MM to be operational by 2003. The UK marketplace is expected to feature one of the fastest growth rates; though the market only featured 300,000 online accounts in 2000, Allegra Strategies estimates that 2.4MM accounts will be in use by 2004. Other growth markets include Sweden, Germany, France, and Switzerland. Leading European online ventures include: Comdirect, ConSors, and Direct-Anlage in Germany; Cortal, I-bourse, B*Capital, Logitel Net, and Fimatex in France; Swissquote, CS DirectNet, and UBS Tradepac in Switzerland, and Lloyds TSB Sharedeal Direct, Natwest Stockbrokers, and Barclays Stockbrokers in the UK. US-based services such as E*Trade and Schwab are also gaining ground in Europe. The online trading model is also moving into parts of Asia, particularly Japan, Korea, and Hong Kong. In Japan, the deregulation of the stock market in October 1999 allowed discount brokers and Internet brokers to form and expand; though certain regulatory constraints remain in place, which are slowing the overall pace of expansion, the trend is clear—by the end of 2000 the local market featured 1.7MM online accounts and considerable growth is expected over the coming years. Japanese market leaders include Monex, E*Trade Japan, Matsui, and Nikko Beans; stalwarts Nomura Securities and Daiwa Securities have introduced their own Internet platforms though they, like the US full service firms, are balancing web operations with traditional brokerage business. In Korea, where technology penetration is reasonably deep and a tradition of retail stock investment well established, more than 50% of retail trades have moved online through platforms operated by securities firms such as Daewoo Securities, LG Securities, Seoul Securities and others. In Hong Kong, 24 of the community's dealers offer online trading and more are expected to become operational in the medium-term. In certain instances local firms have teamed up with international firms to create entirely new platforms; for example, Hutchison Whampoa has created a joint venture with CSFB/DLJ, while Pacific Century CyberWorks has formed an alliance with Chase Fleming known as 2cube. In Australia, ANZ offers customers online trading through a partnership with E*Trade, while Westpac offers services through its online Westpac Broking operation. Canadian online trading is offered by nearly all of the major banks—Toronto Dominion does so through its TD Waterhouse platform (which also has extensive operations in the US, as already noted), Royal Bank through Action Direct, Bank of Montreal through BMO InvestorLine, and CIBC via Investors Edge. In Mexico the two largest banking groups, Banamex and Bancomer, offer online stock trading through AcciTrade and Bancomer.com. It is worth noting that various international platforms allow investors to access domestic as well as global markets (for instance, UBS's discounted Tradepac module permits online trading in seven distinct markets, including Zurich, Frankfurt, London, Milan, NASDAQ, NYSE and AMEX, while Commerzbank's Comdirect allows trading in five global markets); the same is not necessarily true of US domestic platforms. In most cases online trading in the US is still limited to the US markets, unless special arrangements or alliances are concluded with other international ventures, or individual subsidiaries are established in local markets. For instance, in order to offer customers international access, E*Trade has created separate subsidiaries in the UK and Japan to deal in those markets, Goldman Sachs has created the PrimeAccess platform in Europe to deal in six European bourses, Merrill Lynch has created MarketEdge along similar lines, and Web Street Securities has concluded alliance agreements with online brokers in Germany, Hong Kong, Chile and other countries in order to penetrate those local markets.

Comprehensive features, ease of use and low cost have been the keys to altering the customer value proposition and attracting consumers online. A large number of retail investors have found the 'do-it-yourself' method of transacting very appealing; many of them are interested in developing investment strategies, doing research, following markets, entering trades, monitoring execution, and managing portfolios. Features offered by most online trading platforms include real-time quotes, trade execution, research alerts, IPO access, portfolio tracking, stock filtering, financial planning, position updates, buying power notification, trade history, profit and loss accounting, multiple account access, and headline news. Trade execution modules typically let investors select the type of buy/sell order desired, including limit orders (executing at a specified price), market orders (executing at the prevailing price), marketable limit orders (executing at no worse than the price specified), good-till-cancelled orders (keeping an order 'alive' until it is executed or cancelled), fill-or-kill orders (filling the entire order or none at all), and so on. While certain online trading platforms feature customized portfolio management tools to help users track their trades, others include links into third-party money management software such as Microsoft Money or Intuit Quicken. Investor interest has also been heightened by the advent of certain retail-oriented ECNs, such as Island and Archipelago, as discussed in Chapter 4. These ECNs have helped inject price transparency and cost savings into the trading process and given small investor orders equal footing in montages. The relatively low cost of executing trades has certainly helped lure consumers to the web. By early 2000 the average cost of executing a standard equity trade through an online firm was $16, much less than the amount charged by discounters or full service brokers through their traditional operations. Deeper discounts, to $5–10/trade, are becoming increasingly prevalent—full migration to free execution in the medium-term appears as a likely scenario, though not until service providers redefine their business models to generate revenues from alternate sources.

Since not every retail customer expects, or demands, the same type of service from an Internet platform, a fairly broad range of models has developed. While some platforms provide only basic execution and tracking, others have strong links into research, monitoring and analysis; still others allow access to financial brokers for advice or guidance. Active traders who are primarily interested in execution and basic tracking can use 'stripped down' platforms which offer very low commissions and little in the way of 'extras' such as research, alerts, and so on; these platforms often lack customer service/support capabilities (which can be vital when trying to resolve trade errors or disputes). Large brokers offer a range of services designed to complement and balance traditional broker-driven business—offering clients an entire spectrum of services, with differential pricing, allows large brokers to more accurately direct business flows and minimize channel conflict. For instance, Merrill Lynch offers clients a choice of several alternatives—one service charges clients full commissions for online execution and permits access to all services, including financial advice; a second charges clients an annual fee based on assets in the account and allows unlimited free online execution and access to all services, including financial advice; and a third service charges clients a discounted online execution rate and allows access to a limited number of value-added services, but not financial advice. Similarly, E*Trade offers standard execution and research services to its typical clients, and larger discounts and preferred IPO access to its most active clients.

With more than 100 online trading firms in operation in the US, and a similar number active abroad, competition is considerable. As the competitive environment intensifies, online trading ventures need to keep their margins buoyant. Since online trading commissions are already comparatively low, these ventures prosper primarily through high order volumes (though they may also generate incremental revenues from other aspects of the business model, such as advertising or subscription). Researchers estimate online platforms need 1.5MM accounts, or $30B in account assets, to generate sufficient volume and revenues to remain viable concerns. Any reduction in volume—as a result of new competitors entering the market, or a market downturn driving investors to the sidelines—immediately impacts revenues. Smaller account balances can also create revenue problems. Since the cost of servicing accounts is the same regardless of balance size, web ventures prefer accounts with larger balances; those that maintain very small balances often generate insufficient revenues to cover basic operating and maintenance costs. Consolidation among platforms, and expansion of value-added services within platforms, thus emerge as strong possibilities in the future. In fact, several pure play, or heavily web-based, platforms have developed new business relationships through partnerships or alliances with wealth management advisors, credit card firms and others; providing more comprehensive services benefits clients and diversifies revenues. By generating revenues from a greater number of sources, these ventures hope to create sustainable business structures that can withstand market downturns. For instance: E*Trade has partnered with Ernst and Young in a wealth management joint venture and has created a retail banking platform known as E*Trade Bank (through its purchase of web bank Telebank); Ameritrade has formed a partnership with MBNA to distribute branded credit cards and has a partnership with NetBank to offer banking services; and Web Street Securities has developed a broad financial portal known as the Financial District which allows customers to obtain credit cards, pay bills, and link into mortgages from LendingTree and insurance from InsWeb; it has also expanded its operations geographically, providing customers with access to international securities trading through alliances with online trading platforms in Germany (ConSors), Hong Kong (SHKOnline), and Chile (CB Capitales).

Other types of value-added services, including extended hours trading and research and IPO access, have been introduced by firms seeking to create a competitive advantage. For instance, in mid-2000 Fidelity and Schwab became the first platforms to offer extended hour pre-market trading to their clients. Though several other platforms already featured after-hours trading on a limited basis (by executing through ECNs from 4.05pm to 8pm EST), Fidelity extended morning trading to allow overseas and domestic investors, eager to act on after- or pre-market news, to execute between 7.30am and 9.15am EST—ahead of the official New York opening of 9.30am. Schwab followed suit shortly thereafter (note that Instinet made the feature available to institutional money managers prior to the Fidelity and Schwab retail practice). Recognizing that pre-market trading is becoming an important dimension of daily activity, NASDAQ developed, in 2000, a new 'pre-market index' to track the performance of 100 major stocks trading prior to official opening; this index provides investors with an early gauge of market direction (and is representative of the gradual moves towards 'around the clock' trading). Ventures without their own research capabilities or IPO access have teamed up with those that feature one or both. For instance, Schwab has developed alliances with CSFB and Chase for research and IPOs, Fidelity has done the same with Lehman Brothers, E*Trade with BancBoston and Wit Soundview/ E*Offering, TD Waterhouse with S&P ComStock and Wit Soundview/ E*Offering, and so on. IPO access, in particular, is seen as an important way of attracting retail customers. The small investor has traditionally been unable to tap into the market for new issues on a regular basis. Institutional investors are generally given preferential treatment by underwriters—particularly on 'hot' new issues—and have been able to capitalize on the sometimes significant gains which can follow the launch of a new stock. In order to give retail customers greater opportunities to participate in this segment of the market, a number of platforms have created specific retail IPO access. For instance, DirectIPO, WR Hambrecht, Friedman Billings Ramsay, Merrill Lynch, Wit Soundview/E*Offering, and select others allow retail investors to submit online IOIs which they then attempt to fill based on bids and book size. During 2000, when this practice became increasingly noticeable, US retail investors actively participated in more than 200 IPOs—demonstrating that there is true demand for the service. Abroad, HSBC has created a similar online retail IPO platform; individual investors can subscribe through the Internet for shares listed on both the HKSE main board and the Growth Enterprise Market (GEM). Though retail access to IPOs is not yet a 'flawless' process, it appears to be moving in the direction of giving individual investors a more equal chance to participate.

Day trading, in which investors execute dozens, or hundreds, of trades in the hope of capturing small spreads, has been in existence since the early 1980s. Most 'professional' day traders, who typically trade in 500–1000 share blocks, have historically relied on electronic direct access trading (EDAT) platforms that include dedicated communications lines, guaranteed instant access to a marketplace and rich, real-time quotes. (Other small investor orders not flowing through EDAT platforms have been routed through the Small Order Execution System (SOES) since the mid-1980s. SOES, introduced in 1984 by the National Association of Securities Dealers (NASD) to give retail investors more equal representation in the market, routed sub-500 share orders directly to market markers with the best quotes. Unfortunately, a new breed of 'SOES bandits' actively interceded in the market, picking off quotes which dealers had not yet updated. Though more stringent participation was reinforced after the 1987 Crash, the system was still less than ideal and was only moderately successful in providing retail investors with proper representation.) With the arrival of the Internet and ECNs such as Island and Archipelago (which readily display real-time order books), the need for dedicated EDAT/SOES dealing has declined. Many day traders (and swing traders, who typically hold positions for a few days rather than a few minutes or hours) have migrated to ventures capable of offering single point-and-click execution routed directly to the ECN or market maker, robust portfolio and trade tracking, sophisticated technical analysis and analytics, deeper quote transparency, and streaming news. Platforms such as AB Watley, CyberCorp (now owned by Schwab), DirectAccess Trader, and others cater to this special segment of the market.

While most web trading platforms focus on stocks, there is a growing list of alternate financial products available to online retail investors. For instance, many of the largest platforms—including Schwab, Merrill Lynch, Ameritrade and E*Trade, allow retail investors to purchase specific fixed income instruments online (from each dealer's current inventory); this includes Treasury, municipal and agency securities, as well as corporate bonds and money market instruments. Certain dedicated retail bond trading services have also emerged, including ventures such as Bonds online, Bondtrac, BondExchange, BondExpress, and others; these firms specialize in servicing retail customers by dealing in small denominations/blocks. B2C ventures offering 'higher risk' products, including futures, options and FX, are becoming somewhat more common, though still out of the 'mainstream'. For example, VelocityTrade, through its Floorpass module, permits online retail futures trading (through a dedicated terminal rather than standard web); other ventures, such as Lind-Waldock, Alaron and Jack Carl Futures, offer retail investors direct futures trading through the Internet. Listed options trading, which can present small investors with considerable risk of loss if not managed with care, can be executed through many of the online trading platforms cited above (once special disclosure has been submitted and approval granted). In the FX market, traditionally the domain of institutional players, web-based offerings have been created to cater to the needs of individuals. For example, Gain-Capital provides retail clients with an FX trading service typically only available to medium and large institutional clients. While minimum dealing size is $100,000, making it unsuitable for the smallest investors, it provides those who wish to participate with execution services within the interbank spread typically reserved for institutions trading in $10MM blocks. Oranda.com is another platform that has established an ECN—Fxchange—that grants retail customers access to the FX market at institutional dealing spreads. As indicated in Chapter 4, E*Trade has partnered with UBS Warburg to give its non-US customers the opportunity to execute FX transactions related to international stock trades through UBS Warburg's FX2B technology platform.

Though online trading platforms have generated considerable benefits and efficiencies for the investing public, they have also created certain problems. For instance, the ease of communicating via the Internet has forced regulators to deal with so-called 'pump and dump' schemes—'hot tips' are amplified through online trading 'chat' rooms and bulletin boards, investors are lured into buying a target stock until it rises to a point where the 'originator' of the hot tip sells out—leaving small investors with potentially large losses. They have also had to contend with Internet scams where online investors are duped into buying the stock of fictitious companies; this tends to occur through online OTC 'bulletin board' trading, where controls are lax (or non-existent) and dealing is on a 'caveat emptor' basis. Examples of these scams include the sale of $50MM of stock to investors in a non-existent entity known as First Zurich National, $7MM of stock in Royal Meridian International Bank, $2MM of stock in Internet Casino Sports Gaming, and so on. Difficulties in controlling the boundaryless web and tracking perpetrators make such schemes an ever-present danger. The ease of online trading has also given birth to a generation of short-term Internet traders who may believe they are sophisticated day or swing traders—but are not. Misuse of online trading capabilities can add to market volatility and lead to personal financial difficulties for such aggressive 'traders'. Online trading during extended hours, prior to market open or after market close, has also caused some concern among exchange and regulatory officials. Since liquidity in off-market hours is low, even modest trades can skew opening prices (causing them to 'gap' up or down) and lead to broader investor losses. Over-reliance on, or belief in the infallibility of, technical platforms can also create complications. When there is a sharp market move and a great deal of activity flowing through an online trading platform, delays in filling an order can occur—depending on the order execution specified, a fill at a very unfavorable price can result.

Though the move to online trading has been embraced by many firms, the question of whether it needs to form a part of every securities firm's business model is still being debated. While many new and established firms are well represented in the sector some, such as Legg Mason and Edward Jones, have opted not to pursue a retail Internet strategy at all, while others, such as Goldman Sachs, have chosen to focus on a very specific segment of the market (i.e. extremely high net worth individuals). Those eschewing a full online trading model generally use the Internet as a platform to provide investors with additional information and research, but not trade execution or portfolio management capabilities. These institutions argue against the need to provide full self-directed, or 'do-it-yourself' (DIY), capabilities and point to the fact that the creation of online trading has not led to the predicted 'demise' of full service firms and their armies of financial consultants. An important segment of the market continues to demand, and value, financial advice and personal service (a fact that some pure online traders have started to recognize, as evidenced by their partnerships with financial advisory firms). Some in this camp believe that the DIY model is a bull market business that will contract during each bear market cycle—leading to 'disgruntled' DIY retail traders, lower volumes and sector consolidation. Firms choosing to offer full Internet capabilities contend that in the 21st century there are ever increasing numbers of investors who want to handle their own financial affairs—online trading (as well as other online personal financial services) helps meet the demands and requirements of an increasingly 'wired' society; as technologically savvy investors come to form a growing segment of the investing population, those unable to offer and deliver online capabilities will lose business. Even established firms that have adopted web-based capabilities have come to view the web as an enabler, not a threat; they have successfully managed channel conflict and turned the Internet into a powerful tool—financial consultants/brokers and Internet communication/distribution mechanisms have thus become interdependent. The debate continues—in the end, there is likely to be room for both structures as long as different types of customers demand particular services.

ONLINE BANKING

Online banking is a broad sector that covers checking/savings/deposits, balance information, fund transfers, payments and credit services. Various models are used to deliver online banking services to the public, including the corporate storefront model (where individual financial institutions provide clients with proprietary banking products/services) and the vertical portal model (where vertical portals operated by banks or non-banks provide customers with banking services in parallel with other services); certain segments of online banking, including mortgages and loans, also make use of the marketplace model. As indicated earlier, even though home PC banking aimed at retail customers commenced in the late 1970s, it remained a rather limited, and cumbersome, process until the commercial introduction of the Internet. Though penetration of online banking remains relatively low compared to other e-finance services, it has gained in popularity and is expected to grow further over the coming years—albeit in a gradual fashion. Some of the growth will come as consumers alter their behavior patterns. For instance, certain studies suggest that purchasers of long-term deposits often like to conduct such business in person, rather than over the web; the same is true for customers taking on large financial commitments, such as mortgages and home equity loans. As these consumers gain greater confidence with the Internet and its delivery mechanisms, they will likely be willing to move more of their personal financial transactions to a web setting. While total revenues derived from online operations remain very small in comparison with those generated through traditional banking operations, they are expected to increase over time as more business is conducted via the web. The economics of offering banking services through the Internet can be compelling, once fixed costs are covered; the low cost of processing incremental web transactions—as compared with standard teller-assisted transactions—is very dramatic. For instance, a Booz Allen study has found that the cost of processing an incremental financial transaction amounts to \$1.07 through branches, \$0.52 through telephone banking, \$0.27 through ATMs, \$0.015 through home PC banking, and only \$0.01 through Internet platforms. Of course, before achieving such marginal cost savings most institutions will have spent considerable sums on fixed cost implementation (i.e. web infrastructure and technology, web marketing, and so on).

While online banking does not possess the 'glamor' and 'excitement' of online trading, it is a business function that lends itself to the tools and technologies of the Internet. Convenience and ease of use—coupled with web-only incentives such as low fees, low balance requirements and high yields—have been drivers in attracting consumers to online banking. e-Banking customers make their overall banking service selection based on a series of factors, including real-time account access and customer support, ease of use, security, range of products/services, and fees/yields. Though many banking customers were slow to migrate their bank accounts away from traditional 'brick and mortar' institutions unable to offer comprehensive e-banking services, there is evidence that such behavior has started to change—technology-oriented consumers are more interested in banking with ventures that are capable of delivering quality web services and are more likely to move their banking relationships in order to accomplish that goal. With growing demand for such services, new and established institutions have been developing, enhancing and expanding their online platforms to meet customer expectations.

Though many major banks now feature sophisticated transaction-enabled services, most have had to revamp their platforms in a major fashion at least once over the past few years and some, like Citibank, have had to completely refocus their efforts. Citibank's original Internet platform, Direct Access, combined web services with full branch and ATM access. In the late 1990s the bank introduced Citi F/I as a separate Internet strategy, brand, and site. Citi F/I was an attempt to offer an independent service, but customers ultimately demanded access to branches and ATMs; after three years in the works, Citi F/I was closed down and all Internet activity was once again channeled through its Direct Access platform. In late 2000 the bank overhauled its platform again, converting the Direct Access service to the new Citibank Online brand, with links into Citibank ATMs and tellers and the Citibank Online Trader discount broker service. Recognizing the importance of the web as a useful and efficient delivery mechanism, most established banks began shifting their strategies in the mid- to late 1990s from purely informational offerings to second generation sites with better GUIs, tighter security, faster access and more comprehensive, transaction-enabled services. Problems that plagued the earliest sites—including unattractive interfaces, limited services and difficult enrollment/access—have been resolved, and new offerings are at the leading edge of technological processes. Pure play banks operated by entrepreneurial outfits and non-bank financial institutions (including some of the online trading ventures discussed earlier) have made some progress in gaining a share of retail banking services, though they face an increasingly aggressive challenge from established institutions that are marrying e-banking capabilities and traditional 'brick and mortar' functions. In most cases pure plays face an incremental hurdle by not being able to offer ready access to branch/ATM services without undertaking separate third-party arrangements.

As indicated in Chapter 2, development of online banking platforms commenced in the mid-1990s. In 1995 approximately 200 banks had web sites, virtually all of them informational in nature; 100 or so were sponsored by North American banks, 80 by European banks, and the balance by institutions from a mix of countries. By 1997 the number of sites had expanded to more than 600, including 200 outside the US; a growing number of these platforms were transaction-enabled rather than informational. In 1999 more than 1000 global banks featured web sites, with nearly half offering transaction-enabled services. According to research firm Dataquest, by early

2000 approximately 600 banks around the world offered interactive online banking services—including fund transfers, electronic bill payment and modified forms of credit application and approval; that number, which excludes information-only sites, is expected to double before the middle of the decade.

The US General Accounting Office (GAO) estimates that by 2001 half of the US's 10,500 banks will feature web sites (many of them still informational rather than transactional). The GAO also indicates that, while only 2.5MM US households made use of home banking services in 1996, a total of 4.5MM households were active in 2000 and 18MM are expected to be active by 2002. Jupiter estimates that 25MM accounts will be operational in 2003, while IDC is more optimistic, forecasting up to 40MM accounts in active use. Most major US institutions, including market leaders such as Bank of America, Wells Fargo, Citibank, Bank One and Chase, have made considerable progress; by 2000 the web platforms of Citibank, Bank of America, Bank One and Wells Fargo featured between 500,000 and 2MM accounts each (some reflecting multiple accounts for a single household). The 11 US pure play banks with no parent affiliations and 15 web-only ventures funded by parent banks (but with charters of their own) have also made some progress, though their rate of growth has slowed. Dominant US pure plays and bank-affiliated web-only platforms that have managed to develop a brand name and sufficient customer trust to operate strictly in the 'ether' include SFNB (associated with Royal Bank of Canada), Wingspanbank (associated with Bank One), CompuBank, First Internet Bank of Indiana, and NetBank. Wingspanbank features one of the largest web-only platforms, counting more than 100,000 retail accounts in 2000; NetBank, a pure play with no particular affiliation, reached 80,000 accounts in 2000. Though these account figures reflect reasonable growth, they are still modest in comparison to the number of web accounts managed by established banks.

The online banking phenomenon is by no means limited to the US—ventures in various other countries are in different stages of development. e-Banking platforms in Europe, Canada and Australia are the most advanced, and are followed by those in various Asian countries; certain Latin American platforms, particularly in Mexico and Brazil, are also quite sophisticated. It is worth noting that, unlike the US, there are very few international pure play banks; virtually all platforms represent hybrid offerings of established institutions (though they may operate under different branding, through the independent structure detailed earlier in the book).

In Europe, research firm Datamation expects 21MM online banking customers will be active by 2004; JP Morgan seconds that view, predicting that more than 40% of households will use online banking services by 2003. Indeed, online banking in the UK, Germany, France, Switzerland, Benelux and Scandinavia is becoming well established. In the UK, Barclays, Royal Bank of Scotland, Lloyds TSB and others feature interactive consumer-oriented web services under their respective brand names. Prudential Assurance has a separately branded, and extremely popular, web platform known as Egg; Woolwich runs the OpenPlan platform; Abbey National operates under Cahoot; Halifax runs the IF Intelligent Finance venture; and HSBC features First Direct. In Germany the major players—Deutsche Bank, Commerzbank, Dresdner Bank, Hypovereinsbank, and the Raiffeisenbank and Sparekassen systems—all have web platforms of their own. Deutsche Bank operates under a separate brand known as DB24 (which commenced as a phone bank several years ago, but has since migrated to the web); Advance Bank, a German web-only bank controlled by Dresdner Bank, has established itself in the marketplace and is a recognized brand. Various French banks have developed a strong full-service presence on the web, including BNP Paribas through BNP Net and e-cortal, Societe Generale through Logitel Net and its own brand name, Credit Agricole Group and the Banque Populaire Group through their affiliates, and so on. The major Swiss banks, as well as several of the smaller private Swiss banks, feature extensive sites. For instance, Credit Suisse operates CS DirectNet with its banking, insurance and trading features, while UBS conducts business through its e-banking classic module. In the Netherlands, ING has developed a successful platform that it has expanded to subsidiaries in Canada and Spain (and is replicating in the US), while ABN Amro has a Dutch presence (as well as a US offering through its group of US banks). In Spain, Banco Bilbao Vizcaya Argentaria reaches clients through its net plus platform (along with Europe's first web-only platform, UnoFirst/First-e, operating out of Dublin, which it owns), while Banco Santander CH offers services through its own corporate storefront. In Scandinavia, online banking is very well established. The population at large is very comfortable with technology, Internet access is high (covering more than 50% of the population in Sweden, Finland and Norway), and online banking services are prevalent. For example, Merita Nordbanken, one of Scandinavia's largest banks, features more than 1MM Internet accounts on its Solo system. SE Banken, a large Swedish bank, has featured a transaction-enabled web platform since the mid-1990s and estimates that 25% of its customers conduct all of their financial business over the web. Most major Scandinavian banks feature integrated platforms, where banking services are supplemented by links to online brokers, bill paying services, and e-shopping.

Canadian banks, like their US counterparts, have developed extensive web-based banking platforms. CIBC offers retail clients e-banking through its Convenience Banking module, Royal Bank of Canada through its Royal Bank platform in Canada and SFNB in the US, Scotiabank through Scotia Online, Bank of Montreal through mbanx.direct, and so on. The largest Australian banks, including Westpac and ANZ, are also well represented online. In Japan, another large consumer banking market, Internet banking services are expanding, though gradually. Deregulation in the financial markets and consolidation within the banking sector are generating more opportunities to offer consumers basic electronic banking. Although retail services are largely confined to fundamental tasks such as balance inquiry, fund transfers and product information, institutions such as Sumitomo Bank, Sanwa Bank, Asahi Bank, Daiwa Bank, and DKB (as part of the new Mizuho Group with Fuji Bank and IBJ) are steadily rolling out new features on their corporate storefronts. In addition, regulatory changes introduced in 1999 allow standalone web banks to be created; Japan Net Bank (a unit of Sakura Bank and Sumitomo Bank) commenced operations in late 2000 as Japan's first pure play. Despite these advances, most other Japanese regional and city banks have limited their web efforts to informational sites. The same is true throughout other parts of Asia, where institutions in Korea, Thailand, Taiwan, Malaysia, India, China and other nations are still focused primarily on informational, rather than transactional, offerings. The main exceptions appear in Singapore, where several banks feature quite sophisticated platforms; for example, DBS deals through its Internet Banking/Investor Online platform, and UOB operates via its CyberBank and UOBS Trader services. In Malaysia, Maybank offers online banking and share trading through its Kawanku web brand, and in Hong Kong global bank HSBC operates through its unified web platform. Latin American online banking platforms are in various stages of development—from purely informational models for banks in most countries, to interactive models for the largest institutions in Mexico, Argentina and Brazil. Mexico's leading banks, Banamex and Bancomer, offer a full range of web services via their Bancanet Express and Bancomer.com units. In Argentina, Banco de Galicia y Buenos Aires offers web banking through e-galicia.com. In Brazil, Unibanco operates through its 30 Horas platform, Banco Bradesco offers a range of services through its corporate storefront, and HSBC affiliate Banco Bamerindus ties into HSBC's own web platform.

While virtually all transaction-enabled banking sites offer standard checking/savings account balance lookup and fund transfer facilities, it is the suite of new offerings—including electronic payments and credit services—that is expected to capture the attention of consumers in the future. Electronic payments are an increasingly important area of focus for banks, merchants and consumers—success in delivering this service in its fullest form is regarded as one of the primary goals of e-finance. Though a system of electronic interbank payments has existed for many years, it has catered primarily to institutional customers making large value payments; the Internet has made it theoretically possible to extend similar functionality to the consumer level, which will aid in the electronic payment of bills and the electronic transfer of small value payments. Though much work remains to be done in improving the retail payment system, progress has been made in EBPP services and electronic micro-payment services. Payment services such as these are rapidly moving from obscure, back-office processes to prominent, value-added, front-office services. Mechanisms that are easy to use, secure and flexible (capable of handling payments for B2B, B2C, P2P and business to government (B2G)) are gaining ground.

In the EBPP sector numerous financial institutions offer consumers the ability to receive and settle bills on a regular basis. Though electronic bill payment—without the use of cash or checks—is more commonplace in certain European and Asian countries (where check payments are infrequent and standing direct debits well established), it remains nascent in the US. In the US alone, 21B consumer and institutional bills are issued every year by more than 3MM merchants and companies (utilities account for approximately 3/4 of all bills generated); more than 70B individual checks are written in settlement of charges. The process is still largely manual and paper-driven, and relies heavily on the physical aspects of the postal service. In instances where payment is made electronically, it has historically been handled through proprietary communication networks, which tend to be expensive and inflexible. According to Forrester Research, less than 3% of online customers currently use electronic bill payment services, primarily because of limitations related to banks or vendors; however, up to 55% of online banking customers have expressed an interest in making use of electronic bill paying services, once the billing cycle can be completed in its entirety online. The billing cycle can be segregated into three distinct steps. The first step is for the vendor to present a bill to the bank (or some other service acting as agent). While this is still a manual and physical process, efforts are underway to have more vendors supply bills in electronic format. The second step is for the bank to engage the customer interactively for action on the bill; this is most often accomplished by e-mail and can be done on a 'per transaction' basis or as a standing authorization. The third step is for the bank to pay the vendor. This may be electronic (involving a credit or EFT to the vendor's account if it is part of an automated clearing system) or physical (sending a check to the vendor if it is not); efforts to complete payments electronically are, once again, a major focus for banks and other agents involved in the EBPP process. The key to success in EBPP comes when the entire transaction can be completed as an electronic 'round trip'—the vendor presents the bill to the customer and/or bank electronically, the customer's account is debited electronically, and the vendor receives payment electronically. Full 'round trip' capability requires vendors to change their systems and internal processes to accommodate the generation/transmission of electronic invoices and the receipt of electronic payments—a process that will take at least several years to implement. To the extent this can be accomplished, the savings associated with paper, postage and manual processing is likely to be considerable. The average cost to physically prepare, process and distribute a bill ranges from $0.50 to $2; the average cost of an e-bill is only $0.35–0.50, and is certain to decline further as more users take full advantage of complete EBPP solutions. Banks and third-party specialists are now seeking to revamp the EBPP market by offering consumers more comprehensive Internet-based services, and by working with vendors to have them present bills, and accept payments, electronically. Various third-party and infrastructure specialists have created a range of EBPP solutions; banks have rapidly joined the marketplace, acting as partners in, or clients of, numerous ventures.

There are presently two different models used in EBPP. Under the first, the service provider (typically a bank, ISP or infrastructure specialist) receives a customer's 'paper bills', scans them and sends an e-mail notification to the customer. The customer reviews the scanned payment on a web site and authorizes the bank to make a payment to the vendor. Platforms such as StatusFactory and PayMyBills/PayTrust follow this model. The second model is similar, except that the service provider does not scan bills—it only accepts electronic bills from vendors equipped to provide such information; Yahoo Bill Pay is an example of this model. Many platforms have chosen to partner with financial institutions and ISPs to provide greater, and quicker, acceptance; for example, PayMyBills/PayTrust is linked with E*Trade, Travelers Insurance, American Express, and GE Financial Services.

As indicated, banks and other EBPP providers often rely on infrastructure companies to provide the underlying architecture and software needed to accomplish the crucial electronic payment tasks; providers such as Cyberbills, CheckFree, Spectrum and others have developed much of the underlying technology used in today's EBPP processes (note that in addition to providing infrastructure solutions some also act as ASPs, providing EBPP services directly to end-users). Cyberbills, funded by numerous VCs, offers technology solutions for integrated consumer and small business EBPP platforms. CheckFree—which is partly owned by Microsoft, Citibank, Bank of America, and First Data—is one of the largest Internet bill payment service providers, linking 3.3MM consumers, 1000 companies, and 350 financial institutions. CheckFree establishes relationships with individual vendors and works with them to transmit electronic bills to a bank or service provider which maintains a relationship with the consumer; the company also provides a turnkey electronic billing solution to vendors. (First Data, one of the partners, has created electronic payment and infrastructure solutions/processes for vendors, credit card companies, mutual funds and others for several years, and so brings considerable expertise to the venture; it has also developed a separate venture with VC firm iFormation to process Internet payments.) Spectrum—which is partly owned by Chase, First Union and Wells Fargo—operates in a similar fashion, but is more flexible in allowing any vendor or financial institution to use its services. Bottomline Technologies is another major EBPP solution provider; through its NetTransact and PayBase modules, Bottomline has been active in US EBPP infrastructure for several years. In addition, in 2000 the company acquired the UK's leading EBPP software provider, Checkpoint, giving it access to 3000 UK and European institutions which provide their own retail clients with EBPP services. Regardless of the specific construct, EBPP services accept payment instructions from customers, collect them at the end of each business day, verify that sufficient funds are available to cover account debits, and determine whether creditors are members of an authorized clearing system (such as the ACH or BACS); members of the clearing system receive funds electronically, while non-members are issued checks. As indicated in Chapter 4, EBPP applies equally to institutional clients. The primary difference is that consumers receive a far greater quantity of short (1–2 page) bills involving small payments, while the institutional sector receives a smaller number of very large (100+ page) bills involving large payments.

In the US, most online B2C payments are handled through credit cards; throughout the rest of the world payment methods vary and include electronic payments, direct debits, and credit cards. While this is cost-effective for most transactions, it is not efficient for smaller 'micro' transactions. Micro-payments are defined as monetary transactions ranging from $0.25 to $10—these amounts are large enough to purchase goods on the Internet but too small for merchants to process through credit or debit card mechanisms in a cost-effective manner. The first generation of micro-payment services, which appeared in the mid-1990s, was not particularly successful as processes were too complex and time-consuming, and acceptance too limited. As a result, micro-payments were largely ignored until the late 1990s. In the past few years service providers have shifted to simpler mechanisms—many employing 'single click' technology—in the hope of attracting more participants. The creation of a workable micro-payment solution through the Internet stands to benefit both consumers and merchants, and represents one of the Internet's areas of 'untapped potential'. According to a Gartner Group research survey, 40% of online merchants claim to have low cost goods that could be sold through the web—they do not currently offer such products, however, given general lack of micro-payment capabilities.

Numerous new micro-payment mechanisms are available in the marketplace, each representing additions to, or variations on, the original 'electronic cash' (or e-cash) theme. These mechanisms include digital currency, digital wallets, virtual escrow accounts and direct P2P payments. e-Cash, in its most basic form, is based on public key encryption. As indicated earlier in the text, asymmetric keys come in public/private pairs—the private key is known only to the 'owner' and the public key is known to all. Any commercial transaction (including e-cash) which is encrypted by a private key can be decrypted by a public key, and vice versa. Banks and customers can thus use their keys for both security and identification. When a bank signs an e-cash transaction with its private key, a customer or merchant can verify the 'signature' using the bank's public key. Equally, when a customer 'signs' for deposits and withdraws e-cash using the private key, the bank or merchant can use the customer's public key to verify identity. Using these security mechanisms, providers have introduced various e-cash payment solutions. For instance, several firms have created bearer certificate systems, which gives the holder of an Internet cash certificate a store of monetary value. When a purchase is made, the holder of the e-cash transfers the required amount to the seller, who then has possession of the value. (An equivalent offline version of e-cash is also available, allowing funds to be stored on a user's smart card; funds can be transferred to another card when a purchase is made.) In addition to bearer e-cash structures, various ventures offer notational certificate systems. Through a notational process a consumer prepays a certain amount of funds into an escrow account; when a purchase is made, the cash is transferred from the account to the merchant; this is effectively a book entry transfer that does not involve interbank clearing and settling.

Digital currency—a form of e-cash which is created through special software and which can only be used/accepted on the web—has increased in popularity over the past few years. In a typical transaction a consumer purchases digital currency from an ASP via a credit card, and then uses that currency to purchase goods/services through the storefronts of participating merchants; alternatively, it can transfer the currency to those who do not have credit cards and want to shop on the Internet. Once a purchase is made, the merchant forwards the digital currency to the ASP, who exchanges it for real currency. In the US, ventures such as Flooz and InternetCash have made some progress in extending this concept; this construct can, again, accommodate smaller value purchases and payments. In the UK, service provider Beenz has created its own form of currency which is based on transferable award tokens that can be earned at particular sites (by performing certain web-related tasks or providing web marketing information), and redeemed for goods and services at other participating sites. Digital wallets are also becoming more widely used in the B2C payment sector. These services are based on software modules that store a consumer's credit and debit card/payment information, along with shipping, product and preference details. When a web purchase is made the contents of the wallet are automatically 'applied' to the payment screen, obviating the need to re-enter/re-access payment information. Major ISPs and ASPs such as Yahoo, AOL and Microsoft all feature digital wallet mechanisms to speed the payment process; several financial institutions, such as Chase, have also introduced their own wallets. Virtual escrow accounts have become another common means of transferring value on the Internet. Through trust platforms such as I-Escrow, Escrow.com, Tradesafe, and others, a buyer and seller can exchange cash and goods in a neutral, web-based escrow setting, including transactions based on relatively small monetary values. The virtual escrow agent verifies that both sides of a transaction are completed before releasing cash and goods to the respective parties, adding security to the exchange process; this has proven particularly helpful in the online auction market, where buyers and sellers are unknown to one another. Direct P2P micro-payment systems are gaining in popularity as the market for financial transactions between individuals expands. These mechanisms, which do not necessarily flow through banking institutions, allow a person to pay another for goods/services or send funds to friends, relatives or colleagues; there are generally no minimum or maximum payment levels. Services typically operate by debiting the sender's credit card for the amount specified and transmitting an e-mail to the recipient, who then registers to have funds deposited in a bank account or delivered in the form of a check (other services bill the charge to the customer's ISP or phone account for collection at the end of each month). X.com (through PayPal), PayMyBills (through PayMe.com), Yahoo (through PayDirect), and online auctioneer eBay (through Billpoint), among others, offer direct P2P micro-payment capabilities. Several major banking institutions have started offering similar services, including Bank One (with its e-money mail product) and Citibank (which joined with AOL to create a proprietary product available through Citibank's platform (via c2it) and AOL's platform (via AOL Quick Cash)).

Credit services are an evolving dimension of web-based retail financial services. The extension of credit—in the form of credit cards/revolving lines of credit, short-term credit facilities, auto loans, mortgages, and home equity loans—is provided by established financial institutions and dedicated credit marketplaces. In the US, firms such as American Express, Citibank, Bank of America, Morgan Stanley Dean Witter/Discover, Chase, and many others provide proprietary credit services through their corporate storefronts. They are joined by a new generation of platforms, such as NextCard, Providian Aria, and Capital One, which provide credit card/revolving credit facilities; these groups operate as pure play or hybrid providers of consumer credit services—not unlike the monoline credit card companies, such as First USA and MBNA, that emerged in the 1980s. Internationally, many major web banks, such as Egg, Cahoot, Lloyds TSB/Loans Direct, and DB24, offer credit services through their sites.

Credit can also be arranged through credit marketplaces, such as E-Loan, LookSmart, Money.net, LendNetwork.com, and eCredit. These marketplaces provide comparative quotes across financial institutions and generate quick credit approvals. Some storefronts and marketplaces use credit scoring technologies from infrastructure companies that permit real-time credit decision-making; providers such as Fair Issac/LiquidCredit accelerate the decision-making process and enable ventures to respond to their customers very quickly. Since the provision of funds under a credit card or revolving line of credit is a straightforward transaction—which needs only to be supported by credit information from the applicant and third-party credit agencies—most platforms can initiate and complete the process online. Turn-around time for application decisions ranges from minutes to hours or days, depending on the particulars of the service and applicant. Credit marketplaces such as eCredit act as general conduits for consumer loans and credit cards, providing instant decisions based on advanced scoring concepts. By establishing relationships with major US lenders, these marketplaces can quickly and easily accept an online application, gather credit information, process it through credit scoring analytics, arrive at a preliminary (and generally final) credit decision, advise the lending institution, receive confirmation, and close the credit facility. Though the lending institution retains the right of refusal, it often synchronizes its underwriting criteria with the web marketplace so that there is a 'common understanding' of which credits are likely to be accepted or rejected. As with other marketplace ventures, those which are likely to be successful over the medium-term will feature compelling business models that can add value as competition increases and markets move through cyclical downturns.

Financing of real property transactions requires a considerable amount of documentation and physical effort related to lien searches, title work, appraisals, and so on. Accordingly, a truly paperless Internet-based mortgage financing process is not yet feasible. That said, many aspects of the mortgage business are well suited to the web—particularly steps related to comparison shopping, pre-processing and post-closing payment and tracking. Consumers seeking a mortgage can search the web for financial institutions offering different mortgage products and rates, select the most appropriate platform and product, complete relevant application questionnaires, obtain pre-approvals, and lock in rates (subject to final approval); post-approval, the consumer can arrange for online mortgage payment and tracking. The mortgage approval process still requires intermediate 'human' contact, as loan officers evaluating requests must deal with a considerable amount of hardcopy documentation, including site plans, appraisals, purchase contracts, titles, and liens. In addition, certain laws still require many documents to be physically signed by the borrower at the closing of the transaction. As regulations governing the process change—through use of digital signatures and electronic filing—streamlining is expected to occur, and more 'paperless platforms' will start to appear; however, some researchers believe the truly paperless model will take a further three to five years to fully implement. According to a survey by the Mortgage Bankers Association of America, less than 1% of the $970B in mortgages originated in the US in 1999 occurred online. However, as regulations change and new platforms are developed, that figure is expected to rise—to as much as 7–10% by 2003. A survey by Federal National Mortgage Association (FNMA), the US's largest mortgage buyer, indicates that 50% of people expect some, or all, aspects of the mortgage process will be handled online by 2003. Indeed, many researchers believe that online mortgage lending will be one of the largest, and fastest, areas of growth in the online financial services sector; service providers with online platforms that cater to this segment of the market stand to benefit considerably. Before achieving such goals, however, consumers will need to become even more comfortable with the online process; since home purchase represents the single largest financial decision most people make, many are still reluctant to abandon the 'physical' dimension of the process (e.g. seeking advice/consultation from mortgage/banking professionals, physically signing documents at closing, and so on)—time and experience will be required before that is likely to change.

There are presently two broad types of online mortgage services available to consumers—those provided by pure play and hybrid banks through corporate storefronts or vertical portals, and those offered by web-based mortgage marketplaces. In the first category, web platforms of banks such as Citibank, Bank of America, and Dime Bancorp, among many others, provide a range of mortgage-related services based on their proprietary mortgage products; these typically include rate/product information, online applications, rate locks, summary closing costs, and automated mortgage bill payment. While full service institutions like Bank of America and Citibank offer mortgages in tandem with other financial products and are thus considered vertical portals, Dime Bancorp and other institutions focus primarily (or exclusively) on the mortgage lending market and are more appropriately considered storefront platforms. Numerous international banks, such as Lloyds TSB, Dresdner Bank, Deutsche Bank, UBS and Bancomer, provide similar mortgage financing facilities to their domestic clients. In the second category, mortgage marketplace platforms such as LoanWorks, E-Loan, OnLoan.com, Loan-Surfer.com, QuickenMortgage, and others provide users with access to mortgage services from a large number of participating institutions. By referencing user-specified details related to mortgage size, type, region, and so on, these platforms search available offerings across dozens, or even hundreds, of banks and mortgage bankers and give consumers the option of selecting from competing quotes. Most marketplaces help customers obtain online rate locks and pre-approvals, and monitor the process through closing; some platforms also provide city-specific closing cost estimates and other value-added services. In certain cases marketplaces are affiliated with particular lending institutions, mortgage bankers or property/real estate companies; most, however, are 'independent' and work with, or represent, offerings from dozens of credit providers. Those supporting a range of institutions are compensated by the ultimate lender for delivering accepted mortgage customers. Within the marketplace segment certain platforms, such as E-Loan and HomeShark, act as mortgage originators by creating loans and then channeling them to the ultimate lender; others, such as LendingTree, act as mortgage brokers, matching borrowers and lenders but not originating mortgage product. Both structures threaten to disintermediate functions performed by traditional mortgage brokers, but must possess business models that can withstand market and refinancing downturns. While the mortgage marketplace concept is expected to remain central to the expansion of online mortgage business, some consolidation will occur over the coming years as users focus their business on a core number of platforms that can provide truly value-added services; early casualties appeared in 2000, when Mortgage.com and CreditLand shut down their operations after being unable to generate a critical mass of business.

Note that at the retail level, consumer credit information—including payment and credit histories for every individual who amasses a financial record—is available on the web. Consumer credit information is of critical importance in the lending process; mortgage lenders, credit card companies, and banks providing credit facilities use personal credit reports to make decisions. While every consumer has the right to see his or her credit report, the process has historically tended to be manual and time-consuming—dissuading many from reviewing their credit histories. Companies that track personal credit information, such as TRW and Equifax, have built online platforms that allow consumers to access their confidential credit files on a 'fee per view' basis. These services also provide additional querying tools that allow problems or discrepancies to be tracked and resolved electronically, rather than by phone or letter.

WEALTH MANAGEMENT

New and established ventures are using the Internet to capture a share of the growing market for wealth management. Online wealth management, which includes private banking services, financial advice and fund management, is expected to increase over the coming years as more individuals accumulate a larger amount of financial assets and generate a greater amount of income. The global economic boom of the past decade, an extended bull market in global equities, and expansion in the technology and financial services sectors have allowed individuals to accumulate greater amounts of investable assets and income—both of which need to be actively managed.

The top end of online wealth management services, targeted towards very high net worth customers, is offered selectively by various financial institutions that are also active in other aspects of online trading and online banking; firms such as American Express, Citibank, UBS, Credit Suisse, Goldman Sachs, and Merrill Lynch provide such wealth management services. Pure plays and hybrids are also participating in the sector through acquisitions (such as Schwab's acquisition of wealth manager US Trust) or partnerships (such as E*Trade's partnership with Ernst and Young to create eAdvisors, or Merrill Lynch's and HSBC's partnership to develop an online bank targeted at high net worth customers). Wealth services are also offered by completely independent web platforms, such as MyCFO, that provide clients with access to financial advisors and electronic products/services for a flat fee; because these ventures are independent they are able to offer wealthy clients the most compelling, and cost-effective, financial services from a range of providers. Most wealth management ventures offer online services to their wealthiest customers as a supplement to, rather than a substitute for, personalized services. Since the essence of wealth management relates to personal financial advice, planning, and execution, many clients do not want these personalized services replaced by web-based products and interfaces. Accordingly, B2C wealth management platforms give clients web tools that promote additional flexibility and convenience. Such ventures allow authorized customers to access account and market information and verify the status of pending/ executed trades and overall portfolios; specific investment, wealth, tax, trust and retirement advice is then provided 'face-to-face' by associated private bankers, investment managers, or financial consultants.

For clients who prefer a 'self-directed' approach, with appropriate guidance as needed, there are platforms that can create an entire financial plan for a flat fee. For instance, financial planning sites such as FinancialEngines, Fin-Portfolio, mPower, and DirectAdvice supply retirement and investment advice based on user-defined inputs and goals. By providing details related to financial assets, liabilities, income, expenses, and future goals, these services generate financial projections/estimates and suggest recommendations related to taxes, tax-deferred plans, investment allocations, savings requirements, IRA/401K and retirement contributions, and so on. Though obviously not as comprehensive or interactive as dealing with a personal financial advisor, these services appeal to a certain segment of the investing public, and are becoming increasingly popular.

Traditional mutual funds and managed, or 'customized', funds are key components of the wealth management sector. Though the mutual fund industry is well established—and somewhat 'set' in its ways—it has gravitated online and is expected to expand its Internet presence further over the coming years. Investment management companies such as Invesco, Fidelity, T Rowe Price, Van Kampen, AXA and others feature interactive corporate storefront platforms that allow investors to purchase their underlying funds and consult information, education and planning modules. (Note that many of the funds managed by these firms can also be purchased through the online trading and banking platforms mentioned earlier in the chapter, which provide links into thousands of funds offered by hundreds of fund families.) Though the mutual fund industry has started moving online, it is expected to transform further as competition forces fund managers to increase disclosure and lower costs. In particular, the managed fund sector—which lets investors create and run their own funds—is presenting established mutual fund companies with significant competitive pressure. Managed funds provide investors with various benefits that mutual funds traditionally have not—transparency, flexibility and competitive costs. Traditional mutual fund offerings tend to be very opaque, publishing their investment holdings publicly two to four times per year on a 'lagged' basis, and highlighting their top holdings only once a month. Many investors are interested in more frequent, and timely, disclosure of portfolio holdings—perhaps weekly or monthly (the extreme example is MetaMarkets' OpenFund.com, which publishes its holdings online every day). In addition, mutual funds by definition are professionally managed, leaving no room for input by the investor; this can be a disadvantage for investors sensitive to the timing of capital gains and losses, or those with a desire to participate more actively in the investment selection and allocation process. Finally, the costs associated with managing traditional mutual funds can be very high. While several years ago mutual funds were the cheapest way for investors to participate broadly in the stock market, the same is no longer true—the availability of online research and execution means costs are now much lower for the investing public, putting certain mutual fund companies at a competitive disadvantage.

Managed funds can help investors overcome these shortcomings. While such accounts have historically been available only to the wealthiest of clients, minimum balance requirements have dropped below $50,000 and are attracting a far broader audience; managed funds accounted for $425B of the $7T fund market in 2000 and are expected to expand at $500MM to $1B per year in the near-term. In a typical mutual fund, an investor owns shares in a company that owns the underlying securities. In a managed fund (also known as a folio or basket) an investor creates an investment strategy and then purchases individual shares directly; the investor thus owns the underlying securities and can alter strategies and holdings at will—being totally aware of portfolio holdings at all times. Customized strategies can also help investors optimize financial requirements as related to tax liabilities, capital gains and losses, and cash flows. Depending on portfolio composition and trading frequency, costs are also very competitive. Though managed funds can be created and managed 'offline', they can also be developed online (for a monthly/ annual fee) through storefront platforms such as Folio(fn), Unx.com, Netfolio, RunMoney, NetStock, and Privateaccounts, among others. For example, Folio(fn) allows customers to create, hold and trade baskets for a fixed annual charge; depending on the size of the portfolio, stocks held and trades executed, such charges can be lower than those on traditional funds. Stocks can be selected from 'pre-packaged' folios by risk, sector, growth or income, and then adjusted, or they can be created from 'scratch'—with up to 50 stocks from a total pool of 2500 stocks. Up to three folios can be created for a single fee, and unlimited trading can be performed within each folio (though executions are swept into the market only twice a day, rather than real-time). (Note that Barclays, through its iShare platform, allows investors to buy/sell online any one of 50 different index funds (effectively portfolios of stocks) which can be selected by style, size, sector, region, industry, and so on; though customization is not possible, a large number of target portfolios are available for purchase and sale. Various other firms, such as Merrill Lynch, State Street, and Morgan Stanley Dean Witter, offer similar types of programs—all are variations on the same theme, giving investors the chance to trade in targeted 'mini-portfolios' of stocks; since these are quoted securities traded on exchanges, they can be bought and sold through online trading platforms.) Other customized portfolio services abound. For instance, SmartLeaf provides investors with individualized portfolio advice/tools, and allows investors to create their own portfolios and manage capital gain/loss timing to maximize tax benefits. Other services, such as MyMoneyPro.com, provide customers with professionally managed funds, but allow for a small amount of flexibility in reallocating portions of a portfolio; since these services combine the best of the professionally managed and DIY models, they tend to cost somewhat more than conventional mutual funds. Given the rate of growth in the managed fund market, many established financial companies are offering, or planning to offer, similar services; in such instances they need to be sensitive to channel conflict. Self-directed funds are, of course, not suitable for all investors. There are many investors who prefer to take a passive role when it comes to asset selection and management, and are therefore unlikely to want such products; they may ultimately benefit, however, from greater transparency and lower costs if mutual funds respond to the competitive pressures imposed by the managed fund sector.

In a separate segment of the 'wealth management' category, accredited investors—those with net worth in excess of $1MM or annual income in excess of $200,000 for two consecutive years—can participate in higher risk investments and ventures, including hedge funds and venture capital funds. Since such investments are very high risk in nature, they are limited to those who can afford to sustain any potential losses that may arise. Certain dedicated sites, such as HedgeFund.net, provide accredited investors with access to a range of leveraged investment products. VC funds, which invest in many of the Internet platforms that are driving B2C, B2B and infrastructure, are also available through the web to accredited investors.

INSURANCE AND ANNUITIES

Insurance, like EBPP and mortgages, is a nascent, but promising, sector of B2C financial services. Though migration of insurance services to the web has been very slow compared with online trading (and even online banking)—in 1999 only 12% of US insurers sold product equal to 1% of their total output through the web, and internationally the amount was even smaller—there is considerable movement underway to migrate more aspects of the insurance business to the web. This is expected to accelerate as consumers gain comfort with the process, and insurers determine how to manage channel conflict and resolve regulatory issues. Researchers estimate that by 2003 approximately 10–15% of US insurance will be sold online—primarily auto insurance (which must be renewed annually), but also including life and property/casualty insurance. For instance, Forrester Research expects online US auto insurance sales to increase from the $500MM achieved in 1999 to $11.8B by 2004. Similar growth rates are anticipated in select Western European nations. To date, online efforts have focused primarily on 'simple' products like term life insurance and auto insurance. More complex offerings, such as health insurance, deferred annuities and other investment-like products, will form part of the 'second wave' as institutions and consumers benefit from further experience.

There are two different methods for delivering insurance online. The first is for established insurance companies or new 'virtual' insurers (associated with established companies) to sell products through the corporate storefront model—these can be thought of as Internet insurance carriers. The second is for ventures to do so through the insurance marketplace model, where each marketplace acts as a network of 'virtual agents'. Both methods demand management of channel conflict—this involves striking a balance between new distribution mechanisms based on the web and established sales mechanisms centered on agent networks (independent agents and direct marketers for life, and independent agents, exclusive agents, and direct response insurers for property/casualty). It is vital for insurance carriers that create their own web distribution mechanisms or partner with insurance marketplaces to achieve a balance between the two networks. Agents are responsible for selling a great deal of insurance on behalf of the major insurers, and account for approximately 25% of the cost of a typical policy. Replacing traditional networks of agents and phone marketing representatives with web/marketplace links is redefining the business and generating savings and efficiencies for both consumers and insurers; at the same time, it is disrupting business flows coming from agent networks. The trend towards greater Internet distribution is expected to continue—albeit gradually, in order not to destroy, in the short-term, business generated by agents. Internet distribution is also likely to expand as companies contend with various regulatory issues. Regulations surrounding insurance coverage and sales, within the US and between countries, are complex. Selling insurance between jurisdictions, while often possible, is not always straightforward; this added dimension of regulatory complexity will remain a hurdle until greater harmonization occurs.

Internet insurance carriers exist primarily as web-based storefronts of traditional insurance companies; as indicated in Chapter 2, true pure plays are limited in number (and include Esurance, with insurance policies backed by Argonaut and General Re, and eCoverage, which carries the financial backing of Softbank and E*Trade). Internet insurance carriers offer consumers a range of features which generally includes instant online quotes for proprietary insurance products (including auto, homeowners, renters, life and health insurance), online premium payment capabilities (primarily via credit card charges), online policy review and claims initiation, and web-based educational material. Some web platforms confine their offerings to specific segments of the insurance market—particularly if parent companies are monoline—while others are broad-based. Certain vendors offer interesting features like online binding for auto insurance in select states, while others have partnered with Internet insurance marketplaces or vertical portals to serve as preferred carriers and widen distribution. Key platforms include the web offerings of Progressive Insurance, GEICO Insurance, AIG, Amica, Allstate, John Hancock, State Farm Insurance, Prudential Insurance and Zurich Direct. Many international companies are active in this arena as well. In the UK, for example, Lloyds TSB provides its customers with auto, home and travel insurance through its InsureDirect offering, while Halifax does so through its e-sure platform; in France, AXA operates a comprehensive corporate storefront, while Societe Generale conducts business through its dedicated Sogecap and CGI storefronts.

Insurance marketplaces give consumers access to product pricing and analysis from a broad range of insurance companies. Marketplaces allow consumers to input desired parameters (e.g. amount, type, coverage, and so on), and review competing quotes from different carriers capable of supplying coverage per the criteria specified. This saves much of the time and energy a consumer or independent agent would normally face in researching the offerings of multiple companies. Consumers can also review policies online and pay lump sum or periodic premia via the web. Note that certain marketplaces act primarily as referral parties for the insurers associated with their sites, receiving fees from an insurer once a consumer has selected the insurer's policy. Others act as online agents, processing applications once the consumer has made a selection and receiving a commission fee from the insurer selected to provide coverage. Examples of insurance marketplace platforms include QuickQuote (which provides quotes and information on a range of insurance products from various carriers), QuickenInsurance (which offers instant online life and auto insurance quotes from numerous carriers), InsWeb (which provides quotes and information on term life, auto, renters, homeowners, and health insurance from 40 carriers (and links the consumer with a 'live agent' once a selection has been made)), Insurance.com (which offers online life and auto insurance quotes from various carriers), and Quotesmith (which offers instant online life and health insurance quotes from over 250 carriers).

The annuity sector is an emerging facet of the web. Annuities, which can be relatively complex, allow investors to receive income from an insurer over an extended period of time in exchange for lump sum or periodic payments; the shifting of income into future time periods results in tax deferrals. While several of the insurance platforms mentioned above (along with other major players such as American Heritage, ING, The Hartford, and others) provide annuity services, the web also features dedicated marketplace platforms, such as AnnuityScout, Annuitynet.com, finportfolio.com, and variableannuitiesonline, that search for annuities across a range of providers based on details supplied by the user; search results give the consumer information about rates, guarantee periods, and state availability, along with links into annuity providers. Since there are literally hundreds of annuity programs offered by dozens of insurers, this type of service can save investors considerable time and effort; many of the platforms also include educational tools to provide guidance on the right type of annuity program given an investor's particular financial circumstances.

Many of the B2C financial services discussed in this chapter (along with the B2B services described in Chapter 4) make considerable use of informational and analytical tools in delivering the fullest benefit to users; the broad topic of information is the subject of Chapter 6.

TALK OF THE TRADE

After-hours trading—trading which occurs prior to, or after, the official New York trading hours of 9.30am and 4pm; a growing amount of activity is occurring after hours through ECNs and other ATSs.

Day trader—a trader who executes dozens, or hundreds, of trades during a single trading session in the hope of profiting from very small moves; day traders close the trading day without any positions.

Digital currency—an electronic currency, created through special software, that can only be used on the Internet.

EBPP—electronic bill payment and presentment, a service which allows customers to electronically receive and pay bills; true EBPP requires electronic presentment by vendors and electronic payment by banks, on behalf of customers, to vendors.

e-Cash—electronic cash, cash which can be created on, and transported through, the Internet; e-cash can be anonymous (bearer, meaning whoever has the e-cash has the monetary value) or registered (token, meaning e-cash has to be re-registered in order to transfer monetary value).

EDAT—electronic direct access trading, a platform widely used by day traders prior to the Internet, typically featuring direct communication into a broker or exchange for instant execution, along with rich information/ analytics and quotes.

Fill-or-kill order—an order to execute an entire transaction as specified, or none of it.

Good-till-cancelled order—an order kept active until it is filled or cancelled.

Limit order—an order to execute at a specific price.

Managed fund—also known as a folio or basket, a customizable fund enabling an investor to construct and alter a portfolio of stocks at will, based on personal investment and tax criteria.

Market order—an order to execute at the prevailing market price.

Marketable limit order—an order to execute at no worse than a specific price.

Micro-payment—a payment under $10 which has not traditionally been economical for credit card processors or merchants to support; a new generation of web-based micro-payment solutions is giving B2C merchants the chance to offer low priced goods and services.

P2P payment—a direct peer-to-peer payment that allows consumers to transfer funds over the Internet; the P2P payment service provider debits the sender's credit card for the amount specified, e-mails the recipient, and arranges to have funds deposited in a bank account or sent via check.

Pump and dump—Internet-based schemes where investors are lured into buying a stock based on exaggerated news, until it reaches an unrealistically high level; the originator of the news sells at the market peak, typically causing investors to lose money as the stock collapses.

Round trip—a complete electronic cycle of the EBPP process.

SOES—small order execution service, a security trading service which represents small investor orders in the marketplace; SOES was originally introduced in 1984 and reinforced after the 1987 stock market crash.

Swing trader—a trader who holds trades for a short period of time, typically several days; unlike day traders, swing traders close the trading day with positions.

Virtual escrow—a neutral, third-party trust provider that stands between a buyer and seller on the Internet; the escrow agent receives payment from the buyer and goods from the seller and, after verifying both parties have complied with their obligations, releases the payment and goods.

6

The Information of Business

THE INFORMATION VALUE PROPOSITION

The financial services business is an information business. Virtually every aspect of institutional and consumer financial decision-making relies on a core of information centered on prices, rates, indicative data, research, investment analysis, quantitative valuation, and technical analysis/charting; in order for financial participants to make rational and reasoned trading, banking, investing and borrowing decisions, they must have access to this information on a timely and regular basis. Since financial information is vital to so many dimensions of financial activity, it comes as no surprise that the preparation, collation, analysis and dissemination of information has become a major priority for financial B2C and B2B providers. The web allows information to be developed and delivered across multiple customer sectors and geographic boundaries very efficiently, injecting speed and transparency into the decision-making process. It also permits much more precise collection and analysis of data related to the needs and desires of small and large customers. The Internet is the perfect mechanism for understanding how individuals and institutions use information, products and services, how they define their preferences and requirements, and what features they find important or irrelevant—the customer effectively becomes data, analyzable by information and serviceable by the Internet. 'Information profiling', made possible through web-based technologies, creates a powerful tool for those gathering and using data to market products and services. Financial ventures are using data profiling capabilities to identify, personalize and target their services more precisely; this results in genuinely useful information being conveyed to a correctly targeted audience, rather than random information being distributed to 'the masses' (with some vain hope of appealing to a small fraction of recipients). By permitting the development and deployment of different information mechanisms, the web is acting as an 'information equalizer'. Timely, detailed, and customized/personalized financial information, which constitutes the core of financial decision-making, is no longer the exclusive domain of Wall Street bankers, traders, money managers, pension funds, and global corporations. Much of this information is available—either for free or for some nominal charge—to the average user.

Recognizing that the Internet has altered the 'information equation', financial ventures have changed their thinking and strategies. While financial institutions used to profit from the inefficient and fragmented delivery of information—to the disadvantage of many customers—they have reconstructed the value proposition by giving clients timely access to relevant information, data and analytics for use in the financial decision-making process. In conveying information through infomediary, storefront or vertical portal structures, many platforms have adjusted their revenue models to supply much of the required client financial information for free, or at reduced prices; to accommodate this type of pricing model, they have created alternate revenue-generating strategies through advertising, alliance, or subscription processes.

Many of the online trading and banking ventures described in Chapters 4 and 5 offer information and tools as part of their corporate storefront or vertical portal platforms; they are joined by pure web-based information brokers, or infomediaries, operating through storefronts or portals of their own. In addition, established financial information/analytics providers—such as Reuters, Bloomberg, and Thomson, among others—have adapted their business models and strategies to address the demands of B2C and B2B users. Together, these service providers offer a combination of free, low- and high-cost services through both the Internet and dedicated terminals—an entire spectrum of information services is thus available to retail and institutional users. For instance, customers can access free information from platforms such as Yahoo Finance, Clear Station, and Thomson Invest, among many others; these services typically provide news, delayed quotes, basic company information and statistics, and rudimentary portfolio and charting tools. Or, users can choose low-priced information services costing $100–500/month from platforms such as S&P ComStock, Thomson ILX, and Reuters+, among others, which include news, real-time quotes, detailed company information, and comprehensive technical and analytic tools. Alternatively, they can select high-end services costing over $1000/month, from Bloomberg, Reuters, and others, which include extensive news, real-time quotes, rich data and indicatives, and sophisticated pricing and analysis tools.

Though different types of information services are readily available to users, conveying financial information in a standard format remains one of the challenges of the Internet—the ability to adopt and promulgate standards will be central to future growth in web information services. Though there are still no absolute standards, certain meta-languages such as XML (and its variants) are making inroads. Employing a meta-language that defines the meaning of data (rather than its appearance, which is the function of HTML) helps establish a common communication link between platforms and users. Nonetheless, the financial industry still features competing standards which may fragment the market and cause delays or disruptions in achieving truly seamless transfer of data.

INFOMEDIARIES AND VERTICAL PORTALS

As indicated in Chapter 1, certain web platforms—known as infomediary portals—consolidate different dimensions of information—including news, searches, directories, discussion groups, and e-mail—and link them with related services, products and resources. True infomediary portals act only as information conduits; they do not provide products or services of their own, and thus rely on third parties for content. Since they 'own' nothing, their primary function is to act as brokers of information, content, data and intelligence. Those that succeed in providing a compelling information brokerage service can make their sites 'sticky'—attracting new customers, enticing existing customers to return for future visits, and generating broad 'communities of interest'; if the business model is correct, such 'stickiness' can translate into a larger amount of revenues. Examples of these infomediary portals include Financewise, CEO Express, ON24 and Investorama, among others. The vertical portal model discussed at various points in the text typically combines the content and communication features of infomediaries with proprietary or third-party financial products/services; this creates the broadest financial portals. Such platforms provide customers with top level access to news, research, quotes, market commentary, financial products, services, affinity cards, online shopping (including special discounts with approved merchants), EBPP, and so on. Vertical portals sponsored by non-financial companies—such as MSN Money, AOL Finance, Motley Fool, WallStreetCity, CNBC, CNNfn, Silicon Investor, Yahoo Finance, FinancialWeb, SmartMoney, Cyberinvest.com, Bloomberg, and others—are all examples of independent platforms that provide comprehensive financial information and links to third-party financial service ventures. They are joined by integrated vertical portals operated by established financial institutions such as Citibank, Schwab, American Express and E*Trade, among others, which combine information with proprietary financial products/services.

Full service information portals include modules that allow users to 'drill down' to obtain greater information. For example, one module might focus on markets and prices. This can contain various subcategories providing additional levels of detail, including real-time or delayed stock quotes, representative money market rates for savings, checking and deposits, FX rates, interest rates, commodity prices, bond prices/yields and macro-economic indicators. A separate module covering news and related analysis can provide further detail, including streaming headlines and breaking news, recent business and financial news stories, and links into news wires, news services, stock picks and research reports. A third module devoted to communications is typical. This often includes facilities for chat discussions on particular topics, access to previous chat session 'threads' (i.e. ongoing discussion topics), frequently asked questions (FAQs), e-mail, searches, and links into related web sites. A separate module focused on tools is also common in many portals. This provides users with a range of calculators to determine taxes, 401K/IRA contributions, capital gains estimates, bond yields, stock and investment returns, and so on. Certain portal operators also include educational modules that provide explanations, examples, and glossaries on different aspects of finance. Some of the most comprehensive platforms include separate sections detailing special financial offers (i.e. investments with high yields, deals with low fees or other price discounts, and so on). These platforms periodically employ intelligent agents to search the sites of financial providers to generate a list of offers which meet criteria specified by the user; once results are found and displayed, the user can link directly into the offerings selected. Alternatively, the platforms display the best current deals offered by their 'sponsors'. In addition to this range of core services, leading-edge portals allow varying degrees of customization. A user can thus modify the 'look and feel' of the portal to deliver specific information, quotes and portfolio views every time login occurs; this allows instant access to relevant news and financial information, and promotes speed and efficiency. The most advanced infomediaries also incorporate multimedia features, including streaming audio/video coverage of financial news stories, analyst commentary, and so on. By paying incremental fees for certain premium services, such as Level II NASDAQ quotes, real-time research updates, and the like, users can create very powerful information platforms which begin, in many instances, to approximate those available to professionals. Such portals are used not only by B2C customers, but by small businesses, portfolio managers and high-end professional users.

It is worth noting that certain platforms now considered integrated vertical portals commenced as infomediary sites and gradually broadened their scope, functions and presence until they became integrated structures. For instance, platforms such as CNBC and Motley Fool started as pure informational conduits; as customers were drawn to their sites it became apparent that forming alliances with financial service providers could lead to a broadening of the customer base—creating benefits for all parties. For portals that choose to develop into integrated platforms, two alternative models emerge: financial institutions as broad-based portals and non-financial portals as financial service providers. Under the first model, a financial institution may seek to extend its reach beyond traditional financial services by offering clients e-mail, chat sessions/discussion forums, search engines, streaming news/sports headlines, online shopping, travel planning, affinity cards, and so on. Certain platforms, such as those of Citibank, American Express and Chase, have already gravitated towards this structure and are becoming broad portals. Chase, for instance, features a range of traditional and non-traditional services through its platform, including a digital wallet for online purchases (Chase Companion), shopping links/discounts (ChaseShop), B2C currency services/travelers checks (Currency to Go), and so on. However, to be a truly effective and comprehensive portal, an institution must be willing to address all of a customer's needs. To the extent this involves directing a customer to a competitor for particular financial services or products that it cannot offer, or to support services that are out of its traditional 'domain', a bank may resist and limit its scope. From the customer's perspective, the 'financial institution as broad portal' model requires the use of a bank-backed general portal when dealing with a very broad range of services (created internally or obtained from third-party content and infrastructure providers). It is unclear that a financial services venture managing a general portal has any competitive advantage over an ISP or ASP in the provision of e-mail, shopping services, search capabilities, travel planning, and so on. Indeed, the extra burden required in terms of developing outsourcing arrangements or establishing internal customer support may outweigh any incremental revenue derived from bringing in more customers to use the core financial services base. The second model is for non-financial portals to become financial service providers. As indicated earlier, certain portals such as AOL Finance, Intuit Quicken, Bloomberg, Yahoo Finance, MSN Money Central, and a select few others already have excellent brand recognition/trust, provide comprehensive information services (including news, research, quotes), feature useful calculators/analytic tools, and supply links to financial services through partnerships and alliances with financial sponsors. The major drawback for such portals is that they lack the regulatory approvals necessary to act as true financial service providers. Without regulatory authorization—and the attendant scrutiny brings—portals cannot really compete directly against financial institutions in the full provision of financial services. Until they achieve that capability—indeed, should they even desire to achieve that capability—the most realistic option for these portals is to provide a strong base of financial information, tools, and resources, supplemented by links to approved deposit-taking institutions. One example of this model is found in the case of portal Excite-eAtHome, which has an exclusive partnership with Bank One; Excite handles all aspects of information content and communication, while Bank One operates the portal's web banking center. Another example is found in Bloomberg's main portal, which features news, content and data from Bloomberg itself, banking from Everbank and Allied Capital, and insurance from Accu-quote. Evidence suggests these types of partnerships are popular—more joint ventures and alliances between banks and ISP/ASP/technology providers are likely to occur in the future.

INFORMATION AND RESEARCH

Consumers and investors have a multitude of options when it comes to obtaining financial information over the web. Gone are the days when only 'privileged' customers—those maintaining high balances, paying high fees, or enjoying an exclusive institutional relationship—had access to the best financial information, quotes/prices, news, research and trade ideas. Web platforms are capable of providing virtually all users with access to the same base of financial information. While certain information services still command a premium, it is already possible to obtain many former premium services for free, or by providing user information through an online registration process (in exchange for free use of certain premium services, the registration information provided by the user is forwarded to marketing platforms which profile and target customers for additional third-party products/services).

One of the most actively used information services on the web is the quote feature. Investors can readily access stock, bond, mutual fund, currency, commodity and index quotes from many sources, including platforms sponsored by banks, brokers, pure plays, portals, aggregators and non-bank financial institutions. Stock quotes tend to be very popular with retail investors. Anyone can access delayed quotes on the web (with 15 minute delays for NASDAQ stocks, 20 minutes for NYSE and other stocks), and many can now access real-time quotes—by paying modest surcharges, providing registration information, or engaging in some other financial business with the service provider. Richer Level II quotes, which give investors a broad range of bids and offers with associated volume, are available to investors at a premium; day traders, swing traders and professional investors typically require such access in order to trade on a more informed and competitive basis. Though real-time quotes still command a premium, it is almost certain that prices will be driven to zero as the process of information dissemination continues on the web. Streaming quotes, which appear in a real-time, continuously updated fashion, are a relatively new addition to the information scene. Streaming quotes usually command a premium since they are both useful and technologically advanced (indeed, since such quotes require a reasonable amount of network server power they are not yet permitted on certain commercial platforms in Europe).

Though stock quotes tend to be the 'public face' of pricing information on the web, there is a great deal of additional price data available through various platforms. Currency rates, bond prices/yields, yield curves, commodity prices, swap rates, volatility prices and other dimensions of financial data are available to institutional and retail users, either for free or nominal charges. Most major bank platforms supply FX rates, bond dealers and securities firms publish bond prices and yields, and key commodity houses supply sector-specific, as well as general, commodity prices. Futures exchanges such as LIFFE, New York Mercantile Exchange (NYMEX), Chicago Mercantile Exchange (CME), Chicago Board Options Exchange (CBOE), CBOT, SFE, along with independent platforms such as futuresource, DailyFutures.com and TradingTactics.com, provide live and delayed pricing quotes on a range of futures and options contracts. Various specialized platforms, such as e-swappx and iVolatility, provide derivative professionals with current and historical derivative prices, rates and volatilities; the most complete platforms feature live quotes for interest rate and currency swaps, basis swaps, caps/floors, swaptions and equity derivatives. Comprehensive financial information providers, such as Reuters and Bloomberg, typically provide most, or all, of these aspects of financial price/pricing information.

Financial news, including breaking stories related to corporate earnings, interest rate policy, market activity, mergers and acquisitions, IPOs, and so on, is supplied by numerous dedicated financial service platforms. Virtually every major financial publishing outfit has developed a web-based platform to disseminate news information; while this has been particularly vital for hard-copy publications that publish on a weekly or monthly cycle, many daily publications have opted to pursue the same strategy. Established print publications such as the Wall Street Journal, Forbes, Fortune, The Economist, Financial Times, and others now feature comprehensive information platforms which update throughout the day. Traditional electronic news and information providers such as Bloomberg, Reuters, Business Wire, PR Newswire, and others are also at the forefront of disseminating comprehensive news via the web. Since the immediacy of information dominates many aspects of today's financial environment, users demand access to real-time, intraday news; accordingly, numerous infomediary and vertical portals feature streaming news headlines from these electronic news services, and provide links to the news platforms themselves. Certain platforms also feature 'chat rooms' or discussion groups, which are a popular way of 'discussing' information and ideas.

Investment research—a valuable product developed by leading banks—is a key element of the financial information age. Many financial institutions have very experienced, and well-paid, teams of analysts tracking stocks, bonds, currencies, commodities, and overall markets in order to render investment and strategy decisions in a timely fashion. Investors with access to such research can—at least theoretically—profit from the investment guidance of research teams. Established financial institutions with such capabilities have migrated research product to their web sites in order to support their new issue and secondary trading businesses and attract new institutional and retail customers. The research business model takes different forms. While some platforms charge customers for individual pieces of research, others provide the product 'free' to customers who are engaged in some type of business with the institution—online trading or banking at the retail level, new issuance and M&A at the institutional level, for example. The online trading platforms of firms such as Merrill Lynch, Morgan Stanley Dean Witter, UBS Warburg, Deutsche Bank, and others provide trading clients with unrestricted access to company, sector, industry, market and macro research and trading strategies. This generally includes actionable, time-sensitive research, real-time stock upgrades/downgrades, and the results of daily briefing meetings (most often encapsulated in so-called 'morning notes'). In exchange for providing this 'free' unrestricted access, sponsoring firms typically expect to generate revenues in the form of trading commissions, asset management or new issue fees, and so on; the cost of research to the customer is therefore implicit, rather than explicit. In certain cases firms make portions of their research available for free to institutions and individuals who are not clients of the firm, following an 'embargo' lasting several days to several weeks. Under this model, firms give their paying customers access to all research first—allowing them time to act on the recommendations—and then grant access to a wider audience, in the hope of enticing some to open an account or conduct other business. In some instances a financial services platform does not produce research of its own, and must enter into an alliance with another firm in order to distribute information to its own clients. This is clearly a cost-effective mechanism for smaller or mid-tier firms who do not want to run the expense of building, staffing and maintaining a research function; research teams are notoriously expensive and the market for talent extremely competitive. While this reduces their flexibility somewhat—for instance, firms have to convey research views to their clients which may, or may not, coincide with their own and have no say in the scope or depth of coverage—it is a workable alternative for many. Firms such as Schwab and Fidelity, for example, contract with CSFB and Lehman Brothers to obtain research content for their clients.

While research content is vital—good investment calls can, after all, lead to more business—timeliness of distribution and service to the client remain important components of the overall process. Most major institutions have spent considerable time and money developing mechanisms to deliver research content as soon as it is produced, to virtually any device used by investors, with little or no human intervention. This has become the de-facto standard for research platforms—any service that cannot achieve transmission speed and flexibility operates at a competitive disadvantage. Most major Wall Street firms offering web-based research have mechanisms to send automated e-mail research alerts to their clients—including flash announcements, earnings 'whispers', upgrades and downgrades, new reports, and so on. This obviates the need for a client to continuously access a firm's storefront site or enter through a third-party portal to get research-related updates. In addition to timeliness, research providers are increasingly focused on total client requirements, rather than 'topic' or product-specific coverage. Research has to meet the broad needs of the client, incorporating all markets, strategies, recommendations, and topics that are deemed to be useful and relevant. Since research is often produced by different internal teams, output needs to be closely coordinated with client relationship managers; using web-based technology, cross-product research coordination is now readily achievable.

Research aggregation services were developed in the late 1990s to give users a single point of access to a broad range of research products. Aggregation platforms such as Multex, FirstCall, StockHouse, BestCalls.com, TheMarkets.com, and BulldogResearch, among many others, provide users with a cross-section of research views; those using such services can reference all research coverage on a company or market by any analyst providing commentary and analysis. This helps users develop a broader perspective on a particular investment candidate. For instance, TheMarkets.com, an initiative launched in late 2000, brings together the equity research of the largest Wall Street firms—including Merrill Lynch, Goldman Sachs, Morgan Stanley Dean Witter, Salomon Smith Barney, CSFB, Deutsche Bank, and UBS Warburg—through a co-mingled research portal; authorized users can view research coverage from all of the sponsors (and also link into the proprietary corporate storefronts of individual sponsors for additional trade execution and support services). Aggregation pricing structures vary by service and access. Individual investors can generally access basic information, such as consensus estimates and corporate overviews, for free; company- or sector-specific research can be accessed on a 'fee per download' basis (though certain reports can be obtained for free following an embargo period). Institutional investors wanting an aggregate research picture are typically charged and given real-time access. Certain research aggregators employ intelligent agents which can scan all available news and research according to a customer's interests and preferences, and generate automatic e-mail alerts when items of interest are located. Various platforms, such as Multex, also act as outsourcing agents for financial institutions that do not want to be engaged in the research distribution process. Through outsourcing the service provider amalgamates, organizes, maintains and electronically distributes, to all authorized users, relevant research information. Research can, of course, be distributed in any number of formats, including electronic print, audio and video. Electronic print remains the most popular and is available in numerous forms (including PDF, HTML, XML, and so on, none yet an 'industry standard' (though XML is seen as promising as it is very flexible and can be targeted at a range of hardware, including wireless devices)). In an effort to take advantage of the multimedia capabilities that are increasingly available through the Internet—streaming audio and video, for instance—certain dedicated services have been created to transmit live online research panels, discussions and seminars. Platforms such as Sage provide investors and analysts with an opportunity to interact in a live web forum. Audio clips of conference calls, analyst comments and breaking news are now routinely available in web-based form over PCs and workstations using applications such as RealAudio. A trader, salesperson or institutional client can thus listen to spoken commentary directly from a terminal.

In addition to company-specific equity research and general investment strategy, many web users are keen to tap into information services related to more specific segments of the global economy and financial markets. As one might imagine, there is no shortage of platforms offering very focused and targeted news, analysis and research; there are many specialized services that offer retail and institutional users access to areas such as earnings estimates, corporate financial statements, federal filings, economic statistics, domestic and international investment analysis/ideas, IPO investment opportunities, credit/risk and mutual fund rankings, and so on.

Earnings estimates, which drive a great deal of stock market activity, are tracked closely by analysts and investors. Numerous ventures bring together consensus earnings estimates and provide comparisons against past periods and future expectations. In addition to the research aggregation platforms mentioned above, dedicated web platforms such as Zacks and Earningswhisper.com provide a wealth of earnings information, including earnings calendars, new earnings warnings/estimates, positive and negative earnings surprises, income statement information, and current news on earnings reports; they also include discussion forums and links to Wall Street research sites covering particular companies. Insider buying and selling by company directors and officers is another dimension of market research analyzed by professionals and small investors. While data on restricted purchases and sales is tracked through official filings, it is also available online through specialist services such as InsiderScores. Many of the underlying financial statements which investors and researchers use to analyze earnings and make decisions are available online through private and regulatory platforms. Annual reports and associated financial statements (such as 10-Ks (annual reports) and 10-Qs (quarterly reports)) are generally made available by individual corporations through their web sites. SEC documents related to corporate filings and registrations—including S-1 registration statements—are also available online; the EDGAR (Electronic Data Gathering, Analysis and Retrieval) database and web platform, for instance, acts as a central repository for all federally-filed documents. SEDAR, the Canadian equivalent of EDGAR, provides similar financial detail on Canadian institutional registrations. International corporate coverage is provided by platforms such as

Wright Investors' Service, as well as regulatory sites maintained by government and exchange officials in various countries.

Investment and trade ideas are of interest to many investors. Those searching for trade ideas can access special platforms designed to summarize and analyze proprietary or third-party investment strategies. For instance, web ventures such as Validea, iExchange, BestSignals, InvestorLinks, and others provide users with access to a range of fundamental trade ideas across individual securities, industries, markets and macro-strategies. These services aggregate recommendations from different industry sources and allow investors to search, sort and filter by pre-specified criteria. They also evaluate or rate specific ideas generated by institutions and analysts, and provide statistical information such as best/worst returns achieved by published ideas. Certain services categorize recommendations by investment strategy so that investors can quickly link to those most suited to their investment style (such as momentum, growth, price strength, valuation, 'bottom fishing', and so on). A number of these platforms, such as BestSignals, cater to international investors by providing coverage of, and ideas from, major international markets. Platforms also exist for those interested in more specific aspects of a given market. For example, stock option traders can consult informational sites such as Schaeffers Research, OptionInvestor, or Optionetics for trade ideas related to options. Investors interested in analyzing and participating in forthcoming IPOs can turn to dedicated sites that provide information on the global IPO calendar, deal specifics, 'price talk', research views, and so on; ventures such as IPOcentral, IPOdata, IPOmonitor, IPOmaven, and others cater to this specific sector of the investment information market.

There is a considerable base of international information available to global investors. In addition to local research sites that address the specific language and investing needs of a particular domestic investor base (often sponsored by large local financial institutions through their corporate storefronts), there are numerous global portals which provide multilingual content for international users. These platforms provide company-specific analysis, market trends and news, and broad macro-economic research and strategies. Examples of these ventures include WorldlyInvestor.com and global-investor, which provide a global view of markets and assets, EuropeanInvestor.com and Europe Online, which focus more narrowly on the European markets, and UK-invest, which is dedicated to UK investment news. In the Asian sphere, platforms such as scmp.com, feer.com, and Koscom provide market and economic news and analysis related to China, Hong Kong, Korea, and other countries of Asia; the Nikkei financial press sponsors the Nikkei Net Interactive bilingual platform, which covers activity in the Japanese and Asian markets. In Latin America, sites such as Patagon.com offer coverage of the largest South American markets, and in the Middle East platforms such as MENA.fn provide coverage of local financial markets. In addition to dedicated international platforms, several major Wall Street houses have discovered the wisdom of translating, via the Internet, their proprietary English language research so that it can be used by local investors. For example, Morgan Stanley Dean Witter has made use of the Lionbridge Technology translation platform to quickly and efficiently convert its web-based research into various foreign languages. International government economic/financial statistics are available through many government-sponsored and central bank/monetary authority web sites around the world—the economic/financial statistics of most countries are well represented on the web. Government authorities in the UK, Canada, Australia, South Africa, and various Latin and Asian nations have crafted useful informational offerings which can often be accessed in multiple languages. In the US, researchers can tap into an entire range of economic statistics and data from platforms run by the Financial Management Service of the US Treasury Department, the Department of Commerce, the Bureau of Labor Statistics, and the Bureau of Economic Analysis, among others.

The Internet also provides users with web-based information related to credit, risk and mutual fund ratings. These informational tools allow credit and market risk officers, credit investors, and mutual fund investors to tap into the accumulated wealth of research information produced and maintained by outfits such as Moody's, Standard and Poor's, FitchIBCA, Duff and Phelps, Morningstar, and others. Through their corporate storefront sites, the major rating agencies provide varying levels of free company- and country-specific credit rating information and history, default probabilities, and associated data; subscribers have access to more detailed information. A risk ranking service known as RiskGrades, developed by JP Morgan spin-off RiskMetrics Group, provides investors with a benchmarking tool that compares investment risk across assets, regions, and currencies. The service charts investment risk ratings over a period of time and allows individual assets to be compared to broad markets or relevant subindexes; an entire portfolio can then be 'graded' by riskiness. Similar services are provided by other ventures. Morningstar, which was a pioneer in popularizing the rating and ranking of mutual funds, offers its services online, in a flexible format that allows investors to quickly search and filter mutual funds based on customized parameters such as market sector, expense ratio, management tenure, industry return, and so on. Intuit Quicken, Findafund, Money.com, SmartMoney, Personal Fund, Fundalarm, and other platforms provide ranking, filtering or ratings views of their own. Users interested in monitoring the performance of international funds can utilize the Micropal engine, and those searching for the broadest range of mutual fund information can access services such as Sageoline, Multex's mutual fund portal. While many of these fund ranking tools and information services have been available to retail investors for several years, they have recently been extended to meet the specific needs of institutional investors, such as pension funds and university endowments. For instance, InvestForce.com, backed by Internet Capital Group, CALPERS, Thomas Weisel Partners, Mellon Bank and Merrill Lynch, provides online research tools for institutional investors and pension fund consultants. These tools allow users to tap into databases which rank, rate and track professional money managers; they also permit the development of online 'requests for proposals' that can be channeled electronically to relevant money managers under consideration.

EDUCATION AND ANALYSIS

The web has developed into an excellent medium for financial education. Numerous service providers have created comprehensive, interactive instruction and education modules that can be accessed through the web. These cover varying levels of competency and expertise, from the most basic and fundamental to the most complex and academic. Web platforms can provide either general or specific education and analysis. Broad portals like Motley Fool and Yahoo Finance, along with general investment education platforms such as invest-faq, Investopedia and investing.wsj, cover a range of topics related to home purchase, debt/credit management, investing, online bank/broker selection, tax management, college/retirement planning, IRA/401K optimization, home budgeting, and so on. Certain web sites focus their educational efforts on specific areas of expertise. For instance, AIG's aigdirect.com provides users with insurance-related FAQs, articles, glossaries, coverage tips and advice. Similar specialty education can be found on the Internet platforms of online traders, mortgage providers, banks, and asset managers. Many of the platforms also allow for e-mail queries and operate bulletin boards/chat rooms to promote discussion and exchange of ideas. While there is a great deal of educational information for the novice, there is also a wealth of material for professionals and academics. As one might expect, these offerings tend towards more complex issues, topics and debates, and move into the realm of the highly mathematical and technical. Certain platforms are geared specifically for advanced education on specific topics—for instance, sites such as GARP.com, Numa.com, Equity Analytics, Financial Engineering News, ISDA, RiskCenter.com, FinMath.com, and others focus heavily on technical issues related to risk management and derivatives. Financial infomediary portals with search engines, such as Financewise and Finweb, provide a bounty of links to other educational forums; these can include research articles and papers, educational spreadsheets, live and archived discussion forums, and so on. Links into academic papers maintained at universities are also available online. Major business schools provide a range of educational and academic information related to theoretical studies on financial markets/services, and many university research documents are available on the web.

The web provides retail and institutional users with a broad range of analytical tools to make the job of managing finances, and financial dealings, easier. These include calculators and analytics, wealth planners, filters/ranking devices, and technical research tools. Many consumer-based portals feature a host of useful analytics that let users compute important information, track portfolios, and so on. In many cases tools are divided by product or service. For instance, users seeking information on mortgages can consult portals with 'toolkits' specifically designed to answer mortgage-related questions and solve mortgage calculations. A typical mortgage portal might offer information on current rates, mortgage programs, and pre-qualification criteria, while its toolkit might include calculators which provide rent versus buy comparisons, maximum home affordability, refinancing thresholds, rates versus points tradeoffs, principal amortization schedules, and so on. A portal focused on insurance might include tools related to insurance planning, whole life versus term insurance, automobile risk evaluation, deferred annuity scenarios, and so on. Investment and wealth management portals might include toolkits with a range of investment calculations, including bond price/yield estimates, currency conversion, mortgage and insurance computations, tax liabilities, retirement projections, and so on; these might also feature links into related web sites, including IRS tax forms, mortgage or insurance applications, 401K and IRA platforms, and so on. There are, as one might imagine, hundreds of offerings in this general category; examples include SmartLeaf and FinPortfolio. For instance, SmartLeaf provides investors with the tools necessary to support the investment advisory services it offers; clients can access tools to let them manage tax gains/losses, reduce costs through asset switching, review the risk frontiers of portfolios, and so on. For a fee, users of FinPortfolio can input portfolios and access a suite of calculators and analytics, including asset allocation/selection, portfolio optimization, risk/style/asset analysis, and so on.

Institutional portals generally provide users with access to analytic tools which are far more complex and comprehensive than those offered to the general public. Many major investment banks offer their institutional clients high-end derivative risk and valuation tools through their corporate storefronts; dedicated third-party providers also supply similar tools. Institutional investors and intermediaries have a much greater need to perform sophisticated calculations associated with a range of products which are typically 'off limits' to the general public. For example, institutions active in the derivative market can access, on the web, calculators which create, price or revalue interest rate swaps, currency swaps, vanilla and exotic options, zero coupon and forward yield curves, and so on. Investors trading and hedging in the MBS market can access analytic tools to determine pre-payment speeds and sensitivities, optimal hedge ratios, scenario analyses, and so on. Platforms such as GFINet, Advanced Risk Management Solutions, Measurisk,

Inventure CorporateFenics, and others give subscribers access to a range of security, derivative and risk valuation/management tools to perform these types of computations. Those active in credit derivatives can make use of detailed analytics related to credit default and portfolio modeling from ventures such as KMV, Kamakura, Sungard, Algorithmics, and others. Many other platforms, offering a range of highly quantitative tools, abound. Since many proprietary and third-party analytic solutions demand more sophisticated modeling capabilities and computing power, they are generally only available to users for a fee.

Technical research tools are readily available online from many web sources. Financial charts depicting prices, trading volume, moving averages, and so on are one of the most popular e-finance features of the web. The most sophisticated platforms offering charting capabilities also have comprehensive technical analysis tools which investors can overlay on charts; these tools are intended to alert technical investors to breakout patterns, trendlines, moving average bands, support and resistance levels, and so on. For instance, services such as TraderBot and FalconEye provide intraday technical analysis with graphics and 'market maps' to help investors visualize trade data. Barchart.com, Bigcharts, Wavechart, Stockchart, and others provide a range of user-friendly stock, bond and macro charting tools, employing historical data covering days, weeks, months and years. ClearStation, owned and operated by E*Trade, is a standalone platform which offers investors a suite of portfolio management tools based on both technical and fundamental analysis.

AGGREGATION AND INFORMATION MANAGEMENT

One of the newest information services to be offered to financial customers is account aggregation. Aggregators (or 'screen scrapers' as they are sometimes known)—such as Yodlee, ebalance, OnMoney.com, Corillion, Verticalone, and ezlogin, among others—provide a customized, consolidated view of a client's financial position, which can include multiple accounts carried on multiple web sites. In order to access these fee-based services, a client provides the aggregator with passwords and logins for each individual web banking, securities, research or other subscription account (including non-financial award accounts operated by airlines, hotels, and so on). The aggregator then creates a customized template of the accounts and provides the client with a master password that allows access to the new consolidated view of financial assets and liabilities. The aggregated view permits the client to pay a bill, check an account, or transfer funds by linking into the institution providing the underlying service. Certain platforms, such as CashEdge, provide infrastructure capabilities which let customers transfer funds between different accounts held at different institutions through the aggregated view. Some aggregators, such as ezlogin, are able to convey aggregated views to a user's wireless mobile device; as wireless technology improves, this is likely to become a very useful service (and a possible industry standard). Aggregators thus unify information across disparate accounts, institutions and marketplaces, and add incremental value by incorporating links, information, and transaction capabilities it believes clients will find valuable. The key to successful aggregation lies in the security architecture. Security standards employed by aggregators are state-of-the-art, based on 128 bit encryption between the aggregator and user, and within the aggregator itself; based on this construct, most customers are willing to reveal their individual account passwords and logins. Approximately 800,000 customers had signed up with aggregators by 2000, and over 4MM are expected to be active by 2002; research firm Celent Communications expects nearly 8MM aggregator accounts to be in place by 2003.

Though the first significant aggregators were developed by 'neutral' infrastructure providers and non-financial portals third parties such as Yodlee, Verticalone, and Yahoo Finance, established financial institutions have been quick to join the fray. Most major firms recognize that access to a customer's consolidated financial picture can generate opportunities to cross-sell their own services and products—the ultimate goal is to get many of those customers to redirect their business. Financial institutions are also participating in order to defend brand recognition and marketing ability. If consumers rely primarily, or solely, on an aggregated view of their financial holdings, there is a possibility that the underlying financial service provider will lose some amount of visibility, resulting in a gradual erosion of the very brand equity that is so important to establish and maintain in an Internet business environment. In late 2000 Morgan Stanley Dean Witter announced the launch of its MSDW Net Worth module, a site aggregator which links a client's Morgan Stanley Dean Witter accounts, as well as those a client might hold at other financial institutions, using Yodlee's aggregation technology. Chase introduced a similar aggregation service, at approximately the same time, through Chase Online Plus.

Since individual and institutional investors must deal with an overwhelming amount of information, much of it readily available on the web for free, they face a real risk of being 'inundated'. In order to condense and focus information into a prioritized and usable form, certain portals and financial web platforms provide users with filter and alert mechanisms. A number of service providers use intelligent agents to help investors sift through a large amount of price, technical, and fundamental data in order to identify potential investment candidates based on user-defined criteria. For instance, if an investor is interested in finding all mid-capitalization technology stocks traded on the NASDAQ with a price/earnings ratio under 50 and a price under $25/share, stock filters—such as NetScreen Pro or Morningstar's screening module—can rapidly search comprehensive databases and alert the user to all qualifying candidates. Services can also send users e-mail alerts when certain market events are triggered or new strategies or trade ideas are published; this allows users to prioritize the type and timing of information that is most relevant. The same type of screening and alert mechanisms can be applied to other markets, products and sectors.

While the web has propelled the 'information age' to new heights and granted many users access to cheap, timely, and beneficial information and tools, there is a strong need to manage this wealth of knowledge carefully and employ it in a meaningful and constructive fashion. Since the Internet is such an efficient information distribution mechanism, it can be used to great effect and add considerable value; however, it can also lead to unintentional confusion or be used to intentionally disrupt or defraud. Retail and institutional users of web-based information are always cautioned to approach data, pricing, research, news, commentary and opinion on a 'caveat emptor' basis; this is especially important when information is being used to make economic decisions. Too much information can create confusion and contradiction; those capable of focusing on what is important stand to gain the greatest benefits. While there is clearly a temptation to experiment with different sites as they come onstream, it is equally important for users to remain disciplined in their use of such information. This is particularly true when data, prices, and research are being used to drive economic decisions—such actions have profit and loss consequences that cannot be ignored. In a world of increasing information access, information management is a critical imperative.

TALK OF THE TRADE

10K—an official, detailed annual financial report filed with the SEC; all public corporations are required to file such reports.

10Q—an official, though brief, quarterly financial report filed with the SEC; all public corporations are required to file such reports.

Aggregator—also known as screen scraper, a platform which consolidates financial information from disparate sources; a subscriber provides the aggregator with password/login information for every financial account that needs to be linked/viewed and the aggregator then creates a consolidated, customized view that automatically accesses the information contained in the user's individual accounts.

Bottom fishing—an investment strategy which focuses on out-of-favor securities which appear 'cheap' compared to historical or comparative measures.

Consensus estimates—an average of the per share earnings Wall Street research analysts expect a company to earn in a given quarter.

Earnings whisper—a non-specific 'pre-earnings' announcement discussed days or weeks in advance of an official earnings release, generally designed to 'prepare' investors for positive or negative surprises.

EDGAR—Electronic Data Gathering, Analysis and Retrieval, a database which houses corporate filings and registration statements.

Morning notes—Wall Street research comments/summaries from morning research/sales conference calls.

PDF—portable document format, a popular page description language, used in the Acrobat document system, that is prevalent in the research community.

Price talk—informal discussion regarding the potential price at which a new bond or stock issue will be launched.

S-1—an official corporate registration statement filed by a company with the SEC, in advance of a public securities offering.

Thread—an ongoing e-mail or chat room discussion on a particular topic.

7
The Digital Future

TRENDS . . .

Many aspects of traditional financial supremacy have been challenged by the Internet, and the platforms and tools which give the web its power and reach. As we have noted, the Internet has provided new and established financial ventures with the framework, infrastructure, and impetus to reconstruct the design and delivery of financial products and services. Technology—which is both inexpensive and pervasive—has helped restructure economic and financial processes, forcing adaptation, restructuring and competition. But technology has not been sufficient, on its own, to produce a sustainable competitive advantage for financial ventures. It is one dimension of a broader process that has been, and must continue to be, supplemented by a will and vision to change business methods in order to deliver greater value to the end-user. What we have witnessed during the second half of the 1990s and the early part of the 21st century is only the beginning of broader and deeper changes in commercial processes. We live in an economy based on, and fuelled by, ideas, technology and capital. Together, these will continue to redefine methods of doing business.

Though we can only speculate on what the financial environment will look like in 10 or 20 years, we can be certain that it will look dramatically different than it does today. Perhaps in the next decade we will have large, global, web-based techno-finance organizations supplying retail customers with all of their financial needs—across borders and in multiple languages, at any time of day or night, on mobile and stationary devices with interactive, voice-enabled 'virtual' customer representatives and financial advisors. Perhaps the institutional trading world will become so highly programmed and efficient, and computationally capable, that trading decisions will be made and executed by sophisticated machines rather than Wall Street traders. Maybe the era of decimalization (moving from quoting stock spreads in 1/4 or 1/8 or 1/16 increments to individual 0.01s) and the advent of intelligent trading technology will cause equity market makers to abandon the business or move to automated agency matching with no human intervention. Perhaps the diffusion of technology and the decentralization of financial processes through network mechanisms will lead to a shift away from centralized financial centers such as New York, London and Tokyo, to virtual hubs/markets operating strictly 'in the ether'. Maybe companies and governments will be able to automatically register, issue and place debt and equity securities directly with end-investors, obviating the need for investment banking services and primary syndication facilities. Maybe the age of paperless, error-free electronic global settlement and processing, completed on a near real-time basis without any human intervention, will finally arrive, eliminating the need for armies of operational and administrative clerks to handle data and paper. Perhaps one global financial services 'super-regulator' will emerge to police e-finance activities on a consistent, cross-border basis, in a boundaryless space. Such is all sheer speculation, of course, but it helps illustrate the point that we are in the midst of a radical, and extremely rapid, transformation of the financial services industry that will cause the operating environment of 2010 or 2020 to look very different than it does today. While the industry will not achieve these types of capabilities for years (or perhaps ever), there are clearly certain changes which will appear in the near-term that will take providers and users down the path of greater automation, efficiency, and clarity.

As more institutional and retail customers make use of technology, more business will be conducted in a technological environment. Companies are generating more revenues with less employees, and operating more efficiently, by using technology. The pace of corporate change is fast, and will become even faster. Information is disseminated internally and externally very quickly, leading to the creation of new ideas and opportunities. Traditional corporate structures are giving way to those that have an external focus and are flexible, global, interdependent and efficient. Organizations capable of innovation—some of it quite radical—are becoming leaders. Ventures able to overhaul business methods by forming alliances, partnerships, and joint ventures, and outsourcing select functions, are setting the pace in the corporate world. Personalization and customization of services are part of the new order, and business models that place the customer at the center are succeeding. Vertical integration—owning all aspects of the process, as in the industrial model of the past few decades—is no longer a driving force; the ability to outsource and partner, in order to achieve 'network scale', is replacing vertical integration. e-Commerce and e-finance platforms—in whatever form they take, be it hybrid or virtual, broad-based or market-specific—will need to remain nimble and create a culture which not only adapts to change, but actually thrives on it.

The truth is we do not yet know which e-finance models and ventures will endure in the long run. The web is at a relatively early stage of development, and institutions actively offering Internet products and services are still trying to determine what works and what does not. Further consolidation and change in key sectors of B2C and B2B e-finance, as well as infrastructure supporting such sectors, is a virtual certainty. As in any 'euphoric' market buildup, the pendulum that started swinging in 1995 moved too far in the direction of expansion. There are almost certainly too many infomediaries, online traders, financial portals and exchanges to meet the demands of all users—though that demand is very large and growing. Many of these platforms will fail or merge, and the industry will move through a restructuring phase. Part of that process will involve the selection of winning business models and ventures that appeal broadly to institutional and individual web users, as well as those that provide e-finance companies with relevant infrastructure solutions; these will survive and become the core drivers of e-finance over the next few years, and help reshape the face of the global financial services industry. Entrepreneurs, companies, VCs, angels, public investors, parent companies and strategic shareholders have come to realize that the web is not simply about creating a 'hot' concept—it is about creating sustainable business processes that are unique and valuable, can tap a very large audience, and can achieve profitability (indeed, Internet stock market valuations have already switched from revenue multiples to earnings multiples—as is typical for 'old economy' companies which generate profits, not just revenues). Though the impact of the Internet on financial services is still being felt, certain trends are starting to emerge, including expansion in B2B e-finance activity, automation of customer services, consolidation in local/regional financial operations, growth in international services, migration towards 24 hour global trading, blurring of business and product lines, disintermediation of traditional products/services, and creation of alternative partnerships and alliances.

As indicated, it is still unclear which e-finance models will triumph. Entrepreneurial storefront pure plays 'jump started' aspects of the industry, providing customers with new and valuable services and forcing established players to respond in kind. While some pure plays have been successful, others have been unable to deliver the full suite of products and services demanded by users, putting them at a competitive disadvantage to traditional financial service providers, and forcing them to create alliances and partnerships or to shut down operations. Established financial institutions, in turn, have had to adapt their business strategies in order to cope with the Internet threat—or opportunity. This has been a wrenching and expensive process for most, as it has required a complete redefinition of how to conduct business internally and externally, how to manage customer relationships, and how to adapt new technology to work with legacy systems. All of this has happened in a very short span of time. Many established firms that have adopted hybrid strategies consisting of traditional 'brick and mortar' operations and new web-based corporate storefront platforms have had reasonable success. In many cases they have been effective in rolling out new platforms (often at large cost), though in certain cases they have cannibalized or disrupted existing business; in some instances they have failed to produce a convincing platform and have had to revisit their approach. Numerous marketplaces, integrated vertical portals, and B2B exchanges have been able to offer compelling services. These models, when properly implemented, appear capable of redefining the value chain by delivering financial services and products to end-users in a unique and value-added fashion; first movers and other leaders have certainly succeeded in redefining the value proposition. Though these entities can be value-added, it is becoming apparent that the market may not be able to support so many portals, marketplaces and exchanges—some will invariably close down or merge. There is thus no absolute answer regarding the 'optimal' future strategy or structure for Internet financial services delivery. Much will depend on the development of new technologies, the arrival of new competitors, and the willingness of existing platforms to partner and outsource; it will also be influenced by the changing demands of customers and the imperatives of regulators. It is possible that certain platforms will remain active and profitable as pure play structures, while most others will do better as hybrids. Some elements of the hybrid world may fare better by using parent branding, while others may succeed through new identities and images. Marketplaces and exchanges that specialize in certain areas may be more effective than those that are general, though a core of broad-based exchanges (supported by top institutions) may be able to create and offer compelling services. Though consolidation will occur among storefronts, portals, exchanges and marketplaces, the industry may be able to support more e-finance infrastructure providers. As discussed at various points in the text, these enablers have been central in creating and implementing creative and forward-thinking solutions that allow ventures to port their businesses to the web in a timely, cost-effective manner. As the face of the e-finance sector changes and new products and services are developed, the need for clever infrastructure solutions from dedicated providers is likely to remain strong.

Pricing/revenue generation on the web is a complex issue and promises to remain challenging as the competitive landscape changes. It is quite possible that, over the coming years, many of the fee-based financial products and services currently on offer will become free. Fee-based Internet access and e-mail were once regarded as prime sources of revenue for ISPs and ASPs; these services are now often available for free as providers acquiesce to the demands of customers and alter their business models. It is not difficult to imagine the day when online trading will essentially be provided to customers at little or no charge through a redefinition of the business model. Firms such as FinancialCafe.com and Free-Tradez started offering commission-free online trades in 2000 by shifting revenue generation to advertising; other 'innovative' pricing arrangements for financial services are likely to emerge over the medium-term. This, in turn, will force web-based ventures to redefine their models and offer new products or services that can generate a premium. For established companies the pressure to use the web as a revenue and profit generator, and not just a customer-based 'loss leader', will remain particularly acute. This is especially true when great quantities of human and financial capital are devoted to the creation or expansion of Internet capabilities.

Though the nature and structure of the truly successful e-finance business model has yet to be clarified, it is increasingly evident that the B2B sector will be a focal point for many e-commerce and e-finance endeavors; this will include new economy and old economy companies, alliances, joint ventures and partnerships. With analysts forecasting the size of the B2B market to be up to 10 times that of the B2C market, considerable revenues are at stake. The adoption of Internet technologies around the world, and the implementation of key regulatory measures, such as electronic signatures and cross-border contracts, should help spur further e-commerce growth. In 1999 B2C revenues were estimated to have reached $22B and B2B revenues $157B; by 2003 B2C revenues are expected to approach $200B and B2B revenues anywhere from $1.5T to $3T (depending on the researcher and definition or metric). e-Finance B2B revenues are expected to grow in tandem. Expansion in B2B e-finance revenues does not necessarily mean growth in the number of storefronts or exchanges—given the large number of platforms currently in operation, consolidation, rationalization and redirection of business to a smaller, more powerful, group of ventures, with greater critical mass, surfaces as a more likely scenario. The B2B model appears likely to expand from its current vertical focus—which has been a useful way of buying/selling inventory and products—to a broader horizontal focus, where companies can communicate and deal across an entire spectrum of activities. Thus, while vertical marketplaces will continue to provide an important focus for particular financial products/services, horizontal marketplaces covering front-to-back services should experience greater growth. Outsourcing components of the horizontal process to specialist providers may increase over time, particularly for storefronts or small B2B platforms that cannot otherwise compete on a price basis. Further growth in extranets—private intranets which cross various enterprises—will be a key element of the B2B sector into the future. Meta-networks (or e-hubs or meta-hubs), which bring together B2B exchanges and professional horizontal service providers focused on accounting, escrow, tax, and legal services, should also emerge.

The future of e-finance will invariably focus closely on the 'human element' of financial services—including customer service and financial execution/advice. Service industries, by their very nature, are intended to serve customers in the best and most efficient way possible—such is the 'mantra' of many organizations, and most center entire product and service functions around their customers. In the Internet world some businesses provide customer service through human interaction, others through automated processes, and most through a combination of the two. However, as technology improves and becomes truly capable of aiding users, the 'human dimension' of the service industry will undoubtedly be re-examined. For instance, when an institutional or retail user of financial services is given a technological solution that can quickly and accurately resolve a problem, answer a question, or provide guidance—to the user's complete satisfaction and at considerable cost savings to the provider—the need for human interface may diminish, or even vanish. That perfect technological solution does not exist at the present time, and may not appear for several years. However, variations on the theme are already being employed, suggesting that the optimal model may well appear in the medium-term. Implementation of a purely automated customer service scheme will, of course, depend on the wishes of customers. If a segment of the population remains steadfast in its demand for personalized customer assistance, service providers will have to weigh that desire (and the attendant revenues generated by satisfied customers) against the relative costs of providing the service. Hybrid platforms currently provide customers with the best of both worlds; their support mechanisms are primarily technological in nature, but they have the ability to offer human assistance when, and if, needed. This presents an additional cost of doing business, but one currently deemed valuable and important. Pure plays, in general, do not have the same capabilities unless they specifically establish 'customer service sites'—which some, but not all, are doing. While pure plays offer telephone assistance, most typically cannot offer customers the same level of service available through face-to-face contact via 'brick and mortar' infrastructure. These platforms should demonstrate whether web-based financial services can, in fact, survive and prosper without human customer support. We may look to pure plays as future pioneers in automated customer service, but for now it is unclear that complete lack of human support is a workable solution. For example, recognizing the need for true 'face-to-face' support, E*Trade has established 'E*Trade Zones' at leading retailers; these 'Zones' are staffed with customer service representatives and are able to give an organization that exists largely in virtual space a 'tangible' presence on the ground. Web Street Securities has implemented similar support, creating 'financial service centers' in several major US cities in order to provide customers with personal assistance.

While the future of the customer service representative is debated, the role of the financial services generalist must also be queried. It is conceivable that the days of the financial generalist are limited, and that the core of the 'human touch' will be limited to very specific, value-added, roles. From a user's perspective much of what financial professionals have traditionally done can

be accomplished with greater ease and efficiency on the web. This is particularly, though not exclusively, true for younger consumers, who are eager
and adept when it comes to interfacing and interacting with technology and its
associated products and services. In the coming years a user may choose to
handle the information/execution aspects of a particular service (i.e. gathering
research, quotes or comparative price information, making a decision and
executing the trade, contract or deal) all online, and seek the services of a
financial professional only for very specific advice (especially as related to
wealth management, estate planning, and tax advice—services that are not
readily available online or which can be accomplished more efficiently
through direct interaction). If this ultimately occurs, financial consultants may
well remain in demand, while insurance agents, bank tellers, stockbrokers and
other 'execution' agents may fade from the scene. The same is likely to apply
in the institutional world, where execution will be handled by clients themselves, while advice will be provided by institutional relationship managers.

Regional growth and competition will evolve over the coming years. In
many countries, such as the US, Germany, France, Italy and Japan, local and
regional financial service providers have historically succeeded in capturing,
promoting and expanding local business by catering to the needs of local
customers. This has been a powerful force in the financial sector and has led,
over time, to the creation of hundreds, and sometimes thousands, of financial
institutions in particular countries. While financial sector consolidation has
been evident for the past decade, there are still many areas of the world that
are serviced by a large number of institutions. It is likely, with the dawn of
e-finance, that local and regional financial institutions will come under increasing pressure to adapt or consolidate—or risk failure. The web dissolves
many of the geographic and regional borders that have traditionally given
small, locally-focused institutions their 'raison d'être'. As web-based financial
services take hold and delivery mechanisms adapt to meet the personal needs
of a broader set of customers, it is probable that the local and regional financial sectors will change in a dramatic manner. Mergers, acquisitions, rational-
izations and closures should feature prominently.

The international arena will be an exciting frontier for e-commerce and
e-finance over the coming decade. Development and use of Internet applications and services internationally appears to have lagged the US by at least
two to three years. While being a first mover is generally considered an
advantage, as it gives pioneering ventures the opportunity to establish a presence and gain market share with little or no competition, there are occasion-
ally some advantages in lagging behind the leaders—being, in essence, second
or third movers. In particular, ventures operating in Asia, Europe and Latin
America have benefited from the US's pioneering Internet experience. By
reviewing and analyzing the American process, they have been able to determine which B2B and B2C e-commerce and e-finance models work most

effectively, and have been able to leverage the new technologies and applications developed by first mover infrastructure firms. In addition, they have enjoyed the benefits of cheaper technology—since, as mentioned in Chapter 1, the price of computing and communications power continues to decline rapidly, a delay of two to three years can allow international ventures, that are only now joining the marketplace, to capitalize on considerable cost savings. Though the international arena has lagged in the migration online, the tide is already turning and overseas expansion promises to be powerful—with 70% of Internet traffic expected to be centered outside the US by 2005, the potential opportunities (and pitfalls) of participating on an international scale are considerable. Europe and Asia will collectively feature 450MM Internet users by 2005, and countries such as India, China, Poland, Ukraine and Turkey—which currently have very low PC and Internet penetration but which possess the technological skills and capital to expand both—will feature the highest per capita increases in web access. In certain areas, such as wireless technology and mobile web services, Europe and Asia are already well ahead of the US. Segments of the European and Japanese marketplaces are very advanced technologically, and have made considerable use, particularly at the retail level, of wireless web services—including wireless financial services. International B2B e-commerce is becoming more evident. European investors are recognizing the importance of the Internet in the allocation and distribution of goods and services, and are funding more initiatives through VC and corporate strategic resources. Asia is also of interest to those developing, or expanding, web-based ventures—the region is both technical and entrepreneurial, and features a new generation that has been 'reared' on technology and the Internet. In addition, the region is mobilizing capital to help fund many of the new commercial web ventures expected to be created over the coming years—Asia features a growing VC market which is starting to make capital available to promising projects (this represents a considerable change from previous VC efforts, which were aimed at management buyouts of existing companies rather than funding of new ventures). Certain international stock markets are also changing their listing requirements to allow more flexible access to equity capital. Though the international web is a very promising sector, it remains to be seen whether changes in the international legal and regulatory environment will keep pace with Internet business growth. In order for the Internet to be truly global and boundaryless countries around the world must reach broad consensus on harmonizing the rules and regulations that impact the web and its commercial activities; cross-border contracts supporting Internet activity are one example of an area that requires further clarification from interested parties.

The concept of 24 hour trading by institutional players has been discussed for many years but has not, as yet, become a reality. Though the FX market operates on a 24 hour basis (at least for major currencies like the dollar, Euro, sterling and yen), the same is not yet true for stocks, bonds or derivatives. The best that has been achieved in such markets is extended hour trading days— even then, lack of liquidity means that market prices are volatile and trades cannot get executed with certainty. With the arrival of the Internet, the financial world has moved one step closer to true 24 hour trading. As indicated earlier in the book, the creation of ATSs and ECNs has provided participants with added market liquidity, extended trading hours, and greater access to competitive prices. It has streamlined new issue procedures and made deals available to a wider group of investors. In the process, 'traditional' conduits, such as equity and futures exchanges, have been forced to rethink the way they conduct business. As indicated, most exchanges have abandoned physical, open-outcry trading in favor of electronic trading, and many structures have converted from mutual to public entities, accountable for delivering revenues and profits to shareholders. Many exchanges have realized that their traditional operating structures and methods are under fire. Cooperative partnerships that would have been unthinkable in the mid-1990s have become a reality—even more alliances are likely to appear over the coming years. The need for established exchanges to unite and provide consistent, uniform platforms, with greater critical mass and more responsive customer services, is imperative. The creation of entities such as NASDAQ/AMEX, Euronext, and others is a reflection of the times—the Internet and its associated technologies have challenged traditional mechanisms and the exchanges have had to respond. All of these changes are pointing the way towards 'around the clock' trading. New electronic initiatives designed to bring 24 hour trading to stocks and bonds are planned for the coming years; for example, the NYSE and Euronext are in discussions with numerous international exchanges (including bourses in Japan, Hong Kong, Australia, Canada, Mexico and Brazil) to create 24 hour markets in the largest blue-chip companies of the world, and the development of the A/C/E futures alliance is permitting continuous trading in select futures contracts around the world. Before widespread, global trading can become a reality, however, considerable work has to be done regarding exchange rules and regulations, trading system linkages, dealing procedures, and currency/settlement issues; global movement to a truly 'paperless' settlement system will assist in the process.

Deregulation has prompted further blurring of the business undertaken by banks, brokers, insurers and fund managers, both in the physical and electronic worlds. Global financial deregulation—particularly regulatory changes made during the 1990s—has made it simpler for financial, and increasingly non-financial, institutions to 'encroach' on one another's territory. Consolidated financial groups are, with only certain limitations, able to operate with relative freedom in commercial banking, securities dealing, insurance and fund management. Institutions that have achieved success in pursuing a broad model in the 'traditional' financial world may well seek to duplicate it online;

indeed, a few have already started the process. There is already growing evidence that numerous financial web platforms are becoming broader-based; this approach helps diversify revenues and create a more complete product/ service offering for clients. Those seeking to expand across a spectrum of activities have been particularly sensitive to channel conflict—the ability to effectively manage such conflict remains a priority. Those that have successfully dealt with the issue by creating workable hybrids or alliances are likely to remain in control of the process, promoting the notion of channel confluence. Those which have been unable to balance internal competition between traditional and web-based business will be forced to redefine their strategies, branding, market presence and client/market niche, or withdraw entirely and focus solely on traditional 'bricks and mortar'; in the 21st century, however, failure to provide clients with a meaningful, value-added Internet strategy can be equated with failure to progress.

Disintermediation has been a fact of life in banking for decades. When banks discover a profitable product or market they exploit it until new mechanisms allow participants to deal directly with one another; this disintermediation has occurred in recent years with bank credit, savings deposits, commercial paper, and select capital market instruments. Not surprisingly, Internet-driven disintermediation has increased over the past few years and will accelerate further as many of the services offered by traditional financial institutions are replicated by others and delivered through the web. Once approvals and licenses are obtained from regulators, there is very little preventing other institutions, including non-banks, from replicating e-finance services and end-clients dealing directly with product originators. While various non-bank corporate conglomerates have challenged banks for business for many years (witness the successful financial units of GE and Ford, among others, that sell receivables, bonds, and commercial paper directly to end-investors), technology providers may well emerge as a new threat in the future. Technology companies, ISPs, ASPs and pure infrastructure providers are poised to supply institutional and retail users with many of the same financial services currently offered by dedicated financial institutions by utilizing the very technologies they develop in the standard course of their 'mainstream' technology-oriented business. As we have noted earlier in the book, firms like Microsoft, Yahoo, AOL, Intuit/Quicken and others use their underlying infrastructure to operate financial portals, and are moving into other areas of financial services through alliances and partnerships. This model is likely to expand further as it has found a ready audience. Technology companies may also emerge as leading providers of back-end services for financial institutions; they may be able to expand their reach deeper into the financial services sector by delivering efficient, automated, and cutting-edge clearing and settlement solutions. Since this area has traditionally required considerable technological infrastructure, it is a logical area of outsourcing for institutions that prefer to remain focused on their core business applications. As the distinction between these services blurs, it is conceivable that some of these non-financial companies will lead with technology and assume a greater role in some—though not all—financial functions. This will require traditional financial service providers to change the way they analyze and perceive the competitive environment. For example, for Morgan Stanley Dean Witter the biggest competitive threat may eventually come from AOL, Oracle or Microsoft, rather than Goldman Sachs or Merrill Lynch. Instead of competing head-to-head with these organizations, some financial institutions may prefer to work cooperatively. Perhaps truly forward-thinking financial organizations will join with technology companies, software specialists, and technical consulting firms to produce internal state-of-the-art technology platforms and external 'killer financial applications'. This may allow them to reduce their own internal technology costs (a notoriously large component of budgets at most financial institutions) and offer exciting products to customers at a faster pace. Merging the skills and talents of technology and financial services companies can be a benefit to all parties, and may result in the creation of truly global financial/technological ASP alliances. There is some evidence that this is beginning to occur, with financial institutions and technology companies partnering on specific infrastructure, products and services. For instance, Morgan Stanley Dean Witter has a partnership with global e-business and software development house Kanbay International, which provides the bank with legacy/web integration and other technology support/resources. Citibank has an alliance with Oracle through which the bank integrates its payment and settlement functions into Oracle's market exchange and makes use of Oracle's web procurement services; the partnership also embeds Citibank's financial services into Oracle's technology, so that B2B clients can settle goods and services online. Merrill Lynch has partnered with technology venture FinTrack to allow clients to interact with the bank's online institutional trading platform in real-time, while Deutsche Bank has formed a strategic alliance with AlphaBox to promote integration of open web-based business intelligence applications. These are only a few representative examples of the many financial institution/technology alliances that have been struck to date.

It is worth noting that while traditional financial disintermediation will undoubtedly continue, financial ventures active in web services need not necessarily be disintermediated from other aspects of the market. New business models will allow them to participate in different layers/segments of new markets. We have already discussed the example of infomediary portals in Chapter 6—these platforms own nothing, but create an 'extra layer' between a pool of information and the end-user. By intermediating in the information process through the development of useful products/services (such as customization, aggregation, collation, and so on), successful infomedary portals are creating value for the customer, generating revenues for the venture, and proving that, in some instances, value-added intermediation can be a successful paradigm.

Whether the trends highlighted above, fuelled by new technological development, result in the gradual shifting of capital and critical mass from traditional financial centers such as New York, London, Zurich, Frankfurt, Tokyo, Hong Kong and Singapore remains to be seen. It is very clear that technological advances have already led to the creation of 'virtual financial operations' headquartered in many different parts of the world—the gradual dissemination of financial and technological capabilities is causing the financial world of the 21st century to become increasingly boundaryless and diffuse. In order to cope with such diffusion, regulatory authorities will need to adapt their structures, organizations and rules. Since the Internet effectively ignores political and physical boundaries, traditional methods of regulation risk becoming outdated or irrelevant; worse, they may inspire a false sense of security or comfort. Investors and other users of web finance have much broader choices when it comes to dealing in new jurisdictions and in new products/services with different tax, investment, savings, and protection rules—that trend will only intensify. From a practical perspective this suggests two possible alternatives. In the first instance, regulators may choose to relinquish some of their traditional 'protective control' oversight, provided home-country financial service users have the appropriate educational tools to understand the consequences of financial activities they may engage in. Alternatively, global regulators may wish to continue policing all, or at least major, aspects of web financial activity, but agree on a construct of minimum standards so that cross-border harmonization can be established. If harmonization can be successfully negotiated it will eliminate the 'regulatory arbitrage' that might otherwise appear; it should also do away with unnecessary regulatory barriers, reduce costs, and improve the competitive playing field.

While many aspects of e-finance migration have led to positive results in the form of enhanced value propositions for retail and institutional clients (as well as the new and established financial ventures providing the services), the process has not been without downside; conducting business in an electronic environment can lead to difficulties and problems. While these 'negatives' do not appear overwhelming—if they were, the rationale for migrating businesses to the Internet would be called into question—they do exist. For example, operating in an electronic environment by definition means placing more reliance on technology and less emphasis on human intervention, judgement and experience—and the associated wisdom such bring; while there is often no substitute for human experience, extreme dependence on technology can push such experience into the background. Technology-based finance can force more users to abandon professional advice and support in favor of the DIY model; while this brings many advantages and efficiencies, it may not be appropriate for all users—the advice and assistance of professionals is an important dimension of the financial sector, but it risks being squeezed out by those eager to handle all aspects of the process themselves. The ease of dealing in an electronic environment can lead certain investors to act imprudently and create, or compound, financial problems; for example, overtrading through the web is not uncommon among novice investors, and more than a few have suffered losses as a result. Some view technology as a panacea rather than a tool, believing that electronic access somehow creates the wisdom and experience to be a better trader or wiser investor. Advice, education and experience—rather than technology—are the primary determinants in creating better traders and investors. Internet security is another key area of focus—and periodic problems. Though security standards on the network have improved dramatically over the past few years, they are not infallible. Users actively engaged in commercial activities on the web through online payments can be the targets of security problems, breaches and fraud. Credit card fraud, for instance, is more prevalent online than in the physical world; Gartner Group estimates that in 1999 1.15% of online credit card purchases were fraudulent, versus only 0.09% in the physical world. Earlier we noted the power of the Internet to deliver information. While the rapid dissemination of information is generally a positive feature, it can lead to greater market volatility as investors try to react to, or even anticipate, market moves and trade in and out of positions aggressively. Instantaneous delivery of false information can also wreak havoc—investors often have a tendency to 'shoot first and ask questions later'; witness the instance of Emulex, where a false earnings report posted on web bulletin boards and picked up by the mainstream media caused the stock to lose a large fraction of its market value as investors dumped their shares—without first verifying the validity of the story. The sheer quantity of information, as indicated, is a two-edged sword: while users generally welcome more, rather than less, information, they are often bombarded with too much information and are forced to cope with sometimes conflicting signals—which can lead to irrational behavior/decision-making. Some of the challenges and difficulties impact e-finance providers themselves. For instance, certain established companies entering the marketplace have created confusion and disruption within their existing organizations as they attempt to define optimal business models and processes. In addition, the e-finance revolution has taken—and will continue to take—a toll on professionals in both the physical and electronic marketplaces, particularly as consolidations occur and the face of the industry changes. As automation increases, professionals active in physical dimensions of the business, such as trading or processing, may ultimately find themselves without jobs—computers will have taken over their functions. Within the Internet's own e-finance world, the tendency towards overcapacity over the past few years has also become quite evident; the creation and staffing of B2B and B2C e-finance platforms has been very rapid and, as consolidation takes greater hold, professionals supporting many of these efforts may ultimately be displaced and forced to enter new segments of the workforce.

Having witnessed rapid growth over the past few years in the e-commerce sector at large, and digital financial services in particular, further changes in market structure, products, and services are on the horizon. Certain segments of the market will continue to grow, while others will contract or consolidate. Over the next few years, the most promising areas of e-finance growth are likely to include aggregation, insurance, mortgages, credit extensions, mutual funds, EBPP, digital payments, and small business, international, and 'Generation X' finance. Areas likely to feature consolidation are ECNs and other institutional ATSs, online retail trading platforms, and general financial portals. In addition, ineffective web sites that offer users no compelling value proposition will soon disappear.

... GROWTH ...

The aggregator—or information consolidator—is a relatively new application that is gaining ground very rapidly; much deeper penetration is expected over the coming years as users derive full value from such services. Mechanisms which simplify and clarify have a great deal of appeal in an era where there is too much information to absorb; aggregators add value by filtering, unifying and personalizing information. Neutral aggregators, which act as consolidators and conveyors of information, rather than marketers of product, will continue to form a vital link between the user community and the financial community—presuming business models allow them to generate revenues from sources which let them remain neutral. Neutral aggregators will continue to be in an ideal position to select, on behalf of users, the best services at the best prices and make them available on their sites. Non-neutral aggregation services—for instance, those provided by financial institutions—that hope to succeed will have to be receptive to open architecture, posting offerings of competitors, including services/products which may be cheaper or better than their own. This should theoretically benefit users by forcing financial institution aggregators to remain competitive and cutting-edge.

Numerous web financial products/services are set to expand over the coming years. While online retail trading has been the dominant story of the past few years, the future belongs to sectors that have not yet been exploited to a significant degree—including online insurance, mortgages and credit extension. Most of these areas are still governed by rules and 'paper-driven' application processes that have slowed the migration online. Once regulations are homogenized, application flows streamlined, and user experience deepened, considerable growth should follow—services that simplify processes, eliminate paper and deliver decisions on a near real-time basis will meet with ready demand from time-stretched users. The 'traditional' mutual fund sector is also expected to change. After decades of opaque reporting and high costs, the era of self-directed investment will force established fund companies to increase transparency and lower costs—or risk losing business. Investors are in a position to demand, and receive, much more timely and detailed portfolio information from alternate investment vehicles, many of them available through new online ventures; this suggests that unless traditional mutual funds can deliver the same customer-friendly service, they will rapidly lose ground. EBPP and micro-payments are two other areas that will experience growth. As vendors convert legacy billing procedures into electronic mechanisms, and as they begin accepting payments electronically, the prospects for increased EBPP penetration are very strong. According to IDC and Gartner Group, approximately 40% of US banks will allow customers to pay their bills online by 2004—more than 14% of all bills are expected to be paid online at that time, up from only 1% in 2000. Micro-payments, including direct P2P payments, should fill a considerable void that currently exists in the consumer payment arena. For instance, Forrester Research expects P2P auction sales to reach $19B by 2003—the vast majority of P2P auction payments are still handled through checks/money orders, suggesting that effective implementation of electronic P2P mechanisms over the coming years will enable service providers to capture a significant portion of the auction payment market; growth in other areas of e-commerce that come to rely on micro-payments will simply add to the total. Revamped EBPP and payment solutions have generated user interest in their earliest stages of development and, as security and efficiency continue to improve and customers gain intellectual and practical comfort with the process, the market should expand.

Small business web finance will grow through efficiency gains and establishment of critical mass. The sector remains fragmented and inefficient and lends itself to the type of 'service consolidation' that the web can readily offer. By bringing together small companies through an exchange setting, true financial servicing of the sector will occur, generating economic benefits for all participants. The international dimension of the Internet is also expected to experience considerable growth. As indicated earlier, international Internet traffic, which includes international e-commerce and e-finance, will become an increasingly dominant share of overall online activity. While European, Latin, and Asian nations have lagged the US in the implementation of B2C and B2B e-commerce solutions, the trend is changing rapidly—more nations are becoming involved in different dimensions of the Internet and web-based commerce, and the gap between the US and the rest of the world is narrowing. Indeed, some countries, such as Japan and Sweden, are already more advanced than the US in areas such as the wireless web. IDC estimates that in 2000 50% of all Internet traffic came from foreign domains (42% of those operating in languages other than English). By 2003 the online population outside the US will exceed that of the US, and by 2005 the US will only account for 30% of online traffic—the rest of the world will assume a commanding 70% share. With estimates such as these, it is clear that global financial platforms must be increasingly adaptable to the foreign marketplace. If they are unable to adjust business content and services to reflect local language, culture, preferences, and sensitivities, they risk losing revenues to local competitors—who will certainly have the technological capabilities to offer such services. Not only do web business platforms need to provide appropriate translation and conversion capabilities, they must be able to do so on an instantaneous basis. Institutional or retail customers using web-based financial service platforms managed by offshore entities will have no desire to wait for information conversion to take place.

The 'Generation X' sector—which includes people in their 20s—will present interesting e-commerce and e-finance opportunities for many B2C ventures. There is a growing realization that the younger generation of the global population is, in general, a powerful force that is comfortable with technology and armed with disposable income. This segment of the population is heavily 'wired' through PCs, mobile phones, personal digital assistants (PDAs), and two-way pagers, and readily spends money on personal goods and items that are available on the web; in 1999 this group spent approximately $600MM online and, by 2004, MarketResearch.com expects purchases will soar to $14B. It is likely that 'Generation X-ers' will emerge as an important segment of the B2C client base, opening bank accounts or secured credit cards/stored value cards (such as youth-oriented cards from American Express (cobaltcard) and Visa (Buxx)) to support standard and micro-payment transactions. Capturing clients when they are young can generate brand loyalty; by the time these clients are ready to enter the broader world of e-finance (including online trading, banking, and asset management), they may have established relationships with, and created preferences for, particular e-finance web service providers.

As businesses and consumers migrate more of their financial dealings online, many will want to be made aware of product offers, price discounts, and special savings on an ongoing basis; they may also wish to be advised of stock or bond investments that meet pre-specified criteria. Instead of doing this through standard browsers and search engines, as is the current norm, many will employ intelligent agents that can be programmed—simply and efficiently—to continuously scan sites for pre-defined products and services. This type of technology is already being implemented in search engines, where 'spiders' continually roam the Internet to identify, categorize and index new web sites and content; customizing intelligent agents to deliver relevant filtered content is also becoming prevalent. As intelligent agents take greater hold, it is easy to imagine extending such services to include particular financial execution functions—for instance, finding and buying securities, or automatically obtaining, reviewing, and then paying bills.

While much of what the Internet provides is external to an organization—selling goods and services to third-party retail and institutional clients, for example—great efficiencies can also be derived from internal use of the web. Many institutions and ventures that have created 'public faces' on the web have also developed their own internal Internets, or intranets. These private networks represent the new de-facto standard for internal corporate communications, helping distribute information and streamline workflows to promote efficiencies. Intranets are becoming so prevalent within organizations that they are redefining and replacing many of the traditional tasks governing aspects of corporate policy and culture. Intranets are helping create efficiencies, improve response times, and generate core technical competencies—all of which can lead to cost savings. Intranets which link several communities or related companies—so-called private Intranets or external Intranets (extranets)—are also likely to increase in popularity over the coming years; they are an efficient means of linking together those with common interests and goals.

. . . AND CONTRACTION

While certain aspects of the web will expand in the future, other segments will contract. Earlier in the text we cited the high failure rate for Internet ventures—up to 75%, by some estimates. Given the large number of ventures active, or hoping to be active, online, the failure rate is unlikely to decline. During the web market expansion of the mid- to late 1990s there was a tendency for many ventures to develop 'me too' platforms. It was true—and remains true, to a certain extent—that once an interesting, unique, or compelling business model introduced by a first mover made its way through the funding stages and onto the web, it was immediately followed by a host of competitors hoping to replicate the formula. This led, and continues to lead, to overcapacity in particular segments of the marketplace. Though it is too early to determine how many B2C and B2B ventures will ultimately fail, the shakeout process commenced in early 2000. It has impacted the B2C sector severely, primarily because a great number of unproven business models targeted towards retail customers made their way onto the web before true discipline had been instilled in the screening and funding process; relatively low barriers to entry certainly compounded the problem. Platforms that lack a credible business model capable of generating revenues and profits over the short-term are being called into question, and are unlikely to receive the type of funding needed to commence or sustain operations. Those that have not clearly identified their business focus, established a recognizable name and service level, or achieved a critical mass of unique visits and customers also risk failure. While this is a disruptive process, it is a necessary one. In addition to consolidation through failure, consolidation will also occur through mergers and acquisitions within, and across, sectors. This is an important stage that will serve to focus capacity, market share, and liquidity with a smaller group of strong players.

The digital finance sector will go through its own consolidation phase as there are too many providers of web-based financial services in the marketplace; the process has already commenced, but will take several more years to complete. Key areas where closures and consolidations will occur include ECNs and other institutional ATSs, online retail trading platforms, financial infomediary portals, and select marketplaces. The large number of ECNs and other ATSs that have been created since 1996 have been instrumental in consolidating fragmented markets and adding liquidity, transparency, and cost savings. They have altered many of the traditional trading mechanisms so familiar to Wall Street, and forced established institutions to rethink and realign the way they approach business. That said, there are too many ATSs currently in existence to survive, let alone thrive. In the equity markets large players, such as Instinet, Archipelago, Island, Brut and Tradepoint, dominate many aspects of the business and account for the largest share of all ECN trading volume. Smaller ECNs, which need a critical mass of orders in order to function, will eventually be squeezed out of the market; it is thus reasonable to assume that within a few years the sector will feature only a handful of large equity ECNs. The same is likely to be true for other ATSs and B2B exchanges focused on debt, FX and derivative trading. As indicated in Chapter 4, during the late 1990s and early 2000 many institutional exchanges and alliances came into existence. While some of these focused on market niches—such as FX options, US MBS or Asian credits—others were more general in nature, covering the entire gamut of fixed income and/or derivative products; with only a few exceptions, the broadest platforms may find it difficult to continue operating in a very competitive environment, and could narrow their business focus, consolidate with others, or discontinue operations. Niche platforms that offer compelling, value-added services may be the survivors. It is interesting to note that many major financial institutions have backed multiple B2B exchanges, ECNs, and trading alliances by taking stakes in various ventures. This suggests that even these established players—who are the most knowledgeable about the industry—recognize that the marketplace cannot support so many web-based platforms. As expert managers of risk, they hedge their bets by taking equity stakes in multiple ventures in the same marketplace—they will sustain modest losses when some shut down, but will almost certainly benefit handsomely when those that they have backed expand in size and value. More importantly, they will have established a foothold in a new market structure which has successfully redefined an aspect of the industry.

Consolidation in online trading platforms aimed at the retail client base will also occur over the coming years. In the US alone there are over 100 such ventures, offering execution services at an average of $16 per trade; a similar number operate in the international sphere. Though operating costs for many of these platforms are relatively low, revenues are still predicated on strong markets and robust volumes. Since all of these online trading platforms were developed in the midst of strong bull markets, they are unproven in a sharp, protracted market correction or cyclical bear market, when investors typically head to the sidelines. Certain ventures have demonstrated foresight by expanding into other financial services that are less sensitive to downturns; this may help cushion the revenue blow resulting from a market slowdown and may create a viable business model. Earlier we mentioned the example of E*Trade, which acquired Telebank to build a broader 'brick and mortar' platform—the acquisition gives E*Trade Bank, as it is known, a network of newly branded ATM machines and customer service representatives. It has also partnered with Ernst and Young to deliver financial advice to customers, once again hoping to create a value-added dimension to its business that might help insulate it from market cycles. Other leading online traders have adopted similar strategies, perhaps realizing their vulnerability in a market downturn. Ventures that remain strictly monoline are prime candidates for consolidation or closure (unless they are the absolute lowest cost producers and have reasonable brand recognition). Some online trading platforms may not even have to wait until the next stock market correction before closing operations. Platforms that have not established a solid name and presence in the marketplace during buoyant markets will soon be unable to cover the cost of doing business; the cost of acquiring new customers during a market slowdown can be prohibitively expensive. Accordingly, mergers, acquisitions and closures within the online trading sector may well occur prior to the next financial downturn. Leaders seeking to expand into online trading may find opportunities in the consolidation phase to expand their own base of accounts; some may pursue outright acquisitions of second-tier web trading ventures as a preferred route towards building critical mass—this is especially important given the continuous time constraints that characterize the 21st century electronic marketplace.

The same type of consolidation may not occur in online banking, though much depends on how quickly web banks can gain market share. In general, the market appears capable of supporting a larger number of banking institutions because banking is a 'bull and bear market' business and many customers still prefer dealing through platforms with a local or regional focus (though that may change as 'brick and mortar' banking consolidation continues). Companies and consumers have to deposit funds, transfer money, make balance inquiries, and pay bills and mortgages, regardless of the state of the economy and markets; while they may take out smaller mortgages or borrow less through their credit cards, they still need to perform basic banking functions. Accordingly, platforms offering these services may be less suscept-ible to consolidation than their online trading cousins. However, online bank-ing platforms that cannot grow fast enough to cover their fixed costs are at risk of closure or forced merger. In order to gain accounts more rapidly they may have to resort to offering high volume products, such as credit cards, or partner with online trading firms with larger account bases. To the extent a venture forms part of a larger banking group, management will have to deter-mine optimal ways of integrating traditional/web strategies to maximize busi-ness throughput and justify the fixed cost base. The marketplace model, which is of tremendous use and benefit to consumers undertaking 'comparison shop-ping', is a paradigm which will endure—though the number of marketplaces will almost certainly need to be rationalized. Some marketplaces supporting specific aspects of online banking, such as mortgages or auto loans, are likely to consolidate, adapt or fold. As indicated in Chapter 5, segments of the banking market feature numerous marketplace service providers—not all of them will be able to achieve the brand equity, traffic and revenues needed to survive; the same is likely to be true for insurance marketplaces. Continued advances in technology and automation mean that certain aspects of trading, processing, administration, reporting and control will lead to consolidation in the financial services industry. While more internal resources may be required to implement technology solutions, a far greater number of front-, middle- and back-office personnel may be forced into new industries.

Infomediary portals are also likely to consolidate. As with other segments of B2C and B2B, those with strong name recognition and truly value-added services, with viable revenue models, will remain the standouts of the sector and should remain vibrant. Those which have played the 'me too' game, atop a shaky business model, will almost certainly fade away. In the era of 21st century 'information overload', customers will focus their attention on portals which provide information and services that add value; they will spend less time 'surfing' other sites for the sake of curiosity, and that will have an impact on 'lesser' portals.

Consolidation in the digital finance sector is, and will continue to be, a healthy process. By eliminating players who operate at the margin, or who can provide greater client benefits as part of broader platforms, the sector can offer customers better service, improved liquidity and more transparent ac-cess. Customers will not need to worry about the financial standing and se-curity of the venture they are dealing with, and will be able to conduct business with greater confidence. In addition to sector consolidation or con-traction, there is almost certain to be a continuous effort to revamp or disman-tle ineffective web sites or little-used services. Creating a web platform demands ongoing feedback from users, frequent maintenance and constant updating. Information, products, services and links that no longer add value must be discontinued, while features demanded by the user community must be added. Though change is constant in many industries, it has been made more immediate by technology, and must figure into the plans and projects of all successful providers of web services.

NEW TECHNOLOGIES

The pace of new technology development is accelerating, and the next five to 10 years will bring many new ideas to the forefront. While we may not fully grasp all dimensions of what lies ahead (including new frontiers in optical computing, quantum computing, nanotechnology, and so on) one thing is certain—computing in the first decade of the 21st century will be powerful, inexpensive, fast, flexible and pervasive. The market already features micro-processors with over 40MM transistors running at speeds of 1.4 GHz (1.4B electric pulses per second)—a feat that probably could not have been imag-ined as recently as 1970; microprocessors with 150MM transistors running at 12 GHz are expected to arrive by 2005. This will help accelerate computing and data processes and open up new horizons. In many cases technology will be so cheap that it will effectively be disposable—the jellybean chip will be everywhere and will help track, catalog, inventory, price and convey all man-ner of information. Though revolutionary shifts in computation lie some years off, there is already new technology that will become part of the web in the near future—including simpler access devices, enhanced browsers, optical networks/switches, 'fat pipe' access/content, voice recognition/translation, and full-feature mobile computing. Many of these advances will improve the e-fi-nance experience and should help promote further growth in the sector.

At the start of this book we indicated that, although the PC has been a prime mover in bringing the world widespread Internet access, future tech-nologies are likely to render the PC, as we know it, obsolete. PC- and workstation-based browsers, which provide users with a view on the web, will also be radically different mechanisms in the future. There are certainly better ways of accessing and visualizing information, and interacting with the Inter-net, and customers will undoubtedly use these new devices and tools to access network applications over the coming years. Indeed, the Internet itself will make use of these new tools and techniques to convey information and ser-vices to users. The process has already commenced with elemental Internet appliances, which plug directly into the web and feature 'always on' connec-tions; for first-time Internet users, or those interested in having direct access to the Internet without full PC applications, the machine is a simple, cheap and useful device. The simplicity and flexibility of Internet appliances might help promote further home use of, and growth in, e-commerce and e-finance services. Cable set-top boxes, which link into a user's cable system to provide high bandwidth transmission, are an emerging delivery mechanism that will become even more prevalent in the medium-term. Next-generation set-top boxes will resemble simplified PCs (with hard drives and powerful processors) and will be capable of accessing not only standard cable/TV entertainment, but also e-commerce/e-finance and informational web sites, e-mail, on-demand applications, and so on. As prices decline these machines will become part of the 'mass access' paradigm, and should help spur additional e-commerce growth.

The ubiquitous browser, an elemental part of everyday web interaction, will be a substantially different interface mechanism in the future. New versions will merge standard browsing views with documents, e-mail, streaming audio/video and other features, in an integrated manner; sophisticated B2B clients may not even require a browser to communicate, but may choose to link directly from network to network. Browsing devices will be extremely flexible. It is ineffective for technologists to focus on delivering tomorrow's content based on today's web architecture, as it will not be relevant in a future environment. Accordingly, it is more important to understand how users will interact with, and employ, information—this will allow optimal design of delivery mechanisms. The goal is to understand the nature of the information customers want and how they wish to use it—visuals can then be designed to promote optimal use. Common data/communication exchange standards (such as those provided by meta-languages) and architectural flexibility will thus remain vital. As more information and services are ported to the web, browsing will be handled by software agents instead of users. There will be little or no need for users to do any browsing or searching themselves—knowing the preferences and needs of users, these agents will supply information and alerts on an automatic basis. Browsing and searching processes that benefit individuals and institutions will make their way into the e-commerce and e-finance sector in short order, promoting further efficiencies and cost savings.

By the middle of the decade virtually all network traffic will be in the form of data and video, rather than voice; migrating from slow, circuit-switched, voice-driven networks to ultra-fast, packet-switched, data-driven networks is a key area of research, development and deployment. In order to support this transformation, many companies are focused intently on further development of optical networks and other broadband transmission mechanisms. Though fiber optics and optical networks are already being deployed in many parts of the world, a truly cohesive optical network, which covers the stubborn 'last mile', is not yet a reality. Full implementation of a broadband network (through pure fiber optics or a combination of fiber optics, fixed wireless, and other solutions) will give the population of Internet users tremendous access and speed advantages, allowing for quicker data dissemination and service execution. Development continues on many fronts. For instance, various networking companies are testing equipment that transmits data at up to 80 gigabytes per second (gbps), many times faster than current standards. Fiber optic wave division multiplexing technology is moving from a current base of 40 communications channels to 80 channels, and dense wave division multiplexing (DWDM) (currently in beta development at various telecommunications firms), which splits light into dozens of colors to multiply the amount of data the network can carry, promises to deliver more than 1000 channels—this will greatly improve transmission bandwidth. The increased carrying capacity of fiber optic networks will demand improvements in switches; current research is focused on light and mirror-based photonic switches that speed switching, and hence transmission.

Once a true broadband network—featuring fiber, fixed wireless, cable and other broadband links, and supplemented by more powerful servers, compression software and mass storage devices—is in place, the personal and professional Internet experience will improve. 'Always on' fat pipes, featuring constant high speed, high capacity connections between computing devices and the web, will become part of daily business and personal life. Developing a fast, 'always on' connection is likely to fuel e-commerce/e-finance growth, as retail and institutional users will be able to obtain quick and reliable access, response and fulfillment; information retrieval should also expand as users gain instant access to the information they are seeking. Next generation broadband sites, with audio/video capabilities and user interactivity, will deliver a more complete Internet service. It is not difficult to imagine many e-banking functions, such as customer services, electronic roadshows, and analyst presentations, taking advantage of broadband technology to convey information more vividly and effectively.

Wireless networks operating within a home will give users the ability to access the Internet, and its associated functions, from multiple devices throughout a house. Some of this may be accomplished through personal area networks (PANs), such as those making use of Bluetooth technology (which allows 300–400 kbps transmission for distances of up to 10 m and will soon be able to transmit at 720 kbps over 100 m) or wireless LANs (transmitting 11 mbps across distances of up to several hundred meters). Home users will be able to conduct e-banking and trading activities from multiple locations within a house, on a variety of interconnected devices. Voice recognition and activation technologies will replace some, or many, of the processes currently governed by the keyboard and mouse. Comprehensive voice browsers and voice-enabled web sites, which are already starting to appear in very elemental form, will allow users to interact with platforms remotely through phones, adding to overall user flexibility. VoxML beta technology, which makes use of voice activation and XML, allows web-enabled phone users to query web sites verbally and receive responses, converted from text, in audible form; online trading platforms are starting to experiment with the dissemination of stock quotes and other financial information through voice-enabled web sites. Live customer service via a web-enabled device activated during a web session will become a reality through various protocols currently under development; this will allow real-time synchronized customer service while the user is operating a browser. Not surprisingly, voice-enabled web sites are drawing considerable attention and are expected to become a significant factor in future e-commerce endeavors. For instance, Forrester Research expects that $450B in e-commerce transactions will be conducted over voice-enabled web sites by 2003. e-Finance sites making use of voice technologies are likely to become quite commonplace over the coming years.

The international arena is another area of new technology focus—with 70% of Internet traffic expected to come from international sources by 2005, the development of new technologies that focus on cross-communication and data transfer is vital. Promising developments based on XML (and its XHTML hybrid) will allow multilingual sites to draw content from others in correct translation and character display; this will help bridge communication barriers. New security measures based on the developing Internet Protocol Security—which places security in a B2C site or B2B exchange at the network or packet processing level rather than the application layer—are expected to improve e-commerce reliability and performance. More widespread use of digital certificates and biometric devices (such as fingerprint or eye scans) is a virtual certainty as more e-business and e-finance migrates to the web. On the architecture front, the creation of meta-networks, or networks of networks, is another likely area of growth. Creation of meta-networks will allow users to access multiple exchanges simultaneously to obtain the best service or price at a much faster rate. This could create advantages in particular segments of the financial markets; for instance, in filling a large bond order, a client might make use of a meta-network to instantaneously search across multiple ATSs or B2B exchanges and execute at the best price. Portal networks, which aggregate all web services (content, applications, communications) to create integrated/personal customer solutions and connectivity to relevant communities, will also emerge.

Perhaps one of the most exciting dimensions of new technology relates to mobile wireless services—greater computing mobility through comprehensive wireless services emerges as one of the main themes of the future. Accessing the Internet, and its associated services, while 'on the go' or away from landline connections is the new frontier in business technology. Some researchers are anticipating that the wireless web will be up to 10 times larger than the Internet as we know it today, by any number of measures—users, traffic, point connections, and so on. This emerges as a real possibility when considering the global dimension of the web—users in many European, Asian and Latin countries use (and will continue to use) mobile phones/wireless devices more actively than PCs/workstations to access the network. The coming years will see greater use of cheap, mobile Internet-enabled 'mass access' devices (from $100 to $500) which will expand the power of the network—these will include powerful cell phones, PDAs, pagers and similar devices providing 'thin client' technological interface (i.e. any client mechanism that places core computing/communications infrastructure with the service provider and allows the client maximum access and flexibility with minimal equipment and maintenance). Inexpensive wireless devices will be supplemented by cheap, and ultimately free, web access from leading ISPs. Wireless penetration rates are expected to reach 40–50% for many countries in the Americas, Europe and Asia by 2005. Research firm Cahners In-Stat estimates that the number of wireless users will increase to 1.3B by 2004; consulting firm McKinsey shares a similar view, anticipating 1B users by 2003, while research firm Ovum expects 1.6B users by 2005. According to Ovum, an estimated 500MM global users will access mobile web applications by 2005, 25% located in the US and 75% in Europe, Asia and Latin America. The evolution to wireless is, of course, already underway, but remains in a nascent stage—wireless is not yet a true broadband mechanism, as transmission speeds are slow and visual/interface capabilities limited. A great deal of technological work remains to be done before wireless web services (including many of the financial services discussed in this book) can be conveyed in a user-friendly form. Once that milestone is achieved, it is likely that the face of business will change even further. New portable devices, with fast connection speeds and useful interfaces, will allow web customers to conduct business from virtually any location, at any time. Being freed from a stationary terminal provides tremendous space and time flexibility.

In order for mobile e-commerce and e-finance services to become a 'workable reality' at least two things must occur: the technological platform must be global and robust, and the services offered must be accessible and useful. At present, the market for wireless services is fractionalized among competing standards. A mobile customer in Tokyo generally cannot use the same device in New York or London, and vice versa. Lack of 'interoperability' in wireless networks—caused by different transport vehicles, switching elements, connection speeds, and protocols—makes the full migration of web services to the wireless arena very challenging. The Internet has been successful because it has created architecture/protocol that accommodates different networks and machines using different operating systems; the same does not yet exist in mobile communications. As mentioned briefly in the Appendix, there are several competing wireless standards in operation, including Global System for Mobile Communications (GSM), Time Division Multiple Access (TDMA), Code Division Multiple Access (CDMA), and Personal Digital Communications (PDC). Most of Europe is on the GSM standard, the US primarily uses TDMA and CDMA, much of Asia uses GSM, and Japan favors PDC. In 2000 there were 331MM GSM users globally, 48MM TDMAs, 67MM CDMAs, and 48MM PDCs. GSM features the greatest number of users globally, but they are not evenly distributed—215MM users reside in Europe, 90MM in Asia, 7MM in the US, and 18MM in other countries.

In addition to incompatibility in mobile standards there is lack of standardization in the wireless 'microbrowser' area. Just as conventional browsers allow users to view products and services on a PC or workstation, microbrowsers allow mobile users to see information on a small mobile device. The visual capabilities of phones, PDAs and pagers are still very limited, so new standards for designing, transmitting and displaying web pages on mobile devices are required. Since mobile devices cannot display the content and detail typical of HTML-based pages, the marketplace has developed several different microbrowser standards based on handheld device markup language (HDML), wireless markup language (WML), and compressed (or compact) hypertext markup language (CHTML). To the extent an emerging bridge, known as wireless application protocol (WAP), takes hold these differences can be overcome—though not without some technical effort. WAP is an emerging standard being built into a range of mobile devices which allows users to interact with web sites; WAP can be built on any mobile operating system (including PalmOS, Windows CE, OS/9, JavaOS, and so on). In its full implementation, WAP provides message notification, call management, e-mail links, locator services, alerts, news, and internet/intranet access. Though WAP uses WML, it can access web sites using HDML and CHTML if operators of those sites include appropriate translation software (note that the popular Japanese I-mode platform, described below, has been successful in making use of CHTML). Crafting specific mobile views through these markup languages is a critical step in the process; mobile views must give users content they want, in an easily readable format—while some work has been completed in this area, more remains to be done. Though first generation WAP is still burdened by shortcomings that will have to be resolved before it can be employed as a true mobile net solution, it is indicative of the technological efforts that are currently underway. When future generations of WAP-enabled mobile devices are truly operational they will allow for secure and reliable voice and data communications, including storing/ forwarding, instant messaging, and data synchronizing.

Establishing a web connection via a wireless device every time a user wants to tap into the Internet has been a source of frustration. With most devices and services, users have to establish a separate connection each time web access is desired (not unlike the dial-up process required for a standard PC). This leads to delays in accessing information and defeats, to a certain extent, the underlying rationale for having a wireless, instant communications device. This is beginning to change as technology permits the establishment of 'always on' connections. For instance, in mid-2000 NTT DoCoMo of Japan—which controls 70% of Japan's wireless market—introduced the 'always on' I-mode connection, giving users instant access to mobile web pages without a dial-up delay; other service providers are expected to follow suit. Importantly,

I-mode clients are only billed for the information/data they download, rather than the time they are connected to the service. Data transmission speed remains an issue, regardless of the standard employed. Most current generation mobile devices transmit data over the wireless spectrum at a maximum of 14.4 kbps, which is slow by any measure (though adoption of Universal Mobile Telecommunication Service (UMTS) in the near-term will allow data transmissions at 144 kbps). By 2003 more than half of all cell traffic will be based on data, rather than voice, suggesting that transmission speed will be of even greater importance. New 3G devices being developed by companies such as Lucent, Motorola, Nokia, and others will be able to transmit at up to 2 mbps—making them far more useful from an applications standpoint. Once 3G transmission speeds become a reality—around 2005—the power of mobile computing will be considerable. As technology renders these devices more useful, their number will increase and—following Metcalfe's Law of Networking—the power of the network will expand. There is, of course, some theoretical limit to this process, as the wireless frequency spectrum is a finite resource—at some point future demand for frequency spectrum will outstrip available supply.

Once interoperability conversion and transmission issues are resolved, wireless Internet applications which synchronize information across multiple devices and networks, regardless of location, should prove popular for a broad range of retail and institutional users. In late 2000, basic wireless web sites featuring product information were the most prevalent applications (comprising 53% of all sites), followed by news/content (36%), and e-mail/ account access (26%); e-commerce and e-financial services accounted for 14% and 8% of all sites, respectively. As technology and transmission speed improve, wireless e-commerce and e-finance sites are expected to expand in scope and number. In a break with tradition, it is likely that the consumer sector will be the true 'proving ground' for mobile technology and its related applications. Though technological platforms of the recent past have generally been implemented in an institutional setting first, the reverse is expected in the case of wireless applications. Mobile devices are, by their nature, personal instruments that individuals can use for a range of purposes; many new wireless applications are thus being targeted at individuals. Assuming that all technological challenges are resolved and wireless operations become truly global and efficient, financial platforms will need to determine the nature of the services they will offer users. Mobile devices lend themselves to relatively flexible, quick, simple and standard services; many basic financial tasks are text-based and do not require high graphics content or multimedia features. Offerings with any degree of complexity, or those requiring dense content or presentation, are unlikely to be suitable for the earliest generations of wireless finance. Basic services focused on balance information, fund transfers, payments, securities quotes, financial news and trade execution are already available on a limited basis to customers in certain countries, and will roll out to others in the near-term. More complex services, such as loan or mortgage applications, technical charting or financial document review, do not, and will not, feature prominently in first stage mobile financial services platforms—but may follow at a later time, as technology improves.

As indicated, basic wireless financial services are already available to users in certain markets. This is particularly true in Europe, where wireless use is reasonably well established. For example, in Finland, where mobile penetration is very high, bank clients can effect payments and fund transfers through GSM mobile devices equipped with short messaging service (SMS) capabilities; SMS is a text messaging feature found on GSM phones (approximately 3B SMS messages are sent every month and Cahners In-Stat predicts that, by 2004, 250B wireless messages will be sent every month). They can also use the SIM cards in their GSM phones as smart cards, purchasing goods through retailers technologically equipped to handle smart card payments. In Asia, Citibank offers its Singaporean clients access to basic financial services through mobile handsets; it is piloting similar programs in Scandinavia and Spain. In Hong Kong, the HKSE has introduced the AMS/3 trading system that collects stock orders electronically from web platforms and mobile devices, transmits them to a floor broker, executes them and displays them back on the web terminal or mobile device. In the US, wireless financial services remain limited but are gradually growing in scope. Bank of America was the first major US bank to provide basic wireless banking services to customers with PDAs; Harris Bank, based in Chicago, followed shortly thereafter with a wireless platform of its own. In the online trading arena, a number of web ventures made available, in 2000, basic wireless functions, including quotes, account lookup, and trade execution; pioneers of these wireless trading services include Fidelity's PowerStreet, Ameritrade, Celltrader, E*Trade, Morgan Stanley Dean Witter Online, Quick and Reilly, Schwab, Prudential, Suretrade, and TD Waterhouse. Though these services are basic compared to the full Internet offerings available to 'stationary customers', they represent an important step forward in the formation and evolution of wireless financial services.

It is too early, of course, to judge whether mobile financial services will be widespread, but with the era of 'mass access' devices here—and expanding rapidly—it seems reasonable to suppose that such services will be an important dimension of overall e-commerce and e-finance. This is particularly true in countries where users are more reliant on non-PC devices to access the web. Certain researchers and financial institutions believe strongly that essential wireless services will be used by a meaningful segment of the online population; others are somewhat more cautious, suggesting that mobile web finance will be a small 'niche' in the mobile commerce market. Regardless of the view, general mobile commerce, or m-commerce, is expected to be a considerable growth area in the future. By the middle of the decade, Forrester

Research expects m-commerce revenues will reach $38B, while IDC predicts the figure will reach $60B; Strategy Analytics and Ovum are even more optimistic, predicting total revenues will exceed $200B. Though the estimate of m-commerce revenues remains fairly broad, it is clear that the sector is set to expand over the coming years.

Many other dimensions of new technology will appear over the coming years and will add to the products, services, and initiatives currently underway. Many of these will have a direct, or indirect, application to the Internet, e-commerce, m-commerce, and the conveyance of financial services to a range of users around the world. The past few decades in general, and the past few years in particular, have demonstrated that changes in technology impact business processes profoundly—this trend will only accelerate as further advances are made. But in order for technology to remain a driving force it cannot simply serve as a mechanism for conducting business. It must create and expand business by helping users become more efficient and productive.

TALK OF THE TRADE

Beta development—a test version of a technology product or service that is functional but not available to users at large.

CHTML—compressed hypertext markup language, a key markup language used for wireless devices.

Decimalization—the process of quoting stocks in single 0.01 price increments (rather than the traditional 1/16, 1/8 or 1/4 increments common up until 2000).

m-Commerce—mobile commerce, electronic commerce conducted through a mobile wireless device.

Meta-networks—networks of networks.

SMS—short messaging system, a basic text character messaging display system available through GSM phones.

Spider—an intelligent agent that continuously searches the web for new sites/content and then creates catalogs and indexes.

Thin-wire client—any client mechanism that places core computing/communications infrastructure with the service provider and allows the client maximum access and flexibility with minimal equipment and maintenance.

Voice-enabled—technology which permits verbal interaction with a web site by converting audio information into digital, and vice versa.

WAP—wireless access protocol, an emerging communications protocol that provides a link between wireless devices and Internet sites.

WML—wireless markup language, a key markup language used for wireless devices.

Appendix
The Digital Revolution

This book has discussed the electronic revolution in financial services that has been created by a unique convergence of technology, creative thought and capital. In less than a decade, entire structures for conducting financial business—at both the institutional and retail level—have been redesigned and transported to an electronic environment, changing the way users perceive, and interact with, financial services. The revolution has had a profound impact on many dimensions of the industry—new Internet ventures have appeared to challenge the status quo, banks, securities companies, asset managers, and insurers have been forced to restructure methods of conducting business, non-traditional companies, such as technology firms, have become important participants in the financial process, and retail and institutional customers have gained access to more efficient and cost-effective ways of conducting financial affairs.

While creativity and capital have been central to the process, technology has been the driver. Without advances in technology, particularly those evident in the 1980s and 1990s, it is difficult to imagine business processes changing so dramatically—no amount of creative thought or money could transform the business world so fundamentally, without technology. Technology alone has not been, and is unlikely to ever be, a sufficiently powerful force to create sustainable competitive advantages for participants in the 21st century. But it has been the catalyst for change. In the main part of the text we have discussed the creative thought behind new e-commerce models and the driving force of capital, but use this Appendix to provide some background on the technological dimension of the digital revolution. In this brief section (which readers primarily interested in the broader, non-technical topic of electronic finance can omit without loss of understanding or continuity) we highlight two distinct, but ultimately related, strands of technology that have helped transform the business landscape—the development and deployment of increasingly powerful computing and communications devices, and the creation and expansion of computer networks—most notably, the Internet.

COMPUTING: FROM ELECTROMAGNETICS TO SILICON CHIPS

Basic counting mechanisms have been in use for centuries. The abacus, Greek for 'counting table', was employed by Greeks, Romans, and others as a means of tallying quantities and performing basic sums; the Chinese adopted an abacus of their own during the 17th century and used it to perform arithmetic operations. Alternative measuring and counting devices appeared in other parts of the world during the 18th century—all were, of course, manual in nature. Broader concepts of computing emerged in the early 19th century when Charles Babbage, and his lover Ada Lovelace (poet Lord Byron's only legitimate daughter), pursued the theory and practice of mechanical computing. Babbage, recognized as the 'grandfather' of actuarial theory and operations research, developed technical aspects of the card-based mechanical counting machine in order to compute mathematical tables in a simpler fashion. Babbage helped migrate computation from the analog (calculation by measurement) to the digital (calculation by counting). In 1822 Babbage developed and demonstrated a small counting machine for the Royal Astronomy Society that proved the working concept behind his theories. He attempted to follow up with a 'Difference Machine', but the complexity proved too great and he soon turned his attention to the development of a universal calculating machine—which he called the 'Analytical Engine'. Babbage envisioned a machine which could be disassembled and reconfigured in order to perform different types of calculations—additions, subtractions, multiplications and divisions. The 'central mill', or brain of the machine, would be capable of adding up to 50 decimal places and 'storing' up to 1000 numbers of 50 digits each; numbers would be input either through the mill or via punchcards. Though Babbage was unable to produce a functioning working model during his lifetime, his son eventually built a small working prototype that validated many of his underlying theories. While Babbage focused on the development of the Analytical Engine, Lovelace explored theoretical aspects of computing—becoming, in essence, the world's first 'computer programmer'. She wrote sequences of instructions that included subroutines, loops, stored programs, jumps, and conditional 'if/then' branches—all key elements of modern-day programming languages. Lovelace understood that these instructions could be stored and referenced when needed, eliminating repetitive tasks. Unfortunately, she died before implementing any of her theories; Babbage foundered without her help, and was unable to achieve any significant breakthroughs on the mechanical computing engine during his lifetime. While Babbage and Lovelace were working on the Analytical Engine, George

Boole, an English mathematician, was laying the foundations of an algebraic system that would ultimately make its way into modern computing. Specifically, Boole developed an algebraic system that would be used in the 20th century to couple the logic in software with physical operations; Boolean algebra was a key step forward in the logical analysis of a two-state physical device (the only possible results being '1', '0' or 'on', 'off'). Boole's work was advanced in the mid-20th century by Claude Shannon, who published research on machine and relay circuit design based on logical algebra; Shannon's work became central to modern-day computing.

Herman Hollerith, another pioneer of early computing devices, created a punchcard machine that fed data into an electromechanical system. Hollerith's machine featured a copper brush that closed an electric circuit if a hole was not found, allowing for computation and tabulation. In 1900 Hollerith rented his machine to the US Census Bureau, which used it to tabulate statistics from the 1890 US census. Despite early success, Hollerith encountered financial difficulties and sold his invention to the Computer Tabulating and Recording Company (CTR). An enterprising young CTR salesman, Tom Watson, began selling these tabulating devices around the country and, after achieving a modicum of success, gained control of the entire CTR operation. Watson soon decided that CTR was an unsuitable moniker and renamed the company International Business Machines (IBM); IBM's presence and influence in the computing business continues to the present day.

The first generation of modern computers dates back to the pre-World War II period. In 1936 Alan Turing, a British researcher, completed work on the manipulation of tokens according to systematic rules; this gave machines the ability to compute number theory through a formal system. Turing's work led to the development of Robinson, a large electromagnetic computing machine. During the war he developed a new machine, Colossus, based on the same principles, but replaced Robinson's electromagnetic workings with 2000 vacuum tubes; the tubes were used as on/off switching elements to process instructions. Through Colossus, and nine other machines operating in parallel, the Allies managed to break significant military codes transmitted by the Axis powers. Turing's entire body of work influenced subsequent generations of computer scientists—he was the first researcher to focus on the use of software, rather than hardware, to drive a computer's functions (a rather radical idea at the time) and was the first to develop specific methods of 'debugging' computer instructions; he also completed early work on artificial intelligence. Because of Turing's work, British scientists were far closer to developing the world's first electronic computer than their American counterparts. Following the end of the war, however, the British Government curtailed commitments to computer research and Britain lost the computing edge to the US.

Howard Aiken, a US engineer trained at Harvard and employed by IBM, created an all-electronic calculator in 1944 which contained 500 miles of internal wiring; the machine, known as the Harvard IBM Automatic Sequence Controlled Calculator (or Mark I, for short), was an electronic relay computer which used electromagnetic signals to move mechanical parts at three to five seconds per calculation. Though Mark I was a relatively useful machine for its time, the future of first generation computing lay with tube, rather than electromagnetic, machines. Rapid on/off switches were, and remain, the essence of digital computing—vacuum tubes were able to switch on/off 1MM times per second, making them far superior to mechanical switches. In the mid-1940s Presper Eckert and John Mauchly introduced the Electronic Numerical Integrator and Computer (ENIAC); John von Neumann, a professor at the University of Pennsylvania, developed many of ENIAC's key features, including software routines and start/stop capabilities that permitted programming flexibility. The ENIAC—which took two years and $500,000 to build—was 10 feet tall and 150 feet wide, weighed 30 tons, featured 6000 hand switches, 17,000 vacuum tubes, 70,000 resistors, 10,000 capacitors and consumed 160 kilowatts of power; the heat generated by ENIAC frequently reached 120°F, making a cooling system a necessity. ENIAC performed computations 1000 times faster than the electromagnetic Mark I—including more than 5000 additions per second—and was designed to help the US military in numerous projects (including plotting missile trajectories, optimizing supply routes, and so on). A ballistic calculation that had taken 20 hours to perform manually could be completed in a mere 30 seconds by ENIAC. By the time ENIAC came into service the war was ending; accordingly, the machine was put to use in computing thermonuclear reactions of hydrogen bombs. ENIAC's basic underpinnings eventually formed part of Remington Rand's commercial UNIVAC machine.

The Electronic Discrete Variable Calculator (EDVAC) was developed after ENIAC and was the first attempt to build a general purpose computer with stored memory for data and instructions—allowing switches to be discarded. Von Neumann's theories on computer architecture featured heavily in EDVAC, including the logical design of registers and addresses and the creation of a central processing unit (CPU) to act as the main coordinator for all of the computer's functions. Many of von Neumann's architecture standards from 1946 remain in use today. Though EDVAC was the first attempt at a general purpose, stored memory computer, it was beaten to the punch by a British machine. In 1949 Maurice Wilkes at Cambridge University designed and created the Electronic Delay Storage Automatic Computer (EDSAC), a stored memory program computer using binary digits. It could perform 700 additions, or 200 multiplications, per second and remained in active use until the late 1950s. In 1951 Remington Rand, using ENIAC design templates, introduced the UNIVAC 1, a commercial computer. The first generation of modern computers, from the ENIAC to the UNIVAC, represented an important step in implementing theories of computing and automating standard tasks. Nevertheless, early 'big iron' models were extremely rigid and cumbersome, physically large and expensive to build and operate. In addition, each machine featured highly specific and customized operating instructions and had to be programmed in unique machine languages. Storage mechanisms were primitive until the introduction of magnetic tape devices in the early 1950s.

The second generation of computers—defined as those made of discrete electronic components—appeared in late 1947 when three scientists at Bell Labs—John Bardeen, Walter Brattain and William Shockley—developed the transistor. A transistor is an 'on/off' switch which, when charged with electricity or light, changes its state from conductive to non-conductive, and vice versa. The Bell Labs team recognized that transistors could act as switches, replacing the very cumbersome vacuum tubes that formed the core of first generation computers. The transistor fulfilled the functions of the vacuum tube—without the size and heat, and for only a fraction of the cost—and revolutionized the internal workings of computing machines. The Bell team initially developed a 'point contact germanium transistor'—with a semiconduting germanium strip, batteries, plastic and gold foil—but, within three years, Shockley introduced a new bipolar junction transistor which was cheaper and more reliable. Transistors were not widely available to US manufacturers until the mid-1950s, after American Telephone and Telegraph (AT&T, owner of Bell Labs) agreed to supply transistor licenses in settlement of an antitrust lawsuit. Thereafter they were incorporated into the design of new computers—the age of solid state, transistorized computing had arrived. As a result of advances in transistor technology, second generation mainframe computers were smaller, faster, and more reliable than earlier tube machines, and featured superior storage mechanisms. In addition, programmers no longer had to communicate through cryptic machine language routines—new assembly languages provided more programming transparency.

As a result of the flexibility provided by second generation computers, information processing became automated and engrained in the daily processes of governments, companies, universities, and research laboratories. IBM, by then a leader in computers, introduced its massive IBM AN/FSQ-7 in the mid-1950s and the solid state 7090 mainframe in 1959. Digital Equipment Corporation (DEC) introduced minicomputers—including its PDP-1—in the early 1960s. These machines were significantly smaller than mainframes and could be placed 'in the field' for remote operations (linking back to head-office mainframes through modems (devices which converted digital signals to analog and vice versa, so that computer information could be conveyed across phone lines)). Other companies, such as Honeywell, Sperry Rand, Burroughs, and Control Data, joined the mainframe/minicomputer fray and began producing 'corporate' machines. These units featured flexible storage devices and greater memory, and supported new programming languages (including

COBOL and FORTRAN) which let companies program applications to suit their needs; they also featured basic operating systems (OSs) which were used to manage tape/disk storage, timesharing, and task/job sequencing. Corporate applications for mainframes and minicomputers began appearing in the 1960s, and by the end of the decade corporations began using a communications mechanism known as the Electronic Data Interchange (EDI). EDI became a de-facto standard for transmitting corporate information—including purchase orders, invoices, shipping information, accounts payable, and so on—between computers attached to value-added networks (VANs). Compared to today's communication mechanisms, EDI appears cumbersome and inefficient—it could only operate on an end-of-day batch basis through expensive, and closed, proprietary VANs and required significant software implementation at the sites of both suppliers and users. Nonetheless, it helped lower the cost of rote commercial transactions; for instance, the average cost of handling a purchase order declined by an order of magnitude through EDI solutions.

Further technical advances in the late 1950s and early 1960s ushered in the third generation of computers. Though the third generation of computers—defined as those using integrated circuits, disk storage, and online terminals—formally commenced in 1964 with the launch of the IBM System 360 (which cost IBM more than $1B in research and development funds), underlying work had started several years before that. In 1958 Jack Kilby at Texas Instruments developed—but did not immediately publicize—the first electronic circuit containing more than a single transistor. The Kilby integrated circuit (IC, or chip) was less than half an inch wide and contained two transistors mounted on a bar of germanium. Though crude and not particularly powerful, the introduction of this early device paved the way for further IC work. Four months after Kilby created his chip, Jean Hoerni and Robert Noyce at Fairchild Semiconductor completed pioneering discoveries in planar processes and layering techniques on their own IC—which, unlike Kilby's, was based on silicon and had no wires. The advent of ICs enabled computing devices to shrink in size and operate with less heat and greater efficiency. A direct by-product of the smaller size was (and remains) faster computing speed—the shorter the distance a pulse has to travel between two points, the faster it arrives to trip the switch. Once the first IC was developed it was simply a question of time before IC miniaturization became a field of its own. Throughout the 1970s IC designers worked feverishly on inserting more transistors on silicon wafers, a process that continues up to the present day. The design of chips went through various phases, including large-scale integration (LSI), in which up to 100,000 components were placed on a chip, very large-scale integration (VLSI), where placement increased to 1 million components, and ultra large-scale integration (ULSI), where placement exceeded 1 million components. A single vacuum tube from the 1940s, representing a single switch or transistor, can today accommodate billions of modern transistors.

By the late 1960s computer design had started to change. Computer punchcards gave way to keyboards, hardcopy printouts were replaced by display terminals, and large printing consoles evolved into smaller teletype printers. Timesharing of computer resources, which let multiple users access mainframes or minicomputers from different locations at different times, placed a greater emphasis on software. Since hardware could be shared by many users, more time and effort was spent on programming specific software applications; this trend accelerated in the 1980s as networking took hold. The first three generations of computers, which lasted from the mid-20th century to the early 1980s, were aimed at scientific, government and business, rather than personal users. The computing community was focused on mainframes, high level programming languages, and rote data processing, rather than consumer-oriented devices, flexible software, and user-friendly applications. There was virtually no progress in developing machines suitable for use by the average person; indeed, until the mid-1980s, most people could conceive of no particular reason why they might need a computer of their own.

The fourth generation of computing—comprising computers made up primarily of chips, with limited amounts of discrete components—commenced in the early 1970s and continues to the present time. A catalyst in changing the computing world's focus from professional to consumer machines occurred when Noyce and 'Ted' Hoft of Intel developed the first microprocessor. Intel (created in 1968 by Noyce, Gordon Moore, and a dozen other Fairchild Semiconductor engineers) was initially focused on making cheaper and more powerful ICs—however, it soon found itself on a different road. In 1969 Busicom of Japan asked the company to create a programmable calculator with multiple custom chips. Hoft felt that having multiple chips in the calculators was too complex and so developed the idea of a single chip with general purpose logic which would receive instructions from memory. This single 'master' chip marked the birth of the microprocessor—an IC containing all 'essential' computing components, including the CPU, random access memory (RAM), read only memory (ROM), internal clock, and input/output control unit.

Intel introduced its 4004 chip in 1971. The 12 millimeter chip cost $200, featured 2300 transistors and was capable of performing 60,000 operations per second—giving it the computing power of 12 ENIACs. A year later it introduced the 8008 chip, with 3300 transistors, and a PL/M high level language compiler which performed calculations even more rapidly. Both the 4004 and 8008 chips were designed for specific applications, meaning computing flexibility was limited. Not until Intel introduced the 8080 chip in mid-1974 did the world have its first general microprocessor. Other chip companies soon entered the market—including Motorola, MOS, Zilog, and others—and smaller, more powerful, chips followed on a regular basis thereafter. In 1965 Moore estimated that transistor density, and thus computing power, would double every 12 months as technical advances allowed more transistors to be embedded on a silicon wafer; some years later he revised the estimate to reflect a doubling every 18 months. This observation gave rise to what is now referred to as 'Moore's Law'. Even though it commenced as a rule of thumb, Moore's Law has proven useful and accurate. From 1990 to 2000 Moore's Law would predict the number of transistors on a chip to increase from under 1MM to approximately 16MM—in fact, Intel's 1997 Pentium II chip featured 7.5MM transistors and its late 1999 Pentium III chip featured 28MM transistors; its late 2000 Pentium 4 chip featured 42MM transistors. (Note that Moore's Law is bounded by the physical properties of silicon and, after reaching a particular microprocessor gate size, no further speed enhancements can be achieved; based on current estimates, this is expected to occur around 2010.) Today's small chips are approximately 1/16" square and 1/30" thick, while 'large' microprocessor chips are still only 1/4" to 1/2" square. Certain chips are designed to perform very specific functions, while others control entire processes. For instance, logic chips perform a subset of the functions of a processor, RAM chips store data on a temporary basis (while computer power is on), ROM chips (and associated PROMs, EPROMs and others) store data on a permanent basis (whether the computer is on or off), and so on. Many of these chips, referred to as 'jellybeans', are commonly found in other electronic appliances—their cost is so low and their use so widespread they are said to be as cheap and plentiful as jellybeans.

While Intel, Motorola, and others concentrated on developing chips, Xerox (through its Palo Alto Research Center (PARC)) and DEC began research into personal computers (PCs). Alan Kay, a researcher at Xerox PARC, was a central figure in the development of Alto, the first prototype 'personal' computer. Though the Alto appears somewhat primitive by today's standards, it contained a number of features that were well ahead of its time—including a 'point-and-click' mouse, bit mapped graphics, 'pull down' windows, and considerable memory; most of these features did not appear in the consumer market until 1983/1984. Though PARC built 1500 Altos for use by researchers and government offices, it never made the machine available to the home user (though it did introduce a modified version, known as Star, to the office market in 1981—the machine, however, was also a few years ahead of its time).

The potential value of a computer to the individual was not recognized or understood at this early stage. Though scientists at PARC and other research and development 'think tanks' produced very interesting results, major corporations were unwilling to pursue the concept of personal computing; mainframe developers, including Xerox, DEC, IBM and Honeywell, concentrated their resources on minicomputer and mainframe systems. The task of introducing and popularizing PCs thus fell to a group of diverse entrepreneurs. The first breakthrough in personal computing came in 1975 when a small company known as Micro Instrumentation and Telemetry Systems (MITS) introduced a 'home hobbyist' computer called the Altair 8800, based on the Intel 8080 chip. Though it is difficult to imagine in this day and age, the Altair—with 1K (kilobit, or 1000 bits/characters) of memory and no monitor, keyboard, printer, or data storage device—achieved a cult following among hobbyists who wanted to 'tinker' with the machine (flipping a small switch on the console to input computer instructions). The Altair became the first true 'personal' computer in the public market, trumping the much more sophisticated, and powerful, Alto (which remained a 'scientific project'). The Altair operated on a version of BASIC written by Bill Gates and Paul Allen. The duo offered MITS a version of BASIC which did not exist at the time of their original offer—it had to be created on one of Harvard's DEC minicomputers, using a version of public domain BASIC that was enhanced to run in an environment which simulated the Intel 8080 chip. The first time the pair ran their version of BASIC on the Altair was when they delivered the product. The demo was successful; had it not been, the world of software applications and operating systems might have taken a radically different turn—shortly after their work with MITS, Gates and Allen founded Microsoft.

In 1976, Steve Jobs and Stephen Wozniak, ex-Hewlett Packard technologists and co-founders of Apple Computer, created the 'Apple I' computer in a garage. Though the Apple I was more 'user-friendly' than the Altair, it was still a rather crude machine. It took the Apple II—launched in 1977 with a full keyboard, cassette storage device, monitor, color graphics, and sound—to change the face of personal computing. The Apple II was not a powerhouse by today's standards—it featured only 16K of RAM and 16K of ROM in its normal configuration—but it was accessible, non-threatening, and led people to understand that computing was not restricted to scientific research centers, large corporations, and government agencies. The success of the Apple spawned the development of other PCs, including the Tandy Radio Shack TRS 80, Texas Instruments TI99, Atari 400, and the Commodore PET, along with dot matrix printers and other peripherals. Most of these early machines featured an OS known as Central Program for Microprocessors (CP/M), developed by Gary Kildall at Digital Research. An OS acts as a master control program and runs different aspects of the computer. For instance, the OS establishes the user interface (or shell) that enables the user and the machine to interact, creates standards for software/applications which 'talk' to the computer, manages the sequence of jobs and tasks that run on the computer, directs data flow into, or out of, the storage device, and controls communication with peripherals such as printers and storage devices (and, in subsequent years, drivers for sound, network, video capture, hard disk, scanning, communications, and so on). From 1976 to 1980 CP/M was the favored OS on most machines, but compatibility problems remained an issue—new machines from Sinclair, Hewlett Packard, Osborne, Kaypro, and others were not necessarily compatible with one another, despite the use of a common OS.

Software, which let users tap into PC power in ways that were both useful and meaningful, was a driving force behind mass acceptance of new PC technology. Without useful, inexpensive, and available software, the PC would not have had the impact it did with consumers. Users did not have to program their own machines, they could simply buy packages off the shelf that allowed them to play games, write memos, manage data, and so on. Though software titles were still limited in the late 1970s, the release of the first 'killer application' in 1979—Dan Bricklin and Bob Frankston's VisiCalc electronic spreadsheet for the Apple II (and the inspiration for later mega-sellers such as Lotus 123 and Microsoft Multiplan/Excel)—soon led to the release of dozens, then hundreds, and ultimately thousands, of new packages centered on word processing, database management, spreadsheet calculation, entertainment, and so on. The introduction of the floppy disk in 1978 and the hard disk in 1980 led to convenient loading, saving, and running of programs and files. The development and release of software was supplemented by considerable educational efforts. PC companies took the time and effort to acquaint users with new products and help them overcome 'PC phobia', which was still relatively prevalent in the early 1980s.

IBM was notably absent from the PC scene during the 'first wave' and did not enter the market until the early 1980s. When it finally appeared, however, it did so with a vengeance. In 1981 IBM became the first mainframe computer company to validate the PC concept by introducing its IBM PC, the product of more than a year of intensive research conducted under the code name 'Project Acorn'. The company's entry helped business users migrate from mainframes to PC-based platforms. The original IBM PC was an open system that allowed third parties to develop hardware and software for the machine, extending its flexibility, reach and popularity. The new PC featured the Intel 8088 chip, a choice of OS (either CP/M, PC DOS, or UCSD-P), software, expansion cards, and 16K of RAM upgradeable to 256K. In one of the savviest deals in the history of business, Microsoft's Allen purchased, for $100,000, the right to sell Seattle Computer Products' Q-DOS to an unnamed client (IBM), rewrote it, and renamed it MS DOS. Microsoft then got IBM to agree to let the company sell MS DOS to non-IBM projects. MS DOS (or PC DOS as IBM called it) quickly emerged as a favorite and solidified, very quickly, Microsoft's position in the world of operating systems. The IBM PC project was, like Apple's, an almost instant success and was supported by new peripherals, enhanced models, and diverse software titles soon after launch. Within 18 months the enhanced IBM PC XT was created, with a hard drive, 1 megabyte (MB) of RAM, and a new version of MS DOS. IBM clones soon flooded the market, starting with Compaq's 1982 offering, which broadened the market even further. (Note that the Compaq and other clones ran on MS DOS, leading to the eventual demise of CP/M DOS.) Importantly, small and large businesses gravitated to these new machines, marking the emergence of

PC use in a corporate environment. By the mid-1980s the appeal of the PC had grown tremendously. Consumers and businesses recognized the value that could be derived from owning and operating a PC, and the software development community continued delivering a large number of new titles that expanded usage even further. Indeed, by the mid-1980s Apple and IBM boasted 16,000 software titles each. These software 'apps' were supplemented by gradual, though growing, access to online services. In 1981 Hayes introduced a PC-based modem that allowed PC users to communicate with one another through electronic bulletin boards and new dial-up services such as CompuServe and The Source.

The PC market entered a new phase in the mid-1980s as IBM, Apple, Commodore, Texas Instruments, and others launched more powerful machines. Most were designed with faster chips, greater memory capacity, more expansion slots, larger hard drives, and more sophisticated sound and graphics. Some models, such as the IBM AT and Apple II+/e, were successes while others, such as the Apple Lisa, were disappointments. There was, however, a 'silver lining' in some of the most notable failures. For instance, though Lisa was a relatively slow and expensive ($10,000) machine which gained no following, it featured a mouse and a very appealing graphical user interface (GUI), reminiscent of what would eventually appear on the Apple Macintosh and through PCs featuring Microsoft Windows (Microsoft actually commenced work on Interface Manager, the precursor to Windows, in late 1981). Both Apple and Microsoft had visited Xerox PARC in 1979 and 1980 to view Alto's point-and-click, mouse-based GUI, and both ultimately adopted aspects of what they had seen. Using aspects of Lisa's interface, Apple introduced the Macintosh in 1984 with its 'user-friendly' GUI, mouse, and 'point-and-click' technology (and relatively affordable price tag of $2500). The machine revolutionized personal computing and created a divide between Mac and PC users.

Computing accelerated further in the mid-1980s when Intel introduced its new 386 microprocessor (with an astonishing 275,000 transistors), offering new speed capabilities that were perfectly suited for the growing market in interactive GUIs with mouse capabilities. By the middle of the decade numerous new products had entered the market, including Microsoft Word (destined to become the market's most powerful and popular word processing system), the IBM PC jr (an early attempt at a scaled down version of the IBM PC, which was an abject failure), the Hewlett Packard Laserjet (another machine which became an industry leader), and enhanced versions of the Mac. In late 1985 Microsoft finally released Windows 1.0, a full two years after its initial announcement of the product. Though Windows provided PC manufacturers with a product to challenge the Mac, Gates' attempt to interest IBM in Windows was an uphill battle. IBM was initially resistant to tampering with the established and proven DOS system that powered IBM PCs; a substantial, and loyal, following of PC DOS users had grown up around the original OS. As a compromise, Microsoft and IBM jointly began developing OS/2, a more powerful version of the original OS, and IBM ultimately gave buyers the option of loading DOS (and later OS/2) or Windows on their machines. Microsoft and IBM continued their collaboration until 1990, when Microsoft opted to focus its efforts on Windows and DOS, while IBM pursed OS/2. In early 1987 IBM discontinued its original PC line and introduced the new PS2 line, which operated on OS/2. Subsequent releases of Windows, particularly the 3.1 and 95 versions operating on the Intel 486x and Pentium chip sets, gave Microsoft the OS dominance it had long sought.

The introduction of new, more powerful, microprocessors from Intel (486x, followed by the Pentium series) and Motorola (68040, PowerPC6), and from other companies such as Advanced Micro Devices (AMD) and Texas Instruments, followed in the late 1980s and 1990s. The evolution of chip development over the course of nearly 20 years was nothing short of remarkable. While Intel's 8085 5 MHz chip (introduced in 1976) was capable of computing 370,000 instructions per seconds (or 0.37 million instructions per second (MIPS)), its 16 MHz 386 chip (introduced in the mid-1980s) ran at 2.5 MIPS, its 66 MHz Pentium chip (introduced in the early 1990s) ran at 112 MIPS, its 200 MHz Pentium Pro (introduced in the mid-1990s) ran at 440 MIPS, and its 400 MHz Pentium Pro (introduced in the late 1990s) ran at an impressive 832 MIPS. A 1975 IBM mainframe which could perform at 10 MIPS cost $10MM, while a mid-1990s video game player with a Pentium chip could perform at 500 MIPS for only $500. The 1800 square feet representing ENIAC's 1945 computing power can today rest comfortably on an IC the size of a lead pencil tip.

The expansion of onboard memory and hard drives capable of greater storage led to the creation of large and sophisticated 'memory hog' OSs, programs and applications, and the rollout of CD ROM technology resulted in a perceptible decline in the use of diskettes. The early 1990s saw the arrival of the first credible notebook computers; by the end of the decade powerful, ultra light portables were offered by most major computer companies, including Apple, IBM, Compaq, Toshiba, Sony, and others. These machines offered full PC functionality in a small, light, and powerful package, ushering in the era of true mobile computing. The personal digital assistant (PDA), a small, handheld computing device with very basic PC-like functions, was pioneered by Apple through its Newton product in 1993. The Newton, however, was several years ahead of its time—its bulky design and limited functionality acted as barriers to mass use. Not until sleeker, more sophisticated PDAs arrived in the late 1990s (including the highly successful 3Com PalmPilot offerings of the mid- and late 1990s) did the device achieve popularity. PDAs are now a mainstay of mobile and wireless computing. Computer development accelerated throughout the decade, with a steady flow of new desktop and portable models from the major suppliers—including sharply redesigned machines from IBM, Compaq, Dell, and a 'revitalized' Apple. New data storage mechanisms, including disk-sized removable hard drives capable of storing 25–100 MB of information, emerged. Operating systems were upgraded at frequent intervals. Windows became the dominant platform for non-Mac PCs, and Microsoft capitalized on user demand for greater functionality by offering Windows 95, 98, 2000 (as well as the enhanced NT version to run on networks and the CE version to run on PDAs). IBM and Apple continued to upgrade their OS/2 and MacOS platforms. US firms developed most modern PC advances throughout the 1980s and 1990s; while international firms, particularly those in Taiwan and Japan, produced high quality machines during the PC revolution, most were either duplicates or enhancements of technologies developed and marketed in the US.

Though the PC, and its application to personal and business use, will evolve further over the coming years, the machine has already achieved an enormous goal—namely, accustoming personal and business users to technology; this is a significant achievement that has had a tremendous impact on many aspects of modern daily life. The rise of computers during the 20th century—and, in particular, the second half of the 20th century—has been remarkable. From a base of punchcards and manual effort in the 1900s, to electromagnetics and vacuum tubes in the 1940s, to transistors and integrated circuits from the 1950s to the end of the century, the evolution, growth and penetration of computers has been without parallel in human society. The technological and creative powers of hardware and software developers have delivered faster and more flexible machines and applications to businesses and consumers, at ever declining prices, to the point where much of modern life relies on computing infrastructure in order to function. Computing power has, on average, doubled every 18 months over the past 30 years, the average price of a transistor has fallen by orders of magnitude (from $5/transistor in 1950 to less than 1/100th of 1 cent/transistor in 2000), as has the price of the microprocessor (from $230/MIPS in 1991 to less than $3/MIPS in 2000). Little wonder that the considerable advances which have occurred in computing over a relatively short five decades have acted as a catalyst in changing the way the business, among many other disciplines, is conducted.

TALK OF THE TRADE

1st generation computers—computers with switching done through vacuum tubes; these machines were in operation during the 1940s and 1950s.
2nd generation computers—computers with switching based on transistors; these machines were in operation during the late 1940s to late 1950s.

3rd generation computers—computers with switching based on transistors contained within ICs; these machines, in operation from the early 1960s to the late 1970s, were the first to feature terminals and disk storage.

4th generation computers—computers comprised primarily of ICs; with limited amounts of discrete components; these machines were introduced in the late 1970s and exist to the present time.

CPU—central processing unit, the 'brain' of a computer, responsible for coordinating all of the computer's input/output functions.

EDI—electronic data interchange, an early electronic commercial communication protocol between corporations, used for supply ordering, accounting, invoicing/billing, and inventory management.

IC—integrated circuit or chip, a silicon wafer with multiple transistors which acts as a high powered switching device.

Jellybean—a small and cheap IC.

Killer application—killer app, a software or application that becomes so popularly accepted and widely used that it forms part of daily personal/business life.

Microprocessor—an IC housing essential components of a computer's technological capabilities, including the CPU, RAM, ROM, and input/output controls.

MIPS—million instructions per second, a measure of the processing/computing speed of microprocessors.

OS—operating system, the instruction platform that enables a user to interact with a computer; it creates standards for software and applications, manages job sequence, and controls communication with peripherals.

PDA—personal digital assistant, a small, mobile computing device with limited PC-like functionality.

COMMUNICATING: PHONES, CELLS AND FIBER

The telephone was invented in 1876 when Alexander Graham Bell created and patented a functional transmitter that permitted two parties to communicate over an extended copper line. Within a year Bell held a series of public demonstrations to reveal the power of the new medium—shortly thereafter, small telephone networks began developing on the East Coast. Telephone switching was done centrally through a phone exchange; the first such exchange was based in New Haven, and contained 21 lines. While early switching was entirely manual, the introduction of the Strowger electromagnetic switch in the late 19th century helped automate the switching process. The Bell System, named after Alexander Graham Bell and eventually renamed American Bell (and then AT&T), dominated virtually every aspect of 20th century US communications; from 1913 until 1983 it effectively acted as a monopoly, controlling all dimensions of telecommunications. In addition to producing basic telephones and providing infrastructure and service, AT&T controlled important operations related to switch manufacturing (Western Electric) and research (Bell Labs which, as noted above, spawned the transistor). Under AT&T telephone service spread around the country, and then the world, rapidly. In 1915 AT&T created the first transcontinental line, linking New York and San Francisco, and in 1927 it introduced the first trans-Atlantic link, connecting New York and London. Other regions of the world gained telephone access at various points thereafter. Coaxial cables were developed in the late 1930s and the unsightly telephone lines which criss-crossed much of the US (and growing parts of the world) soon moved underground. In 1913 J.N. Reynolds, a researcher at AT&T's Western Electric manufacturing division, designed and patented a new crossbar switch, which improved the switching process; the crossbar switch remained the core of phone exchanges for several decades. During the mid-1950s research commenced into computer-controlled switching based on the transistor work carried out by the Bell Labs team. By the mid-1960s Bell Labs had pioneered digital carrier and switching techniques, and the PBX digital switch was soon being implemented throughout the country; computers and automation soon meant that the switching process was entirely electronic.

In 1927 AT&T combined the transmitter and receiver into a single handset and, by the 1930s, had completely modularized the handset. The basic 'black telephone' model remained unchanged from the late 1930s until 1949, by which time 25MM sets were in use. Models introduced after 1949 featured better audio quality, more robust mechanics, and a somewhat sleeker design (though not, perhaps, by today's standards). The next major feature—the push button 'touch tone' phone—appeared in 1963 as an alternative to the standard rotary mechanism. Touch tone technology was based on dual tone, multiple frequencies assigned by column and row on the keypad; tone signals emitted by each button were translated into digital information and conveyed across the wire to the switching exchange. During the 1970s, as ICs became smaller and cheaper to produce, AT&T removed the wire coils standard in most telephones in favor of ICs that were powered by line voltage. Multiplexing technology, which allowed circuits to carry several calls over one wire simultaneously, became a standard for the telephone business and, by the late 1950s, nearly 80% of intercity communications were multiplexed.

In the late 1940s AT&T began exploring the feasibility of using microwave radio signals to deliver telephonic messages, and in 1951 the company successfully tested, and then implemented, the first transcontinental microwave system. The system, which stretched from New York to San Francisco, comprised 107 relay towers spaced at 30 mile intervals and transmitted signals through electromagnetic radiation in the 1000 to 300,000 MHz range; the development of the cross-country microwave system strengthened the growing market for long-distance telephony. Very elemental mobile radio transmission commenced in the mid-1940s when AT&T introduced its mobile telephone service (MTS), which required devices to be connected to the public switched telephone network (PSTN). MTS of 1946 was very basic—the service was effectively 'simplex' in nature, meaning only one party could speak at a time, and required the mobile user to call from a radiophone on an unused channel, speak to a mobile operator, who then dialed the call over the PSTN. In 1964 AT&T improved MTS by offering duplex operation, auto channel search, and auto dialing. Despite these advances, MTS was still limited by lack of frequencies. A frequency could only be used once in a given area, meaning that only a dozen channels were available in a particular zone. In addition, MTS devices were extremely bulky—base stations transmitted at high power, meaning that radiophones needed large batteries. During the 1970s and 1980s traditional 'landline' telephones and basic MTS were supplemented by more robust wireless services. The first generation of wireless services (so-called 1G) appeared in 1979 and centered on analog devices capable of wireless voice transmission—these services included cordless telephones and cellular radiophones. Cordless telephones were limited mobility, wireless extensions to the standard phone base. True mobile communications were centered on cellular radiophones that operated on radiowaves in the 800–900 MHz range. In a cellular system, geographic areas are divided into 'cells', with each cell connecting to the base station serving that cell. Transmission is re-routed (or 'handed off') as the user moves from cell to cell. When demand for radio channels within a given cell expands until the point of overload, the cell is re-split into a group of smaller cells (each with its own base station); the related frequencies are then rearranged. Through this type of architecture the cell structure avoids the very problems which plagued MTS—namely, limited access.

In the early 1980s AT&T and Motorola created the advanced mobile phone system (AMPS), an analog FM system featuring 666 paired voice channels. AMPS was initially deployed in Chicago and proved an early success since the system provided sufficient channel access—at least for a time. Though AMPS was expanded to 832 channels it soon encountered capacity problems which were not solved until narrowband AMPS was developed in the early 1990s—this created another 2496 channels. In 1990 the second generation of wireless services (2G) arrived; these remain in use up to the present time. 2G services—which are also known as personal communication services (PCS)—cover all forms of wireless transmission connected to the PSTN. While cell phones had historically been voice-only devices, PCS popularized the voice/data combination so prevalent in today's world, allowing both voice and data to be transmitted digitally through very small units with low terminal costs. A key dimension of 2G technology, digital modulation/voice compression with time division multiple access (TDMA), appeared in the early 1990s. TDMA, which divides voice/data into time segments and sends the segments through wireless frequencies, is one of the main cell/PCS standards used today (primarily in the US). In 1994 technology company Qualcomm created another wireless transmission method known as code division multiple access (CDMA), which divides voice/data into packets and sends them through the wireless frequencies. CDMA, which has become another primary cell/PCS standard (used in the US, as well as Korea, Japan and Hong Kong), features digital voice compression with digital modulation, allowing 10–20 times the capacity of standard AMPS. Unfortunately, TDMA and CDMA were, and are, incompatible; both supported, but did not replace, AMPS. Though US companies have been actively involved in developing cell technology, they have not been leaders in deploying cell networks (the lack of standards and the ease of getting landlines are two principal reasons for the slow response). Japan, for instance, created a cell network as early as 1979, most of Scandinavia was cell-ready by 1981, and the UK joined in 1983. European mobile systems, though more advanced than others, were incompatible until the public telephone companies of the European Union decided to support the emerging Global System for Mobile Communications (GSM) platform, another important cell/PCS standard (based on TDMA constructs)—this solved European compatibility issues and has helped propel usage to very high levels.

The wireless industry continues to employ 2G wireless devices (which use digital encoding and feature limited data/messaging capabilities), but has already started developing third generation (3G) technology which is expected to improve the speed, access, and functionality of wireless devices; full deployment of 3G, which will cost an estimated $200B in infrastructure development, should appear by the middle of the decade; in the meantime, certain 2.5G innovations are being introduced as a 'stop gap' measure. Various 3G constructs are emerging, including W-CDMA (wideband CDMA), cdma2000 (a 3G version of CDMA), UMTS (Universal Mobile Telecommunications System, based on W-CDMA), and EDGE (Enhanced Data rate for Global (GSM) Evolution, effectively a 3G version of TDMA). A recent addition to the wireless sector centers on technology known as Bluetooth, which sets the standard for data exchange between mobile devices using shortwave radio signals; though the range is still limited to a maximum of a few dozen meters, it is an interesting wireless standard which is gaining ground in personal area networks (PANs).

Satellite-based communications supplemented terrestrial and radio telephony in the latter part of the 20th century. Satellite signals, when connected to the PSTN, are vital in reaching areas not covered by cell radio signals. The genesis of working satellite communications dates back to the high altitude orbit Inmarsat satellites which provided airborne communication services. The high orbit (35,000 km above the Earth) required high transmission power and introduced a quarter second delay in communications, but allowed for broad territorial coverage with a relatively small number of satellites. The high altitude system was soon supplemented by low Earth orbit (LEO) satellites, orbiting the Earth at only 1500 km. Given their relatively low distance from Earth, LEO satellites have eliminated the communication delay but cannot provide the same type of coverage as their high altitude counterparts. However, the system allows each LEO satellite to pass communication signals off to the next satellite—forming, in essence, a whole band around the Earth. Iridium, a pioneer in developing the LEO satellite communications link in the late 1990s, managed to place 66 satellites in orbit before it encountered financial difficulties and closed down operations. Others are actively involved in similar endeavors.

Telephony and communications are intimately related to computing and networking. Though the invention of the telephone predated the modern computer and, of course, any theory or implementation of networking, it is virtually impossible nowadays to consider telephony apart from computing and networking. Nowhere is this more evident than in the link between multiple computers, and between computers and networks. Such communications links are more plentiful and flexible than ever. Indeed, the entire broadband sector—defined as wide bandwidth equipment and systems which can carry a large proportion of the electromagnetic spectrum—is a key area of focus for communications and networking companies seeking to provide customers with high speed, flexible access.

For most of the 20th century, individual households, businesses, and switches/exchanges have been linked by copper wires (also known as twisted pairs). Copper wire, which began moving underground in the middle part of the century, has been the primary means of conveying voice and data from point to point; coaxial cable appeared in the mid-1900s as an additional underground communications link. While acceptable for standard voice transmissions, unaltered copper and coax have not been the most efficient means of transferring more complex information, including digital signals representing audio clips, text files, and video images. Digital transmission is rapidly replacing standard analog transmission through technology which either conveys an entire stream of binary information (0's and 1's) or samples sound waves and encodes them as binary pulses; once the binary information is transmitted it is converted by the receiver into an audio or visual form. A very efficient manner of transporting this digital information—in terms of speed, size and cost—is fiber optic cable. Cables of optical fiber transmit information via light pulses and can handle very large quantities of information—they are thus said to have considerable 'bandwidth'. For instance, a single strand of optical fiber can transmit the equivalent of 90,000 volumes of an encyclopedia in one second. Fiber cables are much smaller and lighter than conventional copper/coax cables and require very little maintenance; they are also immune to electromagnetic interference and 'cross talk' effects generated by proximate copper wires. Fiber architecture is perfectly suited to the high bandwidth applications that users are increasingly interested in accessing. Active use of data, graphics and visuals is forcing greater conversion to fiber wherever possible, meaning that applications such as interactive video, video on demand, ultra high speed data transfer, digital TV, video conferencing, and home automation/networking are gradually becoming a reality. Since demand for bandwidth has been tripling every year—and is expected to accelerate in the future—fiber optic networking is seen as a critical imperative. Unfortunately, fiber architecture must still cope with a problem known as the 'last mile'. While replacement of twisted pair and coax grid networks has been a successful effort in many areas, communications companies have been unable in many instances to replace the copper/coax connections between the trunk and the user's computer or communications equipment—the 'last mile' into the home or office. Inability to 'fiberize' the entire connection means that transmission speeds are slowed and the full benefit of high bandwidth is unavailable without alternate solutions, such as wireless links. In areas where fiber optic capabilities are not yet available, telecommunication companies are still laying cable for future use—this is known as dark fiber installation. When technology permits fiber communications in an area that has already been prepared, dark fiber installations are 'lit'.

Wireless transmissions, discussed earlier, form another key segment of the broadband spectrum. Communicating through microwaves (rather than copper, coax or fiber) has, of course, been standard practice for several decades—doing so in digital form has simply been a logical progression. Digital wireless technology is a natural mechanism to support various forms of mobile computing—cell phones/PCS, PDAs, laptops, two-way pagers, and so on. In addition, longer distance fixed wireless systems can be used as an alternative to fiber. Certain communication companies are actively deploying fixed broadband wireless networks as they are faster and cheaper to install than fiber links—up to 1/10th of the cost in a metropolitan area. In addition, wireless technology is helping bridge the 'last mile', bypassing twisted pair/coax connections and linking computers to fiber networks running away from the trunk. Three major types of wireless broadband services are currently in use, including local multipoint distribution service (LMDS), which requires line of sight between the transmitter and antenna of 1–4 miles, multichannel/multipoint distribution service (MMDS), which can operate up to 30 miles away, and the PCS service described earlier, which operates primarily in the 1–2 mile 'short haul' range. LMDS, in particular, is often used as a wireless bridge to the 'last mile'.

Transferring voice/data from point to point requires a device which connects to the underlying 'pipe' (whether copper, fiber or the cable infrastructure used to convey cable TV content); this function is performed by the modem, a device that transmits digital data over established communications lines. In its simplest form the modem on a PC (or other computing device) converts digital signals into analog signals, which are then conveyed along the wire, until reaching the destination PC; there, the modem does an analog–digital reconversion so that the PC can correctly interpret the information that has just arrived. If a PC can compress data before transmission, communication speed can be enhanced. Wireless modems, which are becoming increasingly popular for PDAs and other mobile computing devices, operate on similar principles, except that they send/receive information as radio signals. Modems have evolved from simplex devices capable only of one-way transmission, to half-duplex devices capable of two-way, though not simultaneous, communication, to full-duplex devices capable of simultaneous, two-way communication. Transmission speeds for standard dial-up modems have reached 56 kbps (kilobits per second, or 1000 bits per second), making them acceptable for basic transmission. Standard dial-up modems are not, of course, the only means by which computers can communicate. Other mechanisms include integrated services digital network (ISDN) lines, digital subscriber lines (DSLs), T1 (Trunk Level 1) lines and cable modems. In the mid-1980s ISDN lines—digital lines capable of transmitting voice, video and data—were seen as a potential threat to the longevity of modems. Though ISDN lines have not eliminated dial-up modems, they have provided users with enhanced transmission speeds. Using an ISDN modem (a misnomer, in fact, since communication is strictly digital and no modulation/demodulation is required), an ISDN line provides the user with transmission speeds of up to 128 kbps, double that of standard dial-up modems. Actual speed is still impacted by the length of the copper wire running between the customer and the terminating unit; the shorter the distance, the faster the transmission.

A more realistic threat to the conventional dial-up modem—at least for business users—is the DSL and its variants. DSL is a high speed telecommunications service that converts voice and data into packets which are then delivered through digital DSL boxes over standard copper wires; in addition to supporting digital transmission, certain DSLs can also accommodate standard analog voice. DSLs are 'always on'—that is, the connection between the computer and the network never terminates, so the full bandwidth is available to the user at all times, making access quick and transmission rapid. Typical DSLs can transmit data 50 times faster than standard dial-up modems; the downside is, of course, a higher cost, which makes it somewhat prohibitive for the average home PC user. DSL comes in various configurations that dictate transmission speeds; broadly speaking, these include asymmetric DSL (ADSL) and symmetric DSL (SDSL). ADSL allows for fast download rates but slower upload rates. Depending on the distance and configuration, download rates range from 1.5 to 8 mbps (megabits per second) and upload rates range from 512 kbps to 1 mbps; a separate technology, known as very high bit rate DSL (VDSL), can transmit even faster at distances under 1000 feet.

Typical home/small business configuration, known as G.Lite, downloads at 1.5 mbps and uploads at 512 kbps. SDSL allows for both fast download and upload; again, depending on the distance and configuration, transmission rates can range from 768 kbps to 2.5 mbps. It is worth noting that DSL modem equipment already exists to handle speeds of up to 8 mbps; however, DSL is distance-sensitive, and many of the speed features deteriorate for distances beyond 18,000 feet. T1 lines are dedicated, high speed, point-to-point digital lines that can transmit data at over 2 mbps, depending on configuration. T1 lines are typically installed as pairs, with one wire transmitting, and a second receiving, data. As one might expect, their speed and efficiency result in a high cost to the user; charges of more than $1000/month are common.

If dial-up modems reside at one end of the 'speed' spectrum, cable modems occupy the other. A cable modem, as the name suggests, is a modem that connects a computer to a cable TV service that provides network access. While cable modems can increase a user's bandwidth considerably, actual speed is dependent on the number of cable customers using the cable segment at the same time; theoretical maximum speeds can approach 10 mbps, though this presumes little network activity. In the US, 34MM households had access to cable at the start of the 21st century, but only 1.6MM took advantage of the service; further growth, however, is anticipated. (Expansion abroad, where cable access and use are smaller, is expected to be more limited.) To put the 'speed spectrum' into context, consider that its takes a 56 kbps dial-up modem (the standard for most home users) 23 minutes to download a 3.5 minute video clip, an ISDN line 10 minutes, standard ADSL or a T1 line less than 1 minute, a 4 mbps cable modem 20 seconds, and a 10 mbps cable modem only 8 seconds. Given the impediments, limitations, and compatibility issues facing users, it is reasonable to assume that future broadband network access will be accomplished through a mix of wire, fiber, wireless, satellite, and cable mechanisms. Parks Associates, a research group, estimates that in the US, approximately 5MM broadband connections were in use in 2000, and estimates that 24MM will be in place by 2003; cable and DSL are expected to be the largest contributors to 'fat pipe' growth. Broadband expansion is also expected to increase abroad.

TALK OF THE TRADE

1G—1st generation wireless, mobile communication based on analog, rather than digital architecture; 1G commenced in 1979 and was only capable of handling voice communications.

2G—2nd generation wireless, mobile communication employing digital encoding, covering the CDMA, TDMA, PDC, and GSM standards; 2G, which commenced in 1990 and remains in use to the present day, is used for voice and data communications.

3G—3rd generation wireless, mobile communication expected to come onstream by 2005; 3G will feature high speed data handling, high quality audio, e-mail, web access, and global roaming.

Always-on—a network connection which is continuously on, giving the user instant access to the Internet without having to dial-up.

Bandwidth—throughput of the network, measuring the capacity and speed to transmit voice/data (in kilobits, megabits, or gigabits per second).

Bluetooth—wireless personal area network technology developed by Ericsson, IBM, Intel, Nokia, and Toshiba; it has been established as an open standard for very short-range transmission of digital voice and data using radio waves.

Broadband—high bandwidth, high speed communication links that feature 'always on' connections (e.g. no dial-up required); DSL, T1, cable, satellite, and wireless are examples of broadband access mechanisms.

CDMA—code division multiple access, a digital cell/PCS standard used in the US and parts of Asia; CDMA converts voice/data into packets and sends them via wireless frequency.

DSL—digital subscriber line, a telecommunications service that turns voice and data into packets that travel at high speeds over standard copper wire; DSL is 'always on' and comes in various constructs that allow users to send and receive data at different rates.

Fat pipe—the generic name for any communications link which can transmit a large quantity of data very rapidly (e.g. broadband mechanisms).

GSM—global standard for mobile communications, a digital cell/PCS standard used primarily in Europe; GSM is based loosely on TDMA technology.

ISDN—integrated services digital network, digital lines capable of transmitting data at speeds of up to 128 kbps.

Last mile—the short distance between an end-user's communication instrument (phone, PC) and the aggregation point of a common network, such as a cable head-end or telephone company central office; most often this distance is bridged through standard copper wire, resulting in a slowing of data transmission.

Narrowband—dial-up access which features relatively slow transmission speed and capacity compared with other broadband alternatives; it remains the primary form of Internet access at the household level.

PCS—personal communication service, 2G wireless transmission capable of handing voice and data.

PDC—personal digital communications, a digital cell/PCS standard used in Japan.

T-1 (Trunk Level 1) line—a dedicated point-to-point communications line used for high speed data transfer.

TDMA—time dimension multiple access, a digital cell/PCS standard widely used in the US; TDMA converts voice/data into time segments and sends them via wireless frequency.

Twisted pair—standard copper wire used to transmit voice and data.

NETWORKING: THE HISTORY OF THE INTERNET

The Internet—essentially a vast computer network spanning the globe—has become a part of daily life in the Americas, Europe, and Asia. Its presence is felt in nearly every aspect of 21st century life, and its use will undoubtedly accelerate over the coming years and decades; penetration of the Internet will expand as users access the web in new ways and use it for different purposes. Though the Internet is now an established mechanism in its own right it obviously could not have been created without the significant computing and communications advances of the past two decades. A computer network—whether the Internet or any other internal or external mechanism—is broadly defined as a structure that links together individual computers so that they can communicate, share information, and work together on tasks. Two computers sitting on the same desk, connected and communicating, form a network—albeit a small one. If they are proximate to one another they form a local area network (LAN) and if they are separated by a great distance they form a wide area network (WAN). Many businesses operate LANs and WANs as part of their underlying computing and communication processes. LAN computers are most often linked by cables, infrared light signals or radiowave transmissions, while WAN computers are connected by copper/coax/fiber lines, cable or satellite.

While we may take the Internet for granted in this day and age, its development was complex, time-consuming, and fraught with technical hurdles that had to be surmounted. Getting different networks of computers, operating distinct OSs and running different languages, to 'speak' to one another and work together was a significant challenge that was ultimately overcome by the pioneering work of the US Advanced Research Projects Agency (ARPA), founder of the Internet's predecessor. Though the Internet has evolved over several decades—and over the past few years, in particular—we can trace its roots back to the late 1950s when the Soviet Union launched Sputnik I. The 1957 launch of Sputnik caught the US Government and military establishment off guard, leading to the immediate development and funding of ARPA, a Department of Defense arm charged with guiding scientific and technical research. ARPA's mission, when it commenced operations in early 1958, was to restore the US's technical superiority in areas of computing and communications. Though the creation of the National Aeronautics and Space Agency (NASA) in late 1958 removed many of ARPA's original functions, it refocused its efforts on research into computer networks and architecture, alternate nationwide communication mechanisms, and distributed computing. In 1962 J.C.R. Licklider, a MIT professor and researcher at technical research firm Bolt, Beranek and Newman (BBN), joined the Information Processing Techniques Office of ARPA as its head. Licklider's aim was to solve problems by making computers more interactive. He believed that networks of computers operating separately, but able to work together, would help achieve that goal. He was instrumental in laying the theoretical foundation of the computer network that would become known to the world as ARPAnet; Licklider was succeeded by various managing researchers, including Bob Taylor and Larry Roberts, who helped further his vision.

In the mid-1960s, one of the central concepts of distributed computing came into being. In a curious case of near-simultaneous discovery, Paul Baran at RAND and Donald Davies at the National Physics Laboratory in the UK devised the concept of 'packet switching' (though Davies actually coined the term); Len Kleinrock at MIT had also engaged in similar theoretical studies in the early 1960s. Packet switching involves dividing data into small parcels, sending the parcels across the network by the fastest route available, and then reassembling them in the correct sequence at the destination site. The motivation for Baran's work, which was published in 1964, was centered on the establishment of alternative communication methods that could be used in the event of hostilities; he was particularly interested in the 'survivability' of communications systems in the event of military attack. Baran believed that if messages were sent out in parcels and one (or more) of the parcels was interrupted, duplicate parcels could be resent through a different route and assembled with the remaining parcels, allowing the message to be conveyed in its entirety; reassembling the message if it arrived out of sequence would not be a problem as it would be tagged with the correct reassembly sequence. Baran's early work led to thoughts about allocating parcels to all available bandwidth, regardless of route, so that many parcels could share different communication lines simultaneously; this was deemed a logical approach, as not every communication line is in use all the time. After completing his research, Baran felt that large-scale packet switching, based on 128 bit parcels, was theoretically feasible. Davies' work was of a similar nature, with a particular focus on moving packets through a digital 'store and forward' network. Unfortunately, the communications industry remained skeptical about packet switching and refused to support research.

Not until 1967 did the idea of building a network linking computers around the country—and, ultimately, the world—begin to take shape. Roberts and the ARPA team focused on the creation of a network where host computers at each site would manage the network functions; thus, a host computer would put in 'double duty' as both a research computer (its normal task) and a communications router (its network task). Wes Clark, a researcher who began investigating the matter, advised Roberts to remove the host computer from the communications routing function by inserting a small computer which would act as an interface between the host and the network transmission lines; this was not unlike an approach proposed by Davies. This structure would, effectively, create a sub-network of small interconnected nodes, all identical and capable of 'speaking' the same language. Each host computer needed only a single communications link to the interface computer; individual interface computers could then communicate among themselves. The interface machine, to be known as an Interface Message Processor (IMP), would have no host-to-host functions but would act as a messenger and storing/forwarding device. IMPs would disassemble messages into packets, store the packets, perform error checks, route the packets, send receipts when they arrived, reassemble the packets and send them up to the hosts. The host computer only had to communicate with the IMP and read the message that had been received and assembled. Through this architecture, multiple hosts could connect to a single IMP. In order for the network to be effective the average transit time for a packet, wherever it was going, had to be under half a second; in addition, the network needed to operate autonomously—that is, IMPs could not be tied to the host's maintenance schedule. IMPs were, in effect, the precursor of modern-day routers.

With this breakthrough, Roberts sent a detailed proposal to 140 companies capable of creating an IMP. There was a fair amount of skepticism among many of the recipients, including powerhouses such as IBM, Control Data, and AT&T. After narrowing the list down to BBN and Raytheon, Roberts awarded the IMP contract to BBN; BBN was charged with delivering four IMPs for $1MM by late 1969. The University of California Los Angeles (UCLA), in turn, was awarded the Network Measurement Center contract, becoming the first of four original nodes on the network. BBN quickly commenced work on building the IMP—basically, a heavily re-architected Honeywell 516 minicomputer. In September 1969, with deadlines looming, BBN managed to deliver the IMP to UCLA; it was, in essence, the first node of a packet-switched network. Three other nodes were added within months of the successful UCLA test; by the end of 1969 nodes at Stanford Research Institute, University of California at Santa Barbara, and University of Utah were all functional. A variety of computers were used by the hosts and IMPs—Honeywells, IBMs, Digitals, and Xeroxs—but that did not matter, the network communication between these machines had proven successful and the ARPAnet was born. Other networks soon grew up around it.

The original ARPAnet used a communications protocol known as Network Control Protocol (NCP) that allowed the IMPs on the network to communicate with one another. One aspect of NCP, so-called 'file transfer protocol' (FTP), allowed formatting and exchanging of data files over the network; this was of considerable interest to academic researchers, as it let them share research information and ideas with relative ease. In the early 1970s ARPA commenced a program to link together new networks operating under different protocols. ARPA's goal was to develop a standard, and consistent, protocol so that new networks (that is, non-ARPAnet networks) could be 'internetworked' or 'internetted'—hence the origin of the term 'internet'. Two researchers, Bob Kahn and Vint Cerf, began developing the concept of a 'gateway'—a routing computer operating between various networks (e.g. the ARPAnet and other networks). The gateway had to be able to talk to each network it was connected to, suggesting a need to reconcile different interfaces, packet sizes, transmission rates, and so on. With new networks, it was no longer sufficient to rely on ARPAnet's NCP; something more flexible and independent was required. At the end of 1973 Kahn and Cerf published seminal work on connecting gateways through a new protocol, the Transmission Control Protocol (TCP). Without TCP, communications across networks could not occur; with TCP any network with a gateway computer capable of interpreting and routing packets was able to join. In 1978 TCP was broken into two segments: TCP, to disassemble and reassemble packets and provide error checks confirming safe receipt of all packets, and Internet Protocol (IP), to route and guide packets to the correct destination network and site (every client and server attached to a network has a unique IP address that is assigned on a temporary or permanent basis). Formally, 'internet' is defined as a connected set of networks using TCP/IP, while 'Internet' is defined as connected networks of TCP/IP internets—the first piece of the Internet was created in 1975 when ARPAnet linked up with Xerox PARC's Ethernet. In the early 1970s the Xerox PARC research team, under the leadership of Bob Metcalfe, developed Ethernet, an inexpensive way of connecting computers and letting them send information to other machines operating in close proximity—such as the same room or building. Ethernet became the standard computer communication method for LANs, enabling data to travel over twisted pairs at 10 mbps; linked combinations of PCs and UNIX-based workstations form a de-facto standard in today's corporate world. While Kahn and Cerf's TCP/IP emerged as the Internet standard by the late 1980s, Open Systems Interconnection (OSI), an ISO standard for worldwide communications, briefly challenged TCP/IP; the US Government and many European locales adopted the seven-layer OSI protocol in the late 1970s. During the 1980s, however, UNIX programmers sided with TCP/IP and the first UNIX-based Sun workstations supported TCP/IP; TCP/IP eventually won the battle and OSI is now simply another protocol which can be supported.

The early success of ARPA's small network of computers proved that the concept of packet switching and distributed computing was viable, and marked the commencement of a rapid phase of network development that culminated in the Internet so familiar to 21st century computer users. By 1971 ARPAnet featured 15 nodes and by 1977 had grown to 111 nodes. Advances in computing technology made computers more accessible to a wider group of researchers, government agencies, universities and businesses, helping contribute to the expansion. The primary activity on the ARPAnet during its formative years was the exchange of documents and files. This was mainly of interest to researchers and academicians, hence the overwhelming focus of ARPAnet on universities and research laboratories. The 'killer application' that helped popularize the network appeared in 1971. Specifically, Ray Tomlinson created an electronic mail program that allowed users to send messages across the net; this was the forefather of today's popular e-mail application (and featured the ubiquitous @ sign separating the user's name and domain). Though enhancements to Tomlinson's e-mail program appeared over ensuing years (including replying, forwarding, filing, and so on), the concept remained the same—delivering messages in simple, readable format, almost instantaneously. By 1973 75% of ARPAnet's traffic was devoted to e-mail.

Further milestones in networking occurred in the 1970s and 1980s; for example, the first international ARPAnet connections appeared in 1973 (to University College in London and NORSAR in Norway), and the first commercial version of the network was developed in 1974 (through BBN's Telenet). The success of ARPAnet within the government, academic and scientific communities also gave rise to many new networks. For instance, in 1979 Duke and the University of North Carolina founded USENET, and in 1983 Yale and the City University of New York created BITNET, while Purdue, University of Wisconsin, University of Delaware, RAND, and BBN started CSNET. In 1986 the National Science Foundation (NSF) was established and it created a network of its own. In 1990 the NSF assumed management of a network that came to be known as NSFnet and expanded it by connecting to CSNET and EUNET (linking European sites). NSFnet remains an important Internet backbone (a network communication conduit that routes major traffic through high speed transmission paths). In addition to NSFnet, NASA and the Department of Energy built and contributed important Internet backbones during the late 1980s and early 1990s. Throughout the 1980s a growing number of international nodes came online, providing stronger communication links between the US, Europe, and Asia. Popularization of the PC in the early 1980s, as described earlier in the chapter, fuelled further network growth. In 1979 Telecomputing Corporation of America created an online public information utility; Readers Digest purchased the service in 1980 and renamed it The Source. By the end of 1982 The Source had 25,000 PC subscribers, each of whom paid $100 plus $7–22/hour to access bulletin boards, software exchanges, e-mail, news, and games. CompuServe followed suit; these were the forerunners of today's Internet service providers (ISPs)—services which provide Internet access through dial-ups.

In 1983 APRAnet was split into two segments—MILnet, to take over sites containing non-classified military information, and ARPAnet to handle all other aspects of the computer research community. By 1984 more than 1000 hosts were active—the networking world was using e-mail in record quantities, moderating USENET newsgroups, exchanging files and documents, and so on. In order to ensure greater uniformity on the rapidly expanding network, the domain name system (DNS) was established. DNS was designed to manage addresses and registrations, and established the first registered symbolics familiar to today's Internet users—.com (commercial), .org (nonprofit), .gov (government), .edu (education), .mil (military), .net (network service provider), and .int (international treaty organization). As the success of global networks expanded during the late 1980s, ARPA's administrative functions were divided up and shifted to new organizations/boards. The Internet is now broadly guided by the World Wide Web (WWW) Consortium, Internet Architecture Board (IAB), the Internet Engineering Task Force (IETF, which develops technical standards and communications protocols), the Internet Engineering Steering Group (IESG, which approves the IETF's recommendations), and the Internet Corporation for Assigned Names and Numbers (ICANN, which oversees domain names). In 1990, after more than 20 years in operation, ARPAnet, the 'grandfather' of networks, was formally retired. Many of the researchers involved in the development and maintenance of the ARPAnet over its 20 year history went on to form many other key computing ventures, including Sun, Novell, Cisco, and 3Com, among others.

By the late 1980s, growth in hosts exploded. Approximately 10,000 hosts were active in 1987, and just two years later more than 160,000 were operational. 1989 also marked the year in which the Internet and commercial services began mixing: MCI Mail introduced its commercial e-mail package and CompuServe, one of the original dial-up services, introduced its proprietary e-mail system. In 1991 the Gopher application, effectively a primitive search device capable of scanning the network for user-defined files, was released. In the same year Tim Berners-Lee, a scientist at CERN in Switzerland, used a computer with an object-oriented OS to determine how to link and disseminate information across different networks and OSs. He termed his pioneering project the World Wide Web (WWW or web) and effectively created the world's first web server. His contributions were critical in allowing web access as commonly understood and employed today. As the web expanded, the hypertext transport protocol (http)—a communications protocol to connect a web server to a specific 'web page' (referenced by its address, or uniform reference locator (URL))—took hold. Web pages are now created using the hypertext markup language (HTML) and dynamic HTML, which use standard commands, tags and codes. These developments were, and remain, critical in popularizing aspects of the Internet's functionality.

With more than 1MM hosts online in late 1992, the network was ripe for a migration from pure research applications to broader commercial use. This was made possible in 1993 when Marc Andreessen and several colleagues at the University of Illinois Super Computing Center programmed a GUI known as Mosaic, which put a user-friendly face on Berners-Lee's work. Mosaic was the 'front end' which let users look for files and web pages and send e-mail, in a simple manner, using hyperlinks, graphics and sound. Though other browsers predated Mosaic—such as libwww, violawww, Midas, Samba, Arena, Lynx, Cello, and others—Mosaic was far more flexible and accessible, and thus made its mark. Following the release of Mosaic, Andreessen and his team left to form Netscape. In late 1994 they released a new browser, Mozilla, and followed thereafter with a more sophisticated offering, Netscape Navigator, which remained dominant in the marketplace until Microsoft introduced its competing Internet Explorer in 1995. Once web browsers became prevalent, the true potential of the Internet began to appear. By the mid-1990s consumers and businesses began turning to the Internet for information, e-mail and, ultimately, goods and services. The first web shopping malls appeared in 1994, as did the first evidence of mass junk e-mail (or 'spam'). In 1995 Sun Microsystems introduced Java, a new language for writing web applications, that greatly enhanced the content and 'look and feel' of web pages. Java can be run on servers (as 'servlets') or from web pages (as 'applets') and improve web site functionality. Online service providers, including America Online, Prodigy, and CompuServe, began offering Internet access, e-mail, and other tools, and soon drew many customers. Search engines, including those created by new companies such as Yahoo, Excite, Webcrawler, Altavista, and others, became essential for those looking for specific information on the web; by 1998 the Internet was estimated to have between 275MM and 325MM distinct pages, making search engines an essential tool. New aspects of electronic commerce, electronic auctions, and portals (web sites providing services, e-mail, and information) became part of the public mind by the latter part of the decade.

Metcalfe, creator of the Ethernet which helped popularize networking in the corporate world, established a general rule which has become known as 'Metcalfe's Law'. Specifically, Metcalfe's Law says that the value of a network grows by the number of nodes squared—the power of the network is thus much greater than the sum of its individual parts, a fact that is increasingly evident in today's 'networked world'. The Internet, made possible through advances in technology and telecommunications, has indeed changed entire aspects of personal and commercial life. As discussed in this book, many of these changes have impacted the electronic commerce and electronic finance sectors.

TALK OF THE TRADE

Backbone—a network communication conduit that routes major traffic through high speed transmission paths.

Browser—a GUI which lets network users access information, products, and services in a simple, user-friendly fashion.

DNS—domain name system, a framework which manages network addresses and registrations, including the symbolics found in URLs (.com, .org, .gov, .edu, .mil, .net, .int).

Ethernet—a standard LAN connection which allows proximate computers to connect and communicate at very high speeds.

HTML—hypertext markup language, a meta-language which allows for uniform development of web pages through standard commands, tags, and codes.

http—hypertext transfer protocol, a communications protocol used to connect servers to the Internet.

Hyperlink—a linking protocol which transports the user to associated documents and files on the network.

ISP—Internet service provider, a company that provides users with access to the Internet.

LAN—local area network, a network of two or more computers connected and communicating over a small distance (e.g. same room or building).

Packet switching—the technique of decomposing a message or file into small packets, distributing them through the most efficient route on a network, and reassembling them at the destination point.

TCP/IP—Transmission Control Protocol/Internet Protocol, the primary communications protocol of the Internet that allows communication between, and among, networks; TCP disassembles and reassembles data packets, while IP routes packets.

URL—uniform reference locator, the unique identifier or address used to identify a web site.

WAN—wide area network, a network of many computers connected and communicating over a large distance.

Bibliography

PERIODICALS

Miscellaneous printed and electronic issues of:

Business 2.0
Business Week
Euromoney
Fast Company
Financial Times
Forbes
Forbes.com
Fortune
Fortune Small Business
Information Week
Institutional Investor
PCWorld
Red Herring
Risk
The Industry Standard
Upside
Wall Street Journal
Wired

The Economist, *Survey of Internet Banking*, May 2000
The Economist, *Survey of the New Economy*, September 2000
Risk, *Survey of Electronic Trading*, November 1999
Wall Street Journal, *Survey of Online Trading*, June 2000

WEB SITES

Financial institution web sites (major banks, brokers, electronic trading platforms, venture capital firms)
Corporate web sites
Industry-based web sites
Infomediary web sites
Regulatory web sites

SELECTED BOOKS AND OTHER PUBLICATIONS

Cronin, M., ed., 1998, *Banking and Finance on the Internet*, Wiley, New York.
Evans, P. and T. Wurster, 1999, *Blown to Bits*, Harvard Business Press, Cambridge, MA.
Gilder, G., 2000, *Telecosm*, Free Press, New York.
Gompus, P. and J. Lerner, 2000, *The Venture Capital Cycle*, MIT Press, Cambridge, MA.
Hafner, K. and M. Lyon, 1996, *Where Wizards Stay Up Late*, Touchstone, New York.
Hartman, A. and J. Sifonis, 2000, *Net Ready*, McGraw-Hill, New York.
Kelly, K., 1998, *New Rules for the New Economy*, Penguin, New York.
Kurzweil, R., 1999, *The Age of Spiritual Machines*, Penguin, New York.
Levine, R., et al., 2000, *The Cluetrain Manifesto*, Perseus, Cambridge, MA.
Long, M., 2000, *Financing the New Venture*, Adams Press, Holbrook, MA.
Martin, C., 1999, *Net Future*, McGraw-Hill, New York.
Meerschwam, D., 1991, *Breaking Financial Boundaries*, Harvard Business Press, Boston, MA.
Millman, G., 1999, *The Day Traders*, Times Business, London.
Negroponte, N., 1995, *Being Digital*, Vintage, New York.
Neuchterlein, J., 2000, 'International Venture Capital', Council on Foreign Relations.
Office of the Comptroller of the Currency, 1999, *International Banking Comptroller's Handbook*, October.
Pettit, D. and R. Jaroslovsky, 2000, *Wall Street Journal Guide to Online Investing*, Crown, New York.
Rheingold, H., 1985, *Tools for Thought*, MIT Press, Cambridge, MA.
Siebel, T. and P. House, 1999, *Cyber Rules*, Doubleday, New York.

Index

Lightning Source UK Ltd.
Milton Keynes UK
UKOW04n2214180915

258882UK00001B/21/P